MW00575520

TABLE OF CONTENTS

Top 20 Test Taking Tips

1. Carefully follow all the test registration procedures
2. Know the test directions, duration, topics, question types, how many questions
3. Setup a flexible study schedule at least 3-4 weeks before test day
4. Study during the time of day you are most alert, relaxed, and stress free
5. Maximize your learning style; visual learner use visual study aids, auditory learner use auditory study aids
6. Focus on your weakest knowledge base
7. Find a study partner to review with and help clarify questions
8. Practice, practice, practice
9. Get a good night's sleep; don't try to cram the night before the test
10. Eat a well balanced meal
11. Know the exact physical location of the testing site; drive the route to the site prior to test day
12. Bring a set of ear plugs; the testing center could be noisy
13. Wear comfortable, loose fitting, layered clothing to the testing center; prepare for it to be either cold or hot during the test
14. Bring at least 2 current forms of ID to the testing center
15. Arrive to the test early; be prepared to wait and be patient
16. Eliminate the obviously wrong answer choices, then guess the first remaining choice
17. Pace yourself; don't rush, but keep working and move on if you get stuck
18. Maintain a positive attitude even if the test is going poorly
19. Keep your first answer unless you are positive it is wrong
20. Check your work, don't make a careless mistake

Technology Applications Core

System unit and memory component

A computer system includes two major components: the system unit and the memory component. The system unit of a computer contains the central processing unit (CPU), also known as the microprocessor. The memory component includes the random access memory (RAM) and the hard drive. Alongside these major components, a computer will often have a CD/DVD drive and drivers for other peripheral devices. The keyboard, mouse, speakers, and printer are considered part of the computer system as well. The system unit communicates with these peripheral devices through a series of cables running from ports in the system to ports in the device.

CPU

A computer's central processing unit (CPU) is managed by the kernel of the operating system. It delegates tasks to the various programs installed on the computer, and records the locations of data and programs. In order to optimize efficiency, the CPU can place data and programs either in main memory or virtual memory; information needed frequently is kept in main memory. The information stored on the hard drive can be accessed and processed by the CPU. Inside the central processing unit (CPU) of a computer is a control unit that comprehends and follows the CPU instructions. Specifically, the control unit moderates the electronic signals between main memory and the arithmetic logic unit (ALU) where the logical and arithmetic functions of the computer are performed. It also moderates the signals between the main memory and the I/O devices. The CPU also contains registers which hold onto data while it is being processed. A central processing unit also contains buses, occasionally known as bus lines, along which bits are sent to the motherboard. The central processing unit controls the speed and progress of the bits along the bus lines.

Cache

Caches are special memory sections that computers use for frequently required instructions. The presence of cache accelerates processing functions. Processor chips host Level 1 (L1) cache, which moderates essential processing functions. Slightly less essential instructions are contained on a nearby chip as Level 2 (L2) cache. Advanced, expensive computers also contain Level 3 (L3) cache on their motherboards. This kind of memory is also found on computers that require L2 Advanced Transfer Cache. The cache size of a computer is directly tied to the size of the processor.

Dual core processor, hyper-threading technology, and benchmarks

Using a dual core processor is one way to avoid having to use multiple processors. Dual core processors are faster than a single core processor because they contain the circuitry of two microprocessors on a single chip; however, the operating system and software of the computer must be configured for dual core processing in order to achieve optimal speed. New versions of Windows and high-level graphics software support dual core processing. A similar solution, known as hyper-threading technology (HTT), involves the simulation of two processors. This technology is able to achieve the effects of dual core processing. Finally, benchmarks are used by scientists to compare processing speed with known standards in order to measure the speed of microprocessors.

Virtual memory

The hard disk of a computer contains virtual memory where files and program parts are stored until they are needed. Virtual memory is used to store information when the RAM is full. The creation and use of virtual memory drastically slows down the processing of the computer, so overtaxing virtual memory should be avoided. Computer buyers should also make sure to buy a system that has a sufficient amount of RAM for their purposes.

Bits

Sound and image storage
In order to be stored, images and sounds have to be digitized. Images are subdivided into pixels, each of which is assigned a binary number depending on its color. Sounds, on the other hand, are broken down into wave components. The samples taken from various points along the wave are converted into digital values. In order to represent a specific sound in sufficient detail, a computer must digitize thousands of wave samples every second.

Circuits in miniaturization
In a computer, bits are small pulses of electricity that pass through circuits. A bit is the fundamental unit of binary computer data: when it switches on it represents a one, and when it switches off it represents a zero. A one has a voltage of +5 volts and a zero has a voltage of 0 volts. In a microchip, each bit circuit is miniaturized. This enables some electronic equipment to be very small and portable. Microchips are also known as integrated circuits, since they also contain electric devices like transistors,

capacitors, wires, resistors, and logic gates.

Data storage parts

When computer professionals talk about data storage, they typically refer to the storage medium and the storage device. The medium is where the data is stored, whether it be a hard drive, magnetic tape, or a DVD. The storage device, on the other hand, is the apparatus for recording a copy of the data to be stored. For instance, a floppy disk or DVD are storage media, while a floppy disk drive and a DVD drive are storage devices. The storage device, then, is what places data in the storage medium.

Memory chips and the motherboard

Memory chips, also known as RAM, are the most important temporary storage units for data. They are where data is held while it is in use by the operating system or an open application. Modern computers need 128 MB worth of memory chips at the very least. The motherboard, meanwhile, is so called because it is the main circuit board in the computer. All of the computer's various peripherals, like the keyboard and printer, have to be connected to the motherboard. A typical motherboard contains expansion slots in which the user can install new components and peripherals. The motherboard is like the hub of the computer network: it enables the electric power that enters the computer to be evenly distributed to all components.

RAM

Random access memory (RAM) is the short-term storage location for data in a computer. It is typically used to hold program instructions for open applications and the operating system. RAM, which is typically found on the circuit board, is intended only for the immediate needs of the computer. As program instructions are processed, results are stored in RAM before they are applied. Data that is not readily required is stored in long-term memory on a computer's hard disk. Random access memory (RAM) is composed of capacitors, which are small electronic parts that contain bits. Data is stored in bits as a sequence of zeros and ones. A one is considered "on," while a zero is considered "off," or discharged. There are eight capacitors, each of which contains a bit, in each RAM location. Information contained in RAM is considered vulnerable because it is dependent on a consistent flow of electrical power, and so can be lost if the power source is disrupted.

RAM chips used in PCs
Personal computers contain the four types of RAM: DRAM, SDRAM, SRAM, and DDR-SDRAM. Dynamic RAM (DRAM) must be refreshed regularly by the CPU or it will lose some of its data. Spontaneous dynamic RAM (SDRAM) is controlled by the system clock and is faster than DRAM, capable of reaching speeds in the megahertz. Static RAM (SRAM) is also faster than DRAM and does not need to be refreshed by the CPU. Double-data rate synchronous dynamic RAM (DDR-SDRAM) is the most recently developed form of RAM, and is capable of speeds in the megahertz. DDR-SDRAM is common in both PCs and Macs.

ROM

Read-only memory (ROM) is where the initiating routines of a computer system are stored. ROM is permanently stored on an integrated circuit chip and is not dependent on the presence of electric currents; in other words, it does not disappear if the computer is unplugged. ROM is unchanging and cannot be altered by the addition or deletion of data. It is

responsible for the display of characters on the computer screen. It also contains the ROM BIOS (basic input/output system), which directs the computer to the operating system and loads the OS into RAM. The ROM BIOS is also responsible for accessing the hard drive.

EEPROM

Electrically erasable programmable read-only memory (EEPROM) is a chip or set of chips that store basic information like date and time, CPU type and speed, language, RAM capacity, and other configuration settings. This type of memory is classified as nonvolatile because it does not depend on electric current to exist. The user can adjust the EEPROM setup by holding down the F1 or Delete key during the boot process. Whenever the configuration of the computer is changed, the information in EEPROM must be updated. If the information there is inaccurate, the computer may be unable to boot properly.

CMOS chips and flash memory chips

Complementary metal-oxide-semiconductor (CMOS) chips are used to store information like date and time. These chips are powered by batteries, and therefore retain their contents even when power is lost. This is why a computer is able to maintain an accurate date even if it has been off for several days. CMOS chips can be reprogrammed, as for instance to reflect daylight savings time. A flash memory chip, on the other hand, does not require a battery. This kind of memory chip can be reprogrammed many different times. Flash memory chips are used to store programs in cell phones, MP3 players, digital cameras, and computers.

Floppy disk drives and CD drives

In the past, floppy disk drives were installed internally on desktop computers. In the early 2000s, the CD-ROM drive rendered the floppy disk drive obsolete, and took its place in desktop computers. Compared to CDs, floppy disks are fragile and capable of storing much less information. The early compact discs used for storage were designated either as CD-R or CD+R, depending on whether the laser writing on the disc was performed at a high or low frequency. Unlike floppy disks, information could only be etched onto these early CDs one time, and could not be erased. Modern compact discs, known as CD-RWs, can be written to multiple times.

DVD drives and USB flash drives

Digital versatile disc (DVD) drives are capable of placing data on discs that look exactly like CDs, but have much larger storage capacity. A DVD drive is also capable of reading and writing to CD-Rs, CD-RWs, DVD-Rs, and DVD-RWs. However, DVD drives are not capable of rewriting CD-Rs, CD+Rs, or DVD-Rs. A DVD-RW, on the other hand, can be written to several times. A universal serial bus (USB) flash drive, occasionally known as a thumb drive, is a storage device plugged into a special port on the side of the computer. Many people use these devices to back up or transport data. The data on a USB drive is stored electronically.

Specialized expansion ports

FireWire ports, MIDI, and IrDA ports
Apple developed FireWire, a serial bus system, for input devices that generate a huge amount of data. In particular, the system is useful for dealing with digital video cameras. The Musical Instrument Digital Interface, or MIDI, is a system for connecting musical instruments and amplifiers to a computer system. Finally, the Infrared Data Association, or IrDA, allows the peripheral and input devices of a computer system to be connected without wires. In order for the IrDA system to work, the ports of the two devices must be close together with no obstructions between them.

Multimedia ports, Bluetooth, and Ethernet
A Bluetooth port is capable of sending a wireless signal up to thirty feet. It uses radio waves to connect cell phones, headsets, and computers. Although Bluetooth is widely thought of as a common earpiece, the system actually involves numerous parts. An Ethernet port connects a computer to a modem, to another computer, or to a hub. A multimedia port connects a computer to another media device, like a VCR, DVD player, television, or camcorder. Increasingly, modern computers are able to connect to a wide variety of peripheral devices through only a few common port types.

USB port

A universal serial bus (USB) port is located on the outside of a computer; many peripheral devices attach to a USB port. The newest versions of Windows automatically detect when a peripheral device is plugged into a USB drive and, if the computer does not already have a device driver, will find the one it needs on the Internet. USB ports can support mice, keyboards, and even flash drives. Most modern computers have several USB ports, typically located on the desktop computer casing or on the side of a laptop.

Peripherals

Peripherals are nonessential devices that can be attached to a computer. External

- 8 -

peripherals exist outside the physical space of the computer. Some of the most common external peripherals are monitors, headphones, webcams, external hard drives, keyboards, scanners, and microphones. An internal peripheral, on the other hand, is located inside the computer but does not determine whether the computer can operate. For instance, internal modems and DVD-ROM drives are peripheral devices commonly placed inside the body of a computer. They are not essential in the way that a microprocessor is. Peripherals are often described as input/output (I/O) devices because they either bring data into the computer or provide a method of exporting data from the computer.

Mouse

One common peripheral device is the mouse, which is used to move the cursor around the display screen. Many modern mice have two buttons and a scroll wheel on the top. By rolling the scroll wheel, the user can rapidly scroll the onscreen image up or down. Objects onscreen can be selected by moving the cursor onto the object and clicking the left button of the mouse. Objects can be opened or activated by double-clicking the left button. By placing the arrow on an object and clicking the right button once, the user can activate the shortcut menu. By placing the arrow on an object, holding down the left button, and moving the arrow, the user can move the object. The moving object only becomes stationary when the left button is released.

Pointing devices

Increasingly, the computer mouse is being outmoded by several other devices for moving the cursor. For instance, a trackball is a rubber or plastic sphere that can be rotated with the fingers or hand. Trackballs may be mounted on the computer, or may be part of a peripheral

device. Some computers are fitted with a pointing stick, which looks like a pencil eraser and is in the middle of the keyboard. By pressing on the pointing stick, the user can move the cursor. A touchpad is a flat, rectangular surface on which the user drags and taps his or her fingers. A touch screen is a video screen that works in a similar manner to a touchpad. Some computers have a pen-based system, which allows the user to use a stylus to write on a flat surface; the computer will translate these marks into writing.

Input hardware devices

A keyboard is an input hardware device that enables the user to enter letters, numbers, and other characters. The traditional keyboard is currently joined by foldable keyboards and models that prevent carpal tunnel syndrome. A pointing device, like a mouse or trackball, allows the user to point-and-click at objects on the desktop. Other input hardware devices that allow the user to enter data are digital cameras, voice-recognition systems, scanners, webcams, and audio-input devices.

Modem

A modem (short for modulate/demodulate) is a device for converting digital signals into analog waves and sending them over telephone lines. In other words, a modem takes data from one computer and converts it into a sound which can be heard and translated by another computer. With the aid of a modem, computer users can communicate with one another over vast distances. The creation of modems enabled such communication without requiring the invention and implementation of a new communications infrastructure.

Display device options for a PC

The cathode ray tube (CRT), in which electron beams interact with a display surface to produce the colored dots that comprise an image, has grown obsolete in recent years. Instead, most modern computer screens use LCD or plasma displays. An LCD, or liquid crystal display, is less expensive than a cathode ray tube display. These displays work through a series of light and liquid crystal networks. A plasma screen, meanwhile, is a more expensive system that involves fluorescent lighting. Plasma screens tend to be smaller and less energy-intensive than CRTs.

Specialty types of terminals

A computer with only a display screen and a keyboard is called a dumb terminal, or a video display terminal (VDT). This kind of computer cannot process data, but can export text to a mainframe capable of processing it. A similar system, called an intelligent terminal, includes a keyboard, display, and small processor. This kind of computer system, of which an ATM is one common example, is capable of performing simple functions without recourse to a mainframe. Finally, an Internet terminal provides the user with access to the Internet; for instance, many modern televisions are fitted with web terminals that allow the user to view online content.

Circuits, vacuum tubes, and transistors

A circuit is a pathway for the flow of electric current. In order for current to flow, a circuit has to be closed, or complete. A vacuum tube is a small, hollow cylinder containing a tiny wire circuit that enables the flow of electrons. There is no air in a vacuum tube, which allows the electrons to flow more freely. However, vacuum tubes are notoriously unreliable and energy-intensive, and were eventually removed from computer manufacture altogether. The original vacuum tubes used in a computer were given a value of either zero or one, so that they functioned like bits. Vacuum tubes were eventually replaced by transistors, which are little switches capable of alternating between on and off millions of times every second. Transistors are also more reliable and less expensive than vacuum tubes.

Microchip

The miniaturization revolution made it possible to place millions of electric circuits on a single silicon chip. In miniaturization, a photographic image of the network of circuits is created and reduced to a tiny size, at which point it is etched onto a silicon chip through a process called photolithography. The silicon chips are typically between eight and twelve inches in diameter. A number of flat networks of circuits are placed on either side of the silicon chip. The chip is die-cut into several smaller pieces, each about one centimeter square and approximately half a millimeter thick. An eight-inch wafer of silicon produces about 300 chips. After the chips are created, they are tested and fitted with a protective frame. A microchip will also contain metallic pins that make contact with other parts of the computer.

A microchip contains an arithmetic logic unit (ALU) that completes basic arithmetic functions and makes comparisons. Its action is initiated by instructions received in the control unit. These instructions are interpreted by the ALU, executed, and then discarded as the ALU proceeds to its next task. While the task is being performed, instructions are held in computer memory. As the program begins, the location of the first instruction is placed in the control unit. The control unit then moves the information from the instruction unit to the instruction register. The ALU may be instructed to interpret, accumulate, or communicate the information. All of the results of the action taken by the ALU are placed in an accumulator, at which point the control unit moves the instruction pointer to the next instruction in central memory.

Popular current microchips

Intel, which first made microchips in 1971, is currently the largest microchip manufacturer, responsible for producing microprocessors for IBM and other major computer manufacturers. Intel's main competition is Advanced Micro Devices (AMD), which makes a slightly less expensive microprocessor with different features. Apple used microchips from Motorola and IBM until 2005, when they began using Intel chips. The major microchip manufacturers also have products appropriate for notebooks, portable computers, servers, and desktops.

Intel chips, Motorola chips, and PowerPC chips

One of the positive features of Intel chips is that they can run on computers made by other companies as well as those made by Intel. Most computers that run Microsoft Windows have Intel chips. Apple computers, on the other hand, use the Motorola chip, which are manufactured by Motorola and its subsidiary company Freescale Semiconductor. Finally, the PowerPC chip enables the Macintosh computer to run both PC and Mac software so long as the computer is configured correctly.

Power supply, surge protector, voltage regulator, and uninterruptible power supply

The power supply for a computer converts alternating current into direct current, which is required by the internal components of the computer. The power supply is regulated by the on-off switch, and a network of wires carry power to the hard drives, motherboard, and other components. A sudden increase in power can endanger the components of the computer, so most machines are fitted with a surge protector or surge suppressor to prevent damage. In addition, computers often have a voltage regulator that maintains a sufficient level of current. Also, most computers have an uninterruptible power supply (UPS), which maintains computer operations if the power goes out suddenly.

Device drivers

A device driver enables communication between a computer and a hardware component. In order to function properly, the device driver must be compatible with the operating system. In the past, a peripheral device would be accompanied by a CD or floppy disk containing the driver. Most modern computers, however, have "plug-and-play" capability, meaning that they recognize a new piece of hardware (for instance, a printer, modem, or mouse) and automatically download the appropriate driver. In Windows, this process is executed by the Windows Device Manager. Once the Device Manager has found and installed the appropriate program, the hardware should be ready to operate.

Parity bit

A byte is composed of eight bits, but there is an additional bit at the end that enables the contents of the byte to be verified. This additional data is known as a parity bit. Parity bits are classified as either even or odd, depending on whether the sum of the nine bits produces an even number or an odd number. Most computer users never have to think about parity bits, although occasionally a computer will announce a parity error and the computer will need to be repaired.

Mainframe and supercomputer

A mainframe computer is built to run a number of different programs simultaneously. In most cases, users access the mainframe through a dumb terminal, which is connected to the mainframe's processor but does not perform any processing tasks itself. A mainframe can make millions of calculations every second. Supercomputers, on the other hand, can process trillions of calculations every second. This is one reason why a basic mainframe costs about $5000 while a supercomputer can cost more than $1 million. Despite their speed, however, supercomputers are only used to run a small number of programs. Mainframes, on the other hand, usually run a larger range of applications.

Workstations, microcomputers, and microcontrollers

A workstation is a specialized computer built to perform a task like desktop publishing, software engineering, or computer-aided design and manufacturing (CAD/CAM). In most cases, a workstation can only accommodate one user at a time. Workstations are more unique than microcomputers, which are the personal computers most people have at home or at the office. Microcomputers are outfitted with basic programs and utilities, and generally cost between $500 and $5000. Sometimes, a group of microcomputers is joined together to create a local area network (LAN). Desktop computers, personal digital assistants, and laptop computers are all classified as microcomputers. A microcontroller, meanwhile, is a miniature computer chip embedded into a machine, like a car or an oven, to provide special functions.

Network servers

Network servers are centrally-located computers that host basic programs and files for all of the computers on a network. For instance, the network server for an office might contain a set of files that need to be available to all employees. Servers allow the computers in a network to share applications, utilities, and files. In addition to storing files and applications, servers can manage print functions, send and receive faxes, and manage web activities. All of the computers linked into the network are called clients. Clients are connected either through wireless connections or through a series of cables.

Laptop computer

Unlike a desktop computer, a laptop is meant to be portable, and so all of its necessary equipment needs to be contained within one housing. The typical laptop design includes a keyboard, speakers, an LCD display, a touchpad, and storage devices such as a hard drive and CD/DVD drive. Laptop computers do not contain their own printers, and must be connected via cable or wireless connection.

Principles of computer operation

The primary principle of computer function is to take digital data and convert it into information that can be understood by a person. Another general principle of computing is that in order to store large amounts of data, a computer must have an elegant method of compiling, organizing, and communicating. A computer typically has two storage areas: primary storage, also known as memory, is where the computer keeps data while it is in use; secondary storage is where the computer keeps data when it is not necessary. Finally, the third key principle of computing is that hardware and software are fundamentally different. Hardware is physical equipment, like speakers or a printer, which enhances a computer's function. Software, on the other hand, is the programs and applications installed on a computer.

Starting up, logging on, and shutting down

To start a computer, a user must first press the power buttons for the main computer and any related peripherals. The user must then enter a username and password and press ENTER. The system is ready to be operated when the desktop icons and cursor appear. The process for shutting down a computer, on the other hand, depends on the operating system. In Microsoft Windows, a Shut Down or Turn Off Computer command can be found in the bottom-left corner of the desktop. In Mac OS, there is a Shut Down command beneath the Apple icon in the top-left corner. In Linux, there is a power down command. Once a computer is turned off, the peripherals can be turned off as well.

Boot process

The boot process occurs after a computer is turned on but before the user has access to any files or programs. It is essentially the process through which the computer becomes ready for operation. During the boot process, the computer loads the operating system into its main memory. This task is accomplished by the computer's read-only memory (ROM), though the OS itself is loaded into random access memory (RAM). Essentially, a kernel of the operating system is placed in RAM, where it remains while the computer is on. Also, it is during the boot process that the computer runs diagnostic programs and identifies peripheral

devices. The basic input/output system (BIOS) programs in the computer are copied into main memory, and the operating system is configured.

Instructions and performance of microprocessors

Some of the instruction sets in a microprocessor are extremely complex and therefore require numerous clock cycles. Such instruction sets are operated through complex instruction set computer (CISC) technology. However, not all of the functions performed by the microprocessor are complex: there are also some simpler tasks performed through reduced instruction set computer (RISC) technology. These instruction sets take less time to perform, but do not accomplish as much as complex instruction sets.

Ways a processor can process instructions

A processor is said to be serial processing when one instruction must be entirely completed before the processor can move on to the next instruction. Pipelining, on the other hand, is when a processor can begin working on the next instruction before it has finished the prior instruction. In parallel processing, the processor can work on several instructions simultaneously. Due to their design, parallel processing and pipelining are faster than serial processing because it is not necessary to complete every instruction before advancing to the next.

Control structure

In computer programs, control structures are the sets of instructions that establish the order in which instructions are to be executed. The normal order in which a program proceeds is known as the sequential execution. When the computer program follows sequential execution, it is executing instructions in the same order as they were written. An algorithm is capable of rearranging the order of execution or omitting certain instructions entirely. In addition, some programming algorithms command the computer to repeat instructions indefinitely.

Sequence control structure and GOTO command

A sequence control structure rearranges the order in which a computer processor performs instructions. It issues a GOTO ("go to") command, which tells the processor to proceed to another place in the instruction sequence. The user first enters the GOTO command, and then enters the instruction that should be executed next. Once this sequence control structure has been entered, the computer skips over any intervening structures.

Selection control structure

The selection control structure, also known as the IF-THEN-ELSE structure, sets up a contingency plan for a computer program. It establishes that, if one thing is true, the computer should follow a given set of instructions but, if that thing is not true, the computer should follow a different set of instructions. In other words, the selection control structure sets a fork in the path of the program: depending on the status of the given variable, the program will select one of two paths. The presence of these control structures prevents the programmer from having to set up plans for every possible contingency.

Loop

A loop, or repetition control structure, commands a computer program to continue a certain operation until such time as a given condition is fulfilled. The loop, also known as the iteration, is the

section of code that repeats itself until the desired condition is fulfilled. Some of the common repetition control structure commands are DO...WHILE, FOR...NEXT, and DO...UNTIL. Once the condition set by the repetition control structure has been fulfilled, the computer will proceed to the next task. Sometimes, the termination of a loop is also the termination of the program.

Files

There are two basic kinds of files: data files and program files. Data files include spreadsheets, text documents, music files, and images. Program files include word processing programs, spreadsheet programs, games, and media players. A computer keeps track of files by placing them in hierarchies, with root directories, parent directories, and subdirectories, in descending order. Every file has a name so that it can be easily found and identified.

Task management

Multitasking
In computing, a task is a single operation. For instance, a task might be saving a file or printing a document. If more than one task is being completed at the same time on a computer with one central processor, the computer is multitasking. A computer is able to multitask because the operating system can command a processor to divide its time between multiple programs. A processor is not capable of running two programs simultaneously, but it can divide each program into small bits and alternate between them. To the user, it appears as if both programs are running at the same time, even though the processor is only running one set of instructions at a time.

Multiprogramming and time-sharing
When a computer is multiprogramming, it is running more than one program and is

- 14 -

being operated by more than one user. Multiprogramming is made possible by a process similar to that of multitasking: the computer does not actually run programs simultaneously, but instead alternates between programs and users. Computer experts often refer to this process as cycling. In time-sharing, a computer divides up its processing power between multiple users of different programs on the same computer network. The processor spends a fraction of a second on one user's program, and then moves on to the next user and program. This process is also known as time-slicing. Although the speed of each program will be somewhat diminished by time-sharing, users will not be aware of the processor's alternation.

Multiprocessing
When a computer has multiple central processing units working at the same time, it is said to be multiprocessing. Because of the multiple CPUs, multiprocessing is able to achieve speeds much greater than multitasking or time-sharing. Multiprocessing is accomplished either by parallel processing or co-processing. In a parallel processing arrangement, multiple processors share memory and collaborate on the same tasks. Computer systems with parallel processing are resilient and stable even when one processor fails. Co-processing, on the other hand, involves the delegation of tasks among several different processors.

Downloading and uploading

In downloading, data is shifted from a distant computer to one's own computer. For instance, an individual might download information that moves from a mainframe computer to a satellite liaison to his own computer. In general, downloading entails the transfer of data from a large system to a smaller system. Uploading, on the other hand, is the transfer of computer data from one's own computer to another computer. Typically, one uploads data to a mainframe or network server. Both uploading and downloading can be accomplished through a file transfer protocol (FTP) client or a webpage.

Data, information, and data representation

In computing, data is defined as symbols that represent pieces of information. Data and information are distinct from one another; information is data that has been converted into a form that is comprehensible to people. While computers operate according to data and instructions, humans require information. The data on a computer may be digital or analog. Humans understand analog data, such as light and sound waves, while computers understand and communicate through digital data, which is a series of ones and zeros. The language spoken by computer systems is known as binary code. The manner in which data is stored or displayed is called a data representation. Images, numbers, and text are some common representations of data. A computer is capable of storing sound, text, video, and images in binary code.

Binary system

Binary code consists entirely of ones and zeros. All of the complex and detailed information contained on a computer is understood by the system only as a series of those two numbers. The binary system is called a base-2 system because it only has two unique digits (a decimal system, on the other hand, has 10 unique digits and is therefore known as a base-10 system). So, instead of having place values of a base-10 system such as tens, hundreds, and thousands, binary code has place values like twos, fours, eights, and so on.

- 15 -

EBCDIC, ASCII and Unicode

EBCDIC is short for Extended Binary Coded Decimal Interchange Code. It is the binary code developed by IBM in the 1960s for use on mainframes, and represents characters as sequences of eight bits (i.e., one byte). ASCII is short for American Standard Code for Information Interchange. It is a binary code for microprocessors, and represents characters with seven bits. Extended ASCII uses eight bits to represent characters. Extended ASCII is capable of 256 characters, which is not enough for some languages. More complex languages may require Unicode, which was developed in the early 1990s and represents each character as a series of sixteen bits. In Unicode, there are 65,536 character possibilities.

Machine language

Every computer has a machine language, which is the binary system that instructs its basic processing functions. Machine language is the lowest-level computer language, meaning that it is the most dissimilar from English. For humans, then, machine language is the most foreign of the computer languages. However, machine language is also the fastest programming language, since it is the most easily understood by computers. Additionally, personal computers (PCs) have a machine language different from Macs, which is why the software written for one does not work on the other.

Digital data and analog data

Digital data consists entirely of ones and zeros, a system known as binary code. All of the information on a computer, including text, images, and sound, is stored on the hard drive as a series of ones and zeros. Analog data, on the other hand, can be expressed through many values besides one and zero. Analog data is typically expressed in wavelengths.

The visual data a human acquires from the external world, for instance, is made up of light waves with various lengths. Storing and representing this kind of data on a computer would be very difficult, which is why computers instead use the simple binary system.

Conversion of analog to digital in musical recordings

Digital music files are created with the use of an analog-to-digital converter, which translates sound waves into binary code. In other words, a converter translates analog data into digital data. When the music file is played on a computer, the digital data is converted back into analog waves. An electronic converter records tiny samples of the music and then arranges them in order, juxtaposed so closely together that the human ear cannot hear the gaps. In fact, a compact disc contains approximately 44,100 audio samples per second. A similar process is used in the conversion of photography and moving images from analog to digital and back.

Source code

The computer instructions that are comprehensible to people are known as source codes. In order to be comprehensible to a computer processor, on the other hand, source code must be converted into digital data. Source code is often quite similar to human language, which makes it easy for programmers to manipulate. There are two devices that translate source code into machine language (also known as object code): an interpreter and a compiler. An interpreter translates one statement at a time while a program is operating, whereas a compiler translates a group of program statements simultaneously. This process must occur before any programs can run. Machine code is the name for the set of instructions used by the microprocessor. It is composed of

- 16 -

operation codes, which themselves are composed of command words and operands indicating the location of the data required for each particular operation.

Digital representation of words and letters

On a computer, all information is represented digitally as a series of ones and zeros. This includes all of the information used in arithmetic operations, as well as letters, symbols, and numerals. These latter three types of information are known collectively as character data. Though appearing complicated to the human eye, binary code is the easiest way for a computer to store and communicate data. Computers use several different styles of code for character data, including ASCII (American Standard Code for Information Interchange), which represents each character as a seven-bit sequence; Extended ASCII, which represents every character as an eight-bit sequence; EBCDIC (Extended Binary-Coded Decimal Interchange), used formerly by IBM mainframes; and Unicode, which represents every character as a sixteen-bit sequence.

ASCII and Extended ASCII
ASCII and Extended ASCII are used to represent the numerals zero through nine because these numerals are often required for reasons other than arithmetic. For instance, a computer might need to display a telephone number as a seven-digit sequence. In ASCII, each digit in the phone number would be represented in a seven-bit sequence, while in Extended ASCII each digit would be represented by an eight-bit sequence. The digits in a phone number are never added or subtracted, though they are identical to the numbers used for these functions. For this reason, binary

codes need to be able to represent numerals for non-arithmetic purposes.

Word size

In computing, word size is the number of bits that a system can process. When there are more bits in a word, the computer is processing more bits per word and is therefore faster. A 64-bit-word computer, for instance, is processing data eight bytes at a time, with each byte containing eight bits. The 64-bit-word has become the standard for modern computers. The size of the word is also affected by the size and circuit capacity of the registers in the arithmetic logic unit.

System clock

The system clock is a device that controls the speed of computing operations. It is located inside the microprocessor of a computer. The system clock is regulated by quartz crystal vibrations, which create digital pulsations that are sent to the central processing unit. These pulsations, also known as ticks or cycles, set the speed at which data will be processed. When the microprocessor works quickly, computer applications work quickly. The speed of the system clock is measured in hertz.

Speeds measured in megahertz and gigahertz

In the past, the frequencies of microprocessors were measured in megahertz (MHz), or millions of system clock cycles per second. Modern processors, however, are capable of speeds in gigahertz (GHz), or billions of system clock cycles per second. For instance, the Intel Pentium EE 840 dual core, released in 2006, has been measured at 3.2 GHz for each core with a total of 230 million transistors. When a speed is listed as a certain number of gigahertz, it means there are so many billion cycles per second of the microprocessor's system clock. Some computer instructions take many system clock cycles.

MIPS, FLOPS, and fractions of a second

The speed of larger computers, like mainframes and workstations, is measured in millions of instructions per second (MIPS) rather than in hertz. The speed of supercomputers is measured in floating-point operations per second, or FLOPS. A megaFLOP (MFLOP) is a million floating-point operations per second, a gigaFLOP is billions, and a teraFLOP is trillions. The cycle of time for a computer processor is always a fraction of a second. For instance, the processing speed of a microcomputer is measured in microseconds, and the speed of a supercomputer is measured in nanoseconds, which are even smaller than microseconds. The processing speeds of some supercomputers are measured in picoseconds, which are even shorter than nanoseconds.

Expression of RAM speed

RAM speed is typically measured in nanoseconds, which is billionths of a second, or in megahertz, which is millions of cycles per second. The lower the nanosecond rating, the better, since it is a measure of the time it takes the circuitry to handle a piece of data. For instance, 5ns RAM is faster than 10ns RAM. The opposite is true for speeds measured in megahertz, where the higher the number, the faster the operation. For instance, a RAM speed of 400 MHz is faster than a RAM speed of 300 MHz.

Overclocking

Overclocking is a system for accelerating the system clock of a central processing unit. In some cases, the system clock lags behind the speed of some other component in the computer, which creates delays in function. For instance, many video games require overclocking to power sophisticated graphics. One danger of overclocking is that it requires more electricity and therefore generates a great deal of heat. Computers that engage in overclocking should be fitted with extra fans or refrigerants in order to avoid fire or heat damage.

Accelerating data transfer between memory and the CPU

When a CPU alternates between several memory banks, it is said to be interleaving. Servers, workstations, and mainframes engage in interleaving so that data can be processed almost continuously. Another process that streamlines CPU operation is called bursting: this is when the central processing unit anticipates the data that will be needed and withdraws it in advance, thus reducing processing time. Pipelining, meanwhile, is the process of subdividing tasks and performing them piecemeal or simultaneously. Minicomputers have superscalar architecture, which allows the computer to perform multiple instructions in one clock cycle, a process known as hyper-threading. In hyper-threading, the computer alternates between instruction threads almost every nanosecond.

Modem speed

The device that transmits data between computers over telephone or computer cable is called a modem, short for modulator-demodulator. There are both internal and external modems, although it is much more common for modern modems to be located on the inside of a computer. The speed of a modem is measured in bits per second (bps). Old modems transmitted data at around 28,800 bps, but modern modems are capable of reaching speeds of 56 kilobits per second, or Kbps. Modem speeds can also be expressed as millions of bits per second, Mbps, or billions of bits per second, Gbps.

System software

The system software of a computer includes the operating system, utility programs, and device drivers. The fundamental operations of a computer are controlled by the operating system, or OS. The OS manages the basic controls of the computer so that the user can focus on more specific applications. The computer's hardware is also managed by the operating system according to instructions provided by device drivers, which are typically installed on the computer before purchase. Finally, utility programs expand or augment the other programs installed on the computer.

System software components

System software, which enables the operation of a computer, consists of the operating system, device drivers, utility programs, and language translators. The operating system is the most fundamental component of the computer system. The device drivers manage the operation of peripheral devices like the mouse and the printer. Utility programs, like malware protection and file compressors, perform specific functions to support general operations of the computer. Finally, language translators convert higher-level information, like text and numbers, into the strings of binary code comprehensible to computers. There are three types of language translator: interpreters, assemblers, and compilers.

Operating system

Functions
Operating systems multitask so that computer users can perform several tasks

at the same time. The operating system is responsible for processing and storing data, interfacing with the user, and sending information to peripheral devices (e.g., printers or scanners). Most operating systems allow for multithreading, meaning that more than one stream of code can process at the same time. Operating systems also feed information to a computer's microprocessor. Because some computers have more than one processor, a suitable operating system must be able to allocate the pertinent tasks for greater efficiency.

Systems for various tasks
There are different operating systems for different computing tasks. For instance, single-user operating systems (e.g., DOS) can only receive input from one user at a time. Modern operating systems tend to be multi-user, meaning that they can be accessed and used by several different people or programs at the same time. Multi-user operating systems, like IBM's OS/390, are used in mainframe computers. Using network OS programs like Novell NetWare, multiple users can share information, programs, and peripheral device access. Whereas a multi-user operating system processes information from a central computer, a network operating system parcels out information to individual computers which use their desktop operating systems (e.g., Windows) to process the information.

Security improvement
Operating systems primarily mediate communication between the user and the computer, but it is also essential that they have a method for guaranteeing the security of the information that is sent. For instance, most operating systems have at least a rudimentary password protection program. In order to gain access to the computer, the user must provide a recognized name and password.

- 19 -

Otherwise, the user will be barred from accessing the information on the hard drive or using the programs installed on the computer.

Common operating systems

The most common operating system at present is Microsoft Windows, a PC operating system for which there are several editions: Windows XP, Windows Vista, Windows 7, and Windows Server. Apple computers run one of the MAC OS editions. In the past decade, a number of open-source operating systems have emerged as viable alternatives to Windows. The most popular of these alternatives is Linux, which is currently available in a number of permutations.

Interaction with user

The most common medium for interaction between user and operating system is the "desktop" model, in which the various programs available on the computer are represented by pictograms on the monitor screen called icons. The user can decide which programs and files should be accessible from the desktop, and can move files around with programs like Windows Explorer. This and other programs feature extensive help menus to guide novice users. Users have almost complete control over the appearance and configuration of the desktop, from which they can also configure peripherals and hardware.

Handheld operating systems

Personal digital assistants and other handheld devices run off an embedded operating system housed on a single microchip. These operating systems require a CPU chip, but they do not operate like personal computers or laptops. The most popular operating system for handheld devices is Palm OS by Palm, Inc. Some newer devices feature Microsoft Pocket PC or Windows Mobile, sometimes called Windows CE .NET.

These handheld Microsoft programs have many of the same features as Windows has on desktops and laptops. Handheld devices that formerly used EPOC OS now use Symbian OS. In 2009, Symbian was the world's largest producer of smartphone software. Nokia and Ericsson smartphones both feature Symbian operating systems with both multitasking and multithreading capabilities.

Microsoft Windows

Microsoft Windows is the most popular operating system in the world; it is used on 80% of all computers. At first, Windows was called an operating "environment" because it required another operating system, DOS, in order to comprise a functional whole. The first version of Windows was called Windows 1.0 and was released in 1985. The program derives its name from the four-sided planes that appear on screen and within which the user can complete tasks. Windows did not become the dominant operating system until the release of Windows 3.1 in the late 1990s. Subsequently, Microsoft has successfully released the new editions Windows 95, Windows 98, Windows XP (released in 2001), and Windows Vista (2006). The most recent version, Windows 7, was released in 2009.

Strengths

The success of Windows is somewhat self-perpetuating: because it is the most popular operating system, more programs are written for it, thus making it more essential and useful. At the same time, the popularity of Windows has created a large community of users making suggestions and answering questions for one another. Furthermore, the Microsoft website is full of useful information for users and is continuously updated. Windows is also capable of running many different hardware

- 20 -

programs for desktops, notebooks, and mobile devices. Finally, Windows has plug and play capability, meaning that it is able to use a variety of peripherals quickly and easily.

Weaknesses

The factors that make Windows so popular also create some problems. For instance, Windows is considered less secure than other operating systems because so many viruses are written for it. At the same time, the reliability of Windows is low relative to other operating systems. This means that Windows cannot run for a long period without developing glitches. Some of these minor problems can be solved with a simple reboot, but this process can be time-consuming. Over time, Windows tends to slow down and lose the use of certain programs.

Mac OS

The Macintosh Operating System, commonly known as Mac OS, is to Apple computers what Windows is to personal computers. Indeed, Mac OS predates Windows, and also features a graphical user interface (GUI) with icons. Like Windows, Mac OS was based on the GUI of Xerox PARC. Like with Windows, Mac OS users can open several different programs at the same time. Both Windows and Mac OS enable the user to move an arrow around the screen and use it to activate different programs and files. The Mac OS can be differentiated from Windows by the Apple logo in the upper-right corner of the main desktop. Windows has its distinct logo in the bottom-left corner.

The first version of Mac OS, known as Classic Mac OS, was designed to be compatible with the Motorola 68000 microprocessor. This 1984 operating system had a generic user interface as well as the icons and menus that would become standard in later versions. In 1988, the ability to multitask was introduced in the System 6 operating system, and in 1991 the OS acquired virtual memory and file-sharing capabilities. System 7/Mac OS introduced the video program QuickTime. Mac OS 8, released in 1997, was the first to include a colorized interface. Mac OS 9, released in 1999, featured the Internet search tool Sherlock. In 2001, Apple released an all-new version of the Classic Mac OS, called Mac OS X, which was to be run on Macs outfitted with the Power PC chip from IBM. When Macs made the switch to Intel processors in 2006, Apple released Mac OS X version 10.4, also known as Mac OS X Tiger.

Strengths

Mac OS is known for being safe and easy to use, even for novice users. While PC still used a command-line OS, the Mac OS had a point-and-click interface. The Mac OS also has a data-security capability based on UNIX and is known to be extremely secure. One benefit of the Mac OS being less common than Windows is that fewer computer viruses and malicious software (malware) codes are written for it. The Mac OS X has backward compatibility, meaning newer versions have no trouble accessing the files and programs created for past editions of the OS. The newest versions of Mac OS also have dual-boot programs (e.g., Boot Camp) that allow the user to work alternately through Windows XP and Mac OS X. Finally, the Mac OS X is an adept virtual machine platform, meaning that one computer is able to run the hardware and software found on another system.

Weaknesses

Because there are fewer Mac OS users, there are fewer programs written for the system. The forked nature of files on Mac OS can also cause problems when converting to other machines. Mac OS files have two components, a data section containing the bulk of the program, and a resource section containing a summary of the information in the data section. In order to successfully transfer the information in a Mac OS file to another operating system such as Windows, the user needs to have some method of bundling the data and resource forks.

Linux

Differences from UNIX

UNIX and Linux are both operating systems, but they are not the same. UNIX was developed by AT&T's Bell Labs in 1969, while Linux was created by Linus Torvalds in 1991. Torvalds based his OS on MINUX, a derivative of UNIX created by Andrew Tanenbaum. Both UNIX and Linux are considered dependable in multi-user environments, though neither has achieved near the popularity of Mac OS or Windows. Whereas UNIX is owned by the Open Group, Linux is an open-source program that is continuously being modified by volunteer programmers.

Strengths

The distribution of Linux and its source code occurs under a General Public License, meaning that users can make copies and even sell them. The idea behind this licensing arrangement is to encourage users to develop software and spread the program through their communities. The Linux OS is primarily used on personal computers, although it is sometimes used on web servers and LAN servers. Like UNIX, Linux allows multitasking, TCP/IP drivers, multi-user capability, and virtual memory. Linux users have their choice of several generic user interfaces.

Weaknesses

Linux is a collaborative venture, and so it often lacks the organization of Windows or Mac OS. Unless the user has a good working knowledge of computers, he or she may have difficulty running basic programs. Most of the software developed for Linux is related to business and technical purposes rather than general computing tasks. There are very few games designed for the Linux OS. There are also only a few online distributors of Linux packages, which comprise the so-called Linux kernel and the necessary programs for installation.

Community influence

Linux was developed on an open-source model, meaning that it was the result of collaboration by volunteer programmers. Any changes made to the program are kept in the public domain and subject to informal approval by the community. This collaborative spirit has made Linux appealing to many people, including Chinese leaders, who announced in 2000 that Linux would become the standard OS of the nation. In part, this was an effort to avoid domination by Microsoft. In the United States, companies like Red Hat have given Linux packages away as a way to attract attention to their own software products. Also, because Linux was originally developed online, it is actually more reliable for Internet programs than Windows is. Finally, any bugs within the program tend to be fixed very quickly by its community of programmers.

Common network operating systems

Perhaps the most common network operating system is Novell NetWare, which is designed to manage the local area networks (LANs) through which multiple personal computers can share files and programs. Many businesses use Windows 2000 to allow multitasking, including multi-user Internet access, on an office network. The UNIX operating system can be used by computer networks as well. Two popular versions of UNIX are Solaris by Sun Microsystems, which is used by large businesses and online vendors, and BSD, which is given away by the Open Group that owns UNIX. Linux is another network-ready operating system.

Utility programs

Utility programs, also known as service programs, manage the resources of a computer. Some of the most common utility programs recover deleted files, diagnose system problems, configure the operating system, and compress bulky files. Many utility programs are installed before a computer is sold, while others are purchased and installed later by the owner. The most common type of utility program purchased by computer owners is anti-virus software, which must be updated continuously to stay abreast of new viruses and malware. In Windows, the available utilities can be accessed through the Start menu or Control Panel.

The most common sort of utility program downloaded and installed by computer users is the antivirus program. The most popular antivirus programs are AVG, McAfee VirusScan, and Norton AntiVirus. Many computer users also install file-encryption software, like PGP, and privacy software, like 12Ghosts Wash. Net Nanny and other programs filter adult content from the Internet, while Acrobat Reader converts documents into formats that can be easily printed and shared. Other popular utility programs compress data, defragment hard drives, accelerate memory, set up firewalls, filter spam, and block pop-up advertising.

Virus prevention

A computer user should always scan new documents and programs for viruses. Basic virus-scanning programs can be obtained easily, but they need to be updated continuously in order to remain effective against attacks. Another common source of viruses is email attachments, so these should also be scanned before being opened. Computers should also be equipped with a firewall to prevent takeover attempts by hackers. Finally, though this scenario is less common today, users should never start their computers with a foreign disk or CD in the drive.

DBMS utilities

Database management system (DBMS) utilities enable a user to organize records and files in a database. These utility programs keep a record of the files placed in the database and give the user a method for organizing them. In addition, DBMS utilities limit access to the database, sometimes requiring a password to view the data. A DBMS utility prevents the user from storing the same information repeatedly and from misplacing important data. The program is also set up so that any changes to the database must be approved by the user, and so that the computer will routinely create a back-up copy of the database automatically.

Applications and utilities for the Windows operating system

Windows typically includes Internet Explorer, which is a popular program for accessing the Internet. The user can find files and programs on the computer with the aid of Windows Explorer, and can use WordPad to perform simple word processing tasks. Every edition of Windows also contains a basic calculator, and most include Windows Media Player, a simple program for accessing music, video, and images. Newer editions of Windows contain a Security Center, which maintains a firewall, antivirus scanner, and malware guard. Finally, Windows features a Backup utility that enables the user to create safe copies of important files and programs.

Advantages of third-party utilities

In some cases, the utilities installed on an operating system are inferior and should be replaced by third-party utilities. In particular, antivirus programs developed and maintained by third-party vendors like McAfee and Symantec are preferred by computer users. Symantec's Norton SystemWorks maintains computer security, while McAfee's Security Suite guards against malware and harmful viruses. Both programs predate the Security Center on Windows and are generally thought to provide better security. Another utility which many users obtain from third parties is file compression; in particular, WinZip and QuickZip have earned the praise of experts.

Service packs and patches

A service pack, also known as a service release, is a compilation of security and repair files for a computer. Patches, also known as hotfixes, are small-scale adjustments to recently released service packs. Patches are meant to fill the gaps in security between major pack releases. Service packs include all of the previous patches and packs that are still relevant to computer security. One recent example of this system is Service Pack 2 (SP2), released by Microsoft in 2004 to enhance the ability of the Windows operating system to respond to attacks on the Internet Explorer program. SP2 has subsequently been modified by a number of patches.

Interfaces

In order for a person to properly use and communicate with a computer, the computer must have an interface. An interface is a method of translating human actions and text into computer actions. All electronic devices have interfaces, like switches, dials, buttons, or control panels. On a computer, the most common interface is the "desktop" of Microsoft Windows. The relationship between machine and user is known as human-computer interaction, or HCI. Many engineers and scientists spend their entire careers trying to improve human-computer interaction.

User interfaces

On a computer, the user interface is the appearance of the display screen with which a person can access and operate specific programs. A typical user interface is the "desktop" on which icons represent applications or files. The user can access these applications or files by clicking on them with a cursor. Generally, the screen, keyboard, and mouse can be defined as the necessary parts of the interface, although the hardware and software of the computer is also necessary. Some stripped-down computers have command-line interfaces, in which the user must input direct commands. However, it is more common on modern computers to see a graphical user interface (GUI) in which actions that can be taken by the computer are represented on screen as pictures.

Keyboard as the user interface

The keyboard is one of the basic components of the user interface. It has keys for both executing commands and entering data. One of the special-purpose keys on the keyboard is the Escape key (represented on most keyboard with the letters ESC), which exits open programs and terminates whatever action the user is performing. The general function of the Escape key and other function keys remains the same on different programs, so users should be able to navigate through all sorts of situations once they have acquired a basic understanding of the function keys. Some of the other important function keys on a standard

- 24 -

keyboard are the Control, Page Up, Page Down, and Delete keys.

Graphical user interface

Most computers have a graphical user interface, or GUI, which enables the user to select programs and files with the mouse or keyboard. Microsoft Windows is a classic example of a graphical user interface, since it contains rollovers, menus, icons, and a desktop. A rollover is a short label that appears when the cursor moves over an icon on the screen. An icon is a small picture that represents a file or program. A menu is a list of available functions within a specific program. In many cases, a menu will include directions for how to perform the various functions. The desktop is the two-dimensional surface on which the icons and menus are displayed.

Windows XP
In the most recent versions of Windows, the Start button is located in the bottom-left corner of the desktop. When the Start button is pressed, a menu containing programs, files, and control panel options is displayed. Windows also includes a Recycle Bin, where the user can place unwanted files and programs. In order to remove items entirely, the user must place them in the Recycle Bin and then empty the bin. The user's documents are typically stored in a folder labeled My Documents. Windows also has a special email utility, known as Outlook, displayed on the desktop. In addition, the Windows GUI includes information about the network browser and basic control toggles. The bottom of the Windows GUI is a taskbar displaying all of the open programs, as well as a calendar and a clock.

Menus and dialog boxes

One of the user-friendly aspects of the modern graphical user interface is the menu system, in which various options and commands are listed below a series of headings. For instance, a user might open the Windows menu for "recent items," and thus be shown a list of the most recent files to be accessed. The menu system limits the options available to the user, and organizes the files and applications on the computer. Some selections will generate sub-menus with additional choices. In other cases, a selection will open a dialog box indicating the results of certain choices and the possibilities open to the user. A dialog box often opens when the user needs to make a decision before proceeding with a selected action. For instance, when a user closes a program, a dialog box may open reminding the user to save his or her work.

Desktop widgets

A desktop widget is a small computer program that can be easily accessed and operated by the user. Some common widgets are calculators, clocks, calendars, music players, and notepads. Typically, widgets automatically load into the desktop during startup, and remain available until the computer is shut down. These small programs usually take up space along the right border of the desktop. Widgets are an opportunity for users to personalize their computers' operating systems.

Command-line interfaces

Before the graphical user interface became popular, most computers featured a command-line interface, or CLI. Instead of using the mouse, the CLI user typed commands directly into a text window. The commands had to be typed perfectly or else the command would not be understood by the computer. In addition, executing a command required the user to know where each program was located; if a command was initiated in the wrong folder, it would not be executed properly. With modern computers, the introduction of a picture-based interface with menus of available options has greatly simplified the process of using a computer.

Database user interface

A database user interface should be arranged with the most commonly used fields in the most prominent positions. In most scenarios, the most prominent location is the top-left corner of the window. The user should be directed to the appropriate place to enter data through techniques like shading and colored boxes. The type and organization of fields and boxes should be the same for all set-ups to prevent user confusion. The user should be able to cycle the cursor through fields by using the Tab button. When there is too much information to fit on one screen, there should be an efficient way to move between several screens. In addition, users should be able to skip between records quickly. Finally, there should be a clear and well-organized set of instructions to help the novice user.

Windows desktop screen

In Windows Vista and Windows XP, the Start button is located in the bottom-left corner, and is represented by the Windows logo. Activating the Start button grants access to recent files, control panel programs, and other utilities. The Windows desktop is covered by columns of icons, which represent programs and files. Along the bottom of the screen, the Taskbar lists open programs as well as a calendar, clock, and speaker volume control. The Taskbar also contains a Quick Start Bar with shortcuts to commonly-used programs. Whenever the computer is engaged in a pertinent process, like a program download or virus scan, the time

remaining in the process is indicated in the notification area of the Taskbar.

Mac OS X desktop features

In Mac OS X, a basic menu can be accessed by clicking on the Apple icon in the top-right corner of the screen. This menu enables the user to access common programs and shut the computer down. Along the top of the screen is a Menu Bar that varies in content depending on the open programs. Like in Windows, the Desktop of Mac OS X is covered with rows of icons representing files and programs. The bottom of the screen features a dock with icons for common programs. This dock contains shortcuts to commonly-used programs similar to the Quick Start Bar in Windows.

Software suites

A software suite is a collection of several different applications sold together in a bundle. It is typical for the programs included in a software suite to have a similar theme; for instance, the programs in the Microsoft Office suite (including a word processor, an email manager, and a database creator) are commonly used in business environments. The Adobe Creative Suite and CorelDraw Graphics Suite both combine a number of useful image creation programs, including applications for drawing, painting, and three-dimensional design. A software suite usually costs less than the combined cost of the individual programs because the software manufacturer wants to encourage consumers to obtain all of their programs. The various programs in a software suite also typically have a similar interface and menu structure. Finally, software manufacturers try to make it easy for users to transfer data between the programs in a suite.

System requirements listed on software

The packaging for a software program lists the system requirements, which are the minimum specifications a computer must have in order to run the software effectively. For instance, software requires a sufficiently fast processor and a sufficiently large hard drive to operate. Also, software programs will only run on certain operating systems, and may require specific peripherals. Other system requirements commonly indicated on software packaging include network connection (e.g., Ethernet, DSL, LAN) and network protocol (e.g., TCP/IP).

Categories of application software

Application software is divided into five categories. Commercial software can be purchased on the open market. It is protected by copyright and cannot be used, copied, or distributed without a manufacturer's license. Public domain software, on the other hand, is not protected by copyright, so anyone may copy and distribute it. Shareware occupies a middle ground between commercial software and public domain software: it can be tried for free for a limited time, after which it must be purchased. Freeware is protected by copyright, but is also free; it is usually offered as a method of attracting customers for other products. Finally, rentalware is protected by copyright, but it does not have to be purchased. Rather, it can be leased for temporary use.

Commercial software

Commercial software, otherwise known as proprietary or packaged software, is available for sale on the open market. Among the most common types of commercial software are office suites, like Microsoft Office, or graphics programs, like CorelDraw. There are also popular commercial software programs for tax preparation and foreign language acquisition, among other things. Games and music creation applications are both considered commercial software. In the past, commercial software had to be bought in a store and installed on a computer with CDs or floppy disks, although most modern commercial software is available for download from the Internet.

Productivity software

Productivity software is a set of application programs that improve efficiency and quality in the workplace. Applications for spreadsheets, databases, visual presentations, and word processing are all considered productivity software. Perhaps the most well-known set of productivity software is the Microsoft Office suite. All of the programs in this suite have a similar interface, making it easy for the user to navigate between them. Also, it is easy to transfer data between applications in this and other productivity software suites.

Groupware

Groupware is a relatively new form of software which enables multiple users to collaborate on a project from different clients on a local network or across the Internet. Groupware programs like Lotus Notes and Microsoft Exchange provide both an email and document-sharing service so that all of the members of the project team can access and alter the important documents. In addition, the members of the team can cooperate to create a schedule for future work. Another recent version of groupware is the Virtual Learning Environment, in which the students of a particular class gather to exchange notes and ideas. Groupware in which users collaborate in real time are called synchronous, while programs in which users do not are called asynchronous.

Abandonware, pirated software, and custom software

Abandonware programs are still protected by copyright but no longer sold or supported technically. Software copyrights remain valid and enforceable for 95 years after the original publication. Pirated software is any software that is illegally obtained. Software manufacturers try to prevent their products from being pirated, often by requiring registration before the program can be used. Finally, custom software is developed to meet the specific needs of a user. For instance, many bookstores have custom software programs to manage inventory and sales.

Software tutorials and documentation

Software is commonly accompanied by tutorials, which may take the form of a book or manual providing instructions for use of the program. Documentation, on the other hand, is the entire set of written information packaged with a software program. Software documentation may include technical specifications, instructions, and system requirements. With modern software, it is common for both tutorials and documentation to be available on the Internet. This trend reduces paper consumption and makes it possible for the manufacturer to update materials as necessary. Also, web-based tutorials and documentation can be organized in a more user-friendly manner, allowing users to jump directly to pertinent sections of interest.

Data files

In computing, a file is generally defined as a set of data. There are three types of data files: document files, database files, and worksheet files. Document files, which include essays, letters, and lists, are created in word processing programs like Microsoft Word. Database files compile and analyze information; Microsoft Access is a common database management program. Finally, worksheet files are used to organize and calculate large tables of data. Worksheet files are generated in spreadsheet programs, the most popular of which is Microsoft Excel.

Importing and exporting files

When a file is imported, it is converted from an external file format and location into a format appropriate to the user's task. For instance, a user might import a database to a word processing program, in which case the representation of the data may need to be slightly adjusted. Most office suites enable the user to import files with minimal changes. When a file is exported, on the other hand, it requires format conversion before the file is sent by the user to another computer. In other words, imported files are converted by the receiving computer, while exported files are converted by the sending computer.

Application software and system software

Application software performs a specific task, like establishing a database or compressing a file. In order to function, application software must be configured for the user's operating system. In the past, it was typical to acquire application software as a set of floppy disks or CDs. However, most modern application software is downloaded and installed from the Internet. System software, on the other hand, is the fundamental set of programs that enable the computer to operate. The operating system (as for instance Mac OS X or Microsoft Windows) is the most basic piece of system software. Because it is so essential,

- 28 -

system software is typically installed on a computer's hard drive before it is sold.

Word processing software

Word processing software is designed for writing, composing, and editing printable material. The development of word processing software was a major upgrade from the typewriter because it enabled writers to manipulate text and correct errors without retyping. In modern word processing programs, users can create tables, insert pictures, adjust formatting, and check spelling. The user can also store multiple versions of a document. The most popular word processing program is Microsoft Word, although Corel WordPerfect and StarOffice 7 by Sun Microsystems are also well known.

DTP and web authoring software

Desktop publishing (DTP) software is similar to word processing software, with the enhanced ability to add graphics to text documents. Most DTP software enables the insertion of scanned images and documents. The most popular desktop publishing programs are Adobe InDesign and QuarkXpress. These programs are used to create books, newsletters, pamphlets, and magazines. Web authoring software, meanwhile, enables the creation of web pages for professional and personal use. The best known web authoring software package is Adobe Dreamweaver. Web authoring software allows novice users to create web pages; in the past, users needed to know the programming language HTML in order to create web pages.

Most desktop publishing (DTP) programs allow the insertion of text and graphics. The user can adjust the size of the graphics to fit into the document cleanly. The borders and page formatting can also be adjusted to the user's preference. In addition, DTP software enables the user to combine documents from different programs. For example, a DTP user could combine text from Microsoft Word with a spreadsheet from Excel and images from CorelDraw. Most desktop publishing software also has templates for creating common documents like newsletters and magazines.

Word processing document

The top of a word processing document usually has a title bar indicating the name of the file. Underneath the title, a menu bar displays the various functions available to the user. This menu bar includes the lists of formatting, review, view, and file management functions. There are several different views available to the user: print layout view shows how the document will look if printed, web layout view shows how the document will look as a webpage, full screen reading view shows how the document will look as two pages of an open book, draft view shows the document in a way that makes it easy to edit, and outline view initiates the set of outline tools.

Formatting options
In a document, the paragraph style is the arrangement of the margins and the space between the lines of text. The horizontal position of the text is known as the alignment. A document can be aligned along the left margin, along the right margin, in the center of the document, or justified equally along both the right and left margins. Full justification is considered the most formal alignment, and is used in newspapers and magazines. For line spacing, the common choices are single-spacing, in which there is no room between horizontal lines, and double-spacing, in which below each horizontal line there is an equivalent amount of blank space. In addition to alignment and line spacing, a user can adjust the size and style of the font.

Exporting documents

Documents can be exported from a word processing program in a number of ways. For instance, the user can print the entire document or specific parts of the document. The user can also fax or email the document. It is possible to send the document as a lone email or to attach it to another email; recipients of the attachment will be given the option whether to open it or not. In order to open a word processing document as an attachment, the recipient will need to have a compatible word processing program on his or her computer.

Saving and tracking changes

There are a number of ways to save a document. The most common way is to create a copy on the computer's hard drive. Another way to save a document is to make a copy on a CD, floppy disk, or external hard drive. Sometimes, a user or group of users wants to keep a record of the changes made to a document, in which case the Track Changes feature is useful. When this feature is activated, every change made to the document is recorded. Moreover, the changes made by different people can be indicated by different colors. The various contributors can add comments to the document, and they can print out versions of the document with or without the proposed changes.

Template, wizards, and posting online

Modern word processing programs are fully capable of creating web-ready documents. They can convert documents into the Internet-compatible HTML format, denoted either as .htm or .html. Most word processing programs come with templates representing common document types. In these templates, the layout and font style will be pre-selected. Also, many word processing programs contain utility wizards that lead the user through document creation step by step so that the user can personalize a common document type.

Word processing editing capabilities

Word processing software has a number of text-editing features that allow users to manipulate documents in many useful ways. For instance, using the Insert key allows the user to type over unwanted text; if the Insert button is not in use, new text will push existing text to the side. The Delete button removes the text directly to the right of the cursor. The Backspace key erases the text to the left of the cursor. Sections of text can be cut and placed on the clipboard by using the Cut command. This text can then be reinserted into the document by using the Paste command. Text can also be copied by using the Copy command.

Text and program editors

A text editor is a simple word processor used to make changes to text. The most familiar text editor to many computer users is Microsoft Word. Computer programs are written on a program editor, which is very similar to a text editor. Program editors can be obtained from commercial publishers or downloaded as freeware or shareware from the Internet. Many sophisticated program editors include tools like search-and-replace and colorization.

Features affecting text entry

The cursor, the scrolling function, and word wrap capability can all affect the entry of text into a word processor. The cursor, usually represented as a vertical line, indicates where type is being entered. As a word is typed, the cursor moves one place to the right with each successive letter. The cursor can be moved with the mouse, the arrow keys, and the space bar. The scrolling function is the ability to shift the view of an open document up, down, right, or left. The arrow keys, Page Up and Page Down buttons, and mouse can all scroll. Finally, word wrap is the capacity of word processing programs to move to the next line whenever the current line is full. On a typewriter, the user would have to press Return in order to move to the beginning of the next line; word processing programs perform this function automatically.

Document production software

One of the common features performed by document production software is a mail merge, in which a form letter can be customized and addressed to each member of a mailing list. In other words, a standard letter is created, and then the address is changed on each successive copy, making distribution of the letter very easy. Document production software can also be very useful in the creation of labels; for instance, an address list can be integrated with a label style to produce a series of custom labels. A document production program can add a table of contents or set of footnotes to a document, and can also create cover sheets and faxes. Finally, these programs can export documents to the Internet quickly.

Spreadsheets

A spreadsheet is a document that is divided into a grid of rows and columns. Within this grid, the user can enter data, letters, numbers, and formulas. These documents can be used to organize all of the information related to a specific subject. Spreadsheets are most commonly used to provide a quick look at financial numbers, although they can also be used to display information. The data entered into a spreadsheet grid can also be taken by the program and turned into graphs, tables, and charts. The

information visible on the screen is called a worksheet.

Spreadsheet software
Spreadsheet software, of which the most common example is Microsoft Excel, has become ubiquitous in business and personal computing. Users are able to produce graphs and tables from the information in the spreadsheet, and can incorporate colors to provide contrast. Large spreadsheets can be searched for particular records, and the user can print out an entire spreadsheet or only one section of it. Users are sometimes able to forecast hypothetical situations by applying formulas to spreadsheet data. For instance, a financial advisor can determine the effect of a proposed investment decision on a client's portfolio. For this reason, spreadsheet software is especially popular in business and financial environments.

Organization
The visible portion of a spreadsheet, known as the worksheet, is divided into vertical columns and horizontal rows. The column headings, which describe the contents of each column, span the top of the document. The columns are usually designated by capital letters: A, B, C, etc. The row headings, on the other hand, descend along the left side of the document. Rows are represented by numbers: 1, 2, 3, etc. The squares that form the intersection of individual rows and columns are called cells. A cell is designated with the letter of the column followed by the number of the row: A4, D3, or E7, for example. The numbers placed into a spreadsheet cell are called values. A group of cells adjacent to one another, as for instance cells B2 through B6, is known as a range.

Automatic recalculation and relative and absolute references
When a user applies formulas to the data in a worksheet, a change in one value will

affect the results of the calculation. This function is known as automatic recalculation. A reference made to a precise cell is known as an absolute reference. So, a formula might include an absolute reference to cell B2 because it always wants to use the data contained in that exact cell. In other cases, a formula will require a relative reference, meaning that the cell is described in relation to another cell of the formula. For instance, a spreadsheet formula might require all of the values in column 2 to be added to the values directly adjacent to column 4.

Formulas, functions, recalculations, and what-if analysis

Formulas are the mathematical calculations performed in a worksheet's cell. Most formula references are initiated by an equal sign, which instructs the program to perform a calculation rather than display typed values. Functions are simple formulas that are used so often that they are pre-programmed into the spreadsheet software. An example is the calculation of a simple average. Recalculation is the automatic tabulation of values several different times. The ability to automatically recalculate values is one of the major advantages offered by spreadsheet software. What-if analysis is an operation of spreadsheet software in which the user can generate calculations based on hypothetical scenarios
.

Analytical graphs

Analytical graphs, also known as business graphs, are pictures that make data easier to observe and compare. Analytical graphs include bar graphs, line graphs, pie charts, and other pictorial representations of data. Microsoft Excel contains a set of graphic templates that can generate ready-made graphs based on data entered by the user. Newer programs are even capable of generating three-dimensional graphs.

Templates

Most modern spreadsheet software packages contain a set of basic templates. For instance, spreadsheet programs often include a template for a standard invoice, which is useful for many business owners. The template will have the common calculations associated with that document type pre-loaded. Some businesses have spreadsheets pre-made for them in their software package. Large businesses and customers are sometimes able to contract with software programmers to have specialized spreadsheet programs designed to suit their needs.

Software that work with numbers

Many businesses use statistical software to analyze data, particularly when they have massive amounts of information to parse. SPSS is probably the best-known vendor of statistical software. Mathematical modeling software, of which the most popular vendor is Mathcad, is used to graphically depict mathematical relationships. Many businesses and personal users rely on money management software, like Intuit Quicken, to help them manage their personal budgets and financial investments. Finally, tax preparation software is increasingly popular among businesses and private users. TurboTax is one of the more popular programs used for this purpose.

Computer-aided design software and presentation software

Computer-aided design (CAD) software is used to create three-dimensional graphics for engineering and architecture. These highly complex programs are used to create blueprints for products and buildings. The precise dimensions created by a CAD program can be transferred to a computer-aided manufacturing (CAM) program, which delivers instructions to specialized machinery. The objects depicted in a CAD program can also be rotated so as to be visible from all angles. There are specialized computer-aided design programs in a number of fields, but most users get their start with relatively simple introductory programs like AutoCAD.

Presentation graphics software

Presentation graphics software is capable of creating multimedia presentations. These presentations may contain text, sound, video, and animation. The best known of these programs is Microsoft PowerPoint, although Corel Presentations and Harvard Graphics Advanced Presentations are also widely used. The presentations generated with these programs can be projected onto a screen via a simple projector. Also, presentations can be uploaded to the Internet in HTML. Users have the ability to view one slide at a time, or to view a range of slides simultaneously.

Microsoft PowerPoint
The most common presentation software package is Microsoft PowerPoint. With this program, the user has a choice of several view features: outline, slide, notes page, and slide sort. In outline view, the user sees a stripped-down, text-based version of the file, the text of which can be easily edited. In slide view, the user sees each slide individually, and has the ability to edit both text and multimedia. In notes page view, the user sees a small version of the slide accompanied by a form on which he or she can make notes. Finally, slide sort view shows a number of slides at the same time, which the user can arrange in any sequence.

Drawing programs and painting programs
Drawing and painting programs are perhaps the most common examples of graphics software, though they are used

for slightly different purposes. Drawing programs, of which the most common examples are CorelDRAW and Adobe Illustrator, are used to create designs and patterns. Painting programs, on the other hand, are used to edit images and add color to documents and presentations. Two of the most common painting programs are Adobe Photoshop and Corel Photopaint. Images created by painting programs are called bit-mapped images or raster images.

Templates
Content templates and design templates are the most common pre-made forms for presentation graphics programs. In a content template, the basic information to be contained in the presentation is already input. For instance, Microsoft PowerPoint contains content templates for leading a meeting and encouraging teamwork. A design template, on the other hand, only contains the basic layout for a presentation. This layout includes colors, images, and formatting, while content is left for the user to generate.

Visual enhancement
Presentations can be visually enhanced with graphics from the Internet or from clip art. A user can add a three-dimensional look by importing objects, and can adjust the background colors and designs so that they are appropriate for the presentation. Animation or video can also be added to enhance the presentation. Many business presentations contain extensive graphs and charts, which are used to illustrate the points being made by the speaker.

Databases

A database is a set of data or files kept in storage on a computer or a group of computers. Businesses and individuals use databases to keep track of large sets of information such as phone numbers, inventory records, budget projections and many more. In order to be effective, all of the files in a database should be related to one another in some way. Many businesses use databases that can be stored on a personal computer or on a server/mainframe. Many databases also contain sensitive personal information, like bank account numbers or Social Security numbers, and so there are a number of ways to limit access to database contents for security purposes.

Software

Database software, also known as database manager software or database management system (DBMS) software, is used to generate and manipulate the contents of a database. The most popular database software packages for personal computers are Microsoft Access and FileMaker Pro. For servers, the most popular database software packages are Oracle and MySQL. These database management programs allow users to compile and integrate a large set of data, which prevents redundancy and proliferation of documents. Effective databases also allow the user to compare records quickly. The latest trend in database management software is programs that can be used on a personal digital assistant.

Data storage

Databases are made up of records, which themselves are made up of fields containing individual pieces of data. For instance, a database of the customers for a business might contain separate records for each individual customer. Within each record, there will be different fields for the customer's name, address, phone number, etc. Records are typically presented horizontally on a database, so that one horizontal row will contain an entire record. With this format, each vertical column contains all of the fields related to a specific piece of information. For instance, one column might contain all the customer phone numbers.

Queries

Because it is not efficient to examine an entire large database to find a particular piece of information, database management programs have developed a query language that enables users to quickly find and edit data. One example is SQL, or Structured Query Language, which enables the user to enter a simple English question to obtain a piece of data. Another common mode of locating information is QBE, or Query by Example, in which the user performs a short fill-in-the-blank exercise that helps the program locate the desired piece of information.

Use of search results

Once a database search has been completed, the user can save the results to a hard drive or disk. In addition, the results of the search could be converted into HTML format and published on the Internet, exported to another program on the computer, or emailed to other computers. In one common scenario, the user exports data to Microsoft Excel and uses it to create a graph or table. Sometimes, the user will want to take the data and use it to generate a text document which can be easily read and understood by his or her audience. Finally, it is possible with contemporary programs to import data from one database to another.

Relational databases

In a relational database, there are multiple tables containing overlapping sets of data. Relational databases get their names from the fact that the information contained in the various tables is related in some way. Changes made to the information in one table will be reflected in the other tables. Relational databases are helpful because they prevent the user from having to enter the same data multiple times. A relational database must have a key that differentiates its records. The primary key must be a column that has a different value in each field. For instance, if a teacher makes a relational database of student data, the students' last names could be the primary key (so long as no two students have the same last name).

Screen features
In the most common and representative database software program, Microsoft Access, the left-hand side of the screen offers a range of commands: modules, reports, queries, forms, tables, macros, and pages. To the right of that is the table, which is displayed as a grid of rows and columns. When the program is displaying an individual form, all of the data for one record will be shown at the same time. When the user performs a query, the results will be displayed like a spreadsheet. When the user selects the report view, the data will be displayed in a form appropriate for printing. In order to perform more specific and complicated functions with the database, the user must select the modules. Finally, the macros displayed in a database software program represent shortcuts for performing common operations.

Entry of records
When creating a database, a user can enter records into forms or into tables. When creating a database through forms, the user is required to fill a list of information in full; it will then be added as a complete record in the database. Database management software is often programmed to only accept certain kinds of data for particular fields; for instance, the program might not accept a series of letters in the phone number field. The process of entering data into a database table is much like that of generating a spreadsheet: the arrow keys are used to highlight individual fields, and the user fills these fields by entering information into a blank at the top of the screen.

Personal information managers

A personal information manager (PIM) is a software program designed to organize the private and professional life of an individual. Microsoft Outlook and Scheduler are two common examples of PIM software; these programs keep track of appointments, telephone numbers, to-do lists, and contacts. The most recent versions of these programs also contain email access and automatic reminders. Many people use personal information manager programs as they would use a secretary or personal assistant: to handle routine tasks so that the user can maintain focus on long-term goals.

Specialty software

As software development becomes more lucrative, more specialty software programs are designed to perform very specific functions. These programs are often very expensive, in part because they are sold to a small market of highly trained and educated users. Some common specialty software packages are for project management, computer-aided design, animation, financial management, video editing, drawing, painting, and web design. These programs can be extremely complicated, thus requiring the user to be skilled with basic software programs before advancing to specialty software.

Graphics, graphics software, and paint software

Graphics are all of the images displayed on a computer monitor, whether they are animations, drawings, or photographs. Graphics software enables users to generate and manipulate images. As the visual performance of computers has improved, graphics programs have grown more specialized and advanced. For instance, painting programs, of which Microsoft Paint and Corel Paint Shop Pro are among the best examples, can

- 35 -

effectively mimic the performance of paint in the real world.

Photo editing software, drawing software, and 3D graphics software

Many graphic artists use photo editing software to alter or modify photographs. Contemporary programs, of which the most famous is Adobe Photoshop, are able to adjust contrast, add and remove objects in a photograph, and eliminate the red-eye effect. Drawing software, meanwhile, enables the user to generate clean design with a range of colors. Adept users of drawing software, of which the best current examples are Adobe Illustrator and Macromedia Freehand, can effectively insert text and other images. Finally, 3D graphics software is used to generate wireframes and three-dimensional designs, often for engineering purposes.

Graphic file formats

Some of the most common graphic file formats are as follows:
- .bmp: bitmap; created by Microsoft Windows for use on personal computers and in programs like Microsoft Paint
- .gif: graphic interchange format; commonly found on web pages and other online venues
- .jpeg: joint photographic experts group; common format for photographs and websites
- .tiff: tagged image file format; similar to bitmaps, but can be used to create high-resolution, printable images on personal computers and Macs
- .png: portable network graphics; an alternative to graphic interchange format for web pages

Audio editing software

Audio editing software enables the recording, playing, and manipulation of sound. Two of the most common audio editing software packages are Sound Recorder and Audacity. With audio editing software, users can create digital and voice recordings, and can adjust components to generate a desired sound. The typical interface of audio editing software contains buttons for stop, play, record, fast-forward, and rewind. The user also has the option to adjust bass and treble levels. Files created with audio editing software can be stored digitally on a computer or on an audio player like an iPod.

<u>CD ripper and audio encoding software</u>
CD ripper software extracts tracks from a compact disc and converts them into a digital file that can be stored on a computer. In order to be replayed on the computer, the digital file must be converted into a format compatible with the computer's media player. This process is performed by audio encoding software, also known as audio format conversion software. In most cases, the audio file from a CD is converted into .MP3 or .AAC format so that it can be played on a portable device like an iPod. It is common for CD ripper software to be bundled with audio encoding software.

<u>Ear training software, notation software, computer-aided music software, and MIDI sequencing software</u>
- Ear training software: teaches aspiring musicians to recognize musical notes by ear
- Notation software: similar to word processing software, but designed for music composers; allows the user to edit and adjust musical notes as if they were text
- Computer-aided music software: enables non-experts to make

music without reference to musical notation; features a set of simple controls that can be used to create basic beats and melodies

- MIDI sequencing software: used to create sound effects and adjust the sound produced by digital instruments and special MIDI keyboards

Video editing software

With video editing software, a user can import moving images from a video camera or VCR and then make changes to them. Popular video editing software packages, which include Adobe Premiere, Apple Final Cut Express, and Sony Pictures Digital Vegas, allow users to cut out sections of video and arrange scenes in any order. The user can also add special effects and audio to a video. After editing, the user can immediately see the effect of his or her work on the file, and rapidly undo any errors made during the editing process.

Educational software

Educational software packages help users acquire new knowledge and skills. A number of these programs incorporate games to make learning fun. For instance, one popular software package for young students is 3D Froggy Phonics, which uses games to teach lessons about mathematics and reading. There are also a number of educational software programs for adults, particularly in the areas of music theory and foreign language acquisition. There are also programs designed to provide preparation for specific exams, as for instance the LSAT or GRE. Many schools incorporate virtual classroom programs like Blackboard and WebCT to enable remote participation by students.

Reference software

Rather than acquire a bulky set of reference books, people can now obtain reference software packages that contain enormous quantities of information accessible through their computers. Reference software customers can buy access to the contents of a large set of encyclopedias either on CD, DVD, or the Internet. Microsoft Encarta and the Encyclopedia Britannica are both available on CD and online. Computer users can also obtain specialty reference works like telephone books or cookbooks. One advantage of reference software over traditional reference books is that it is much easier to quickly find specific pieces of information.

Computer and video games

In a role-playing game, the user becomes a character in a complex and detailed story. It is very common for role-playing games, of which a contemporary example is EverQuest, to be set in the Middle Ages and to feature fantastic creatures. Action games like Tomb Raider, on the other hand, require the user to move through a series of hand-eye coordination-based challenges. Adventure games, of which one example is Myst, place the user in a fictional world and force him or her to accomplish specific goals. Puzzle games like Tetris require the user to solve increasingly difficult problems. There are a number of popular simulation games, like Flight Simulator, which mimic real-life situations. Sports games are similar to simulation games, except that they simulate athletic competition. Finally, strategy games, of which one example is Starcraft, require users to gather resources, assemble and coordinate troops, and use tactics to achieve military victories.

Multiplayer games

In a multiplayer game, two or more users participate at the same time. The earliest example of a multiplayer game was Pong, in which two opponents used joysticks to move paddles and strike a ball back-and-forth. With the advent of the Internet, the users in a multiplayer game need not be in the same room, or even in the same country. In a popular online multiplayer game like EverQuest, for instance, thousands of people can play at the same time. Modern multiplayer games create virtual worlds that players can enter and leave at their leisure. Users can also communicate with each other through dialog boxes and headsets as they play the game.

Computer animation

Computer animation works in a manner similar to a child's flipbook: a series of images are arranged in sequence, and the appearance of motion is created when the sequence is passed through quickly. An animator works on the individual frames of the picture. The earliest successful form of animation on the Internet was GIF animation. When a file icon was clicked, a sequence of images (GIFs) was initiated at a rate fast enough to give the appearance of motion.

Multimedia authoring software

Multimedia authoring software combines several disparate applications like word processing, animation, and video, to create a single product. Many institutions, like schools and businesses, want to produce instructional or advertising presentations that contain text, audio, and video. Multimedia authoring software packages like Macromedia Authorware or Adobe Director make this possible. The files created with such software can be recorded onto a CD or DVD, or can be uploaded to the Internet. As computers become faster and more capable of multimedia applications, multimedia authoring software is becoming increasingly sophisticated and popular.

Webpage design software

Webpage design software gives non-experts the ability to develop their own websites, complete with multimedia. Some Internet access providers give subscribers utilities to create simple websites, though many people prefer the commercial software packages Adobe Dreamweaver, Adobe Fireworks, and Microsoft Expression Web. With these programs, the user does not have to understand the Internet programming language HTML. Instead, the user fills out a template, and the program converts the given information to HTML format. Although many Internet service providers grant webpage server space for free, there are also inexpensive hosting options offered by commercial businesses.

Novice web designing

A novice web designer may start out using the PageWizard templates offered by Yahoo. With time, the user might move on to the more advanced PageBuilder, which enables the addition of music and a visitor tracker. Simple web design programs for beginners are also offered by Lycos, America Online, and Microsoft. There are a number of tutorials available at the Lycos site, and America Online provides free templates to subscribers. The Microsoft Internet Assistant is also compatible with Microsoft Office, so that a user can upload texts, databases, and spreadsheets to a simple webpage.

Project management software

With project management software, a user can organize and schedule any

- 38 -

project. These software packages, of which two common examples are Microsoft Project and Primavera SureTrak Project Manager, help the user delegate tasks, outline a budget, and schedule meetings. Project management software includes Gantt charts, which help organize task performance sequence; and program evaluation and review technique (PERT) applications, which block out the amount of time necessary for each component of the project. Increasingly, businesses are using open source project management software so that all the members of a project team can contribute over the Internet. The best-known open source project management package is Open Workbench.

CAD software

With computer-aided design (CAD) software, users can create blueprints for objects both large and small. This software is capable of creating three-dimensional images that can be rotated and viewed from any angle. The incredible precision of CAD software means that the images created on it can be transferred directly to computer-aided manufacturing (CAM) programs for accurate physical construction. For instance, fashion designers often use CAD software to create patterns which can be immediately sent to fabric-cutting robots.

Business software

There are two basic types of business software: horizontal and vertical market software. Horizontal market software can be adapted for use in any kind of business. A comprehensive software suite like Microsoft Office is a good example of horizontal market software, as are any individual software applications for word processing, spreadsheets, or databases. Vertical market software, on the other hand, is only appropriate for a specific market or industry. For instance, retail outlets have specialized software programs that contain functions for cash registers and the maintenance of sales records.

Software licenses

Software licenses, also known as license agreements, limit the uses of a program. For instance, a single-user license prevents multiple simultaneous users. A multiple-user license, on the other hand, enables more than one user at the same time. Often, companies will purchase a multiple-user license to cover all of the employees in an office. The price of a multiple-user license depends on the projected number of users. A site license, meanwhile, permits the program to be used in a certain location. If a site license is obtained for an office, for instance, all of the people in that office can use the software. A concurrent-use license permits multiple copies of a program to be run at the same time. The price of a concurrent-use license is dependent on the number of copies required.

EULA

A EULA, or end-user license agreement, appears when newly-installed software is run for the first time. It requires the user to confirm agreement with the license terms by pressing a button. Unless the user agrees with the license terms, the program will not run. By pressing the button that indicates agreement, the user enters into a legal contract with the software publisher. Any failure to observe the terms of the agreement can make the user liable. Typically, the EULA includes the limitations of the license and the terms of the warranty.

Shrink-wrap licenses

A shrink-wrap license is established as soon as the customer removes the software from its packaging. It is a non-verbal agreement which the customer may be unaware of having entered. However, the shrink-wrap license has some legal validity so long as it is indicated by text on the outside of the software package. If there is a clear description of the shrink-wrap license, it does not need to be read by the customer to be valid and enforceable.

Demoware

Demoware is either a trial version or a limited-license edition of commercial software. Demoware is free, but it usually comes with time and use restrictions. For instance, it may only be valid for two weeks. Often demoware is installed on a new computer when it is purchased; the new owner can sample the software for a limited time, after which he or she must pay for it. Some demoware can only be loaded a certain number of times before it must be bought. Furthermore, some versions of demoware do not include advanced program features.

Shareware

Like demoware, shareware is protected by copyright and limited to a certain trial period after which the user must pay a fee to retain access to the program. Unlike demoware, however, shareware does not have disabled features. Whereas demoware is created by major software manufacturers that hope to sell complete versions of the program later, shareware is created by programmers looking to spread their work and make a profit. The licensing agreements for shareware are typically enforced through the honor system. If the user enjoys the program, it is hoped that he or she will feel obliged to contribute money to the creators.

Freeware

Freeware is protected by copyright, but has no time or use limitations. Users of freeware are never required to pay registration fees. Users can give freeware away, but are not allowed to sell or modify it. Programs are typically distributed as freeware because the developer wants to test it and sell a better version of it in the future. Utility programs, games, and device drivers are often introduced as freeware.

Rentalware

Rentalware is leased software, meaning that rather than pay a set fee for ownership, the customer pays a certain amount each time they want to use the program. Application service providers (ASPs), which provide access and support for the Internet, are examples of rentalware providers. Some types of software are best sold as rentalware because they require almost continuous updates. Also, software used only sporadically is best provided as rentalware because the company does not want to update its copy of the software each time it is opened. The application service provider can update the software as necessary and the user can just get the most recent version every time.

Open source software

Open source software, of which Linux is perhaps the best example, can be modified by its users. The source code of the software is available so that amateur programmers can alter, adjust, or tinker with it. Linux is protected by copyright and is not in the public domain, but it can be legally adjusted by any of its users. However, because Linux is a highly complex program that has been assembled by a skilled community of programmers, making useful changes requires extensive knowledge. The program is compiled when it is distributed, though it must be accompanied by the source code. Open source software may be covered by a BSD license or a general public license (GPL), the latter of which is stricter.

Internet

The development of the Internet can be traced to the space race between the United States and Soviet Union during the 1960s. After the Soviet Union launched the satellite Sputnik into Earth orbit in 1959, the United States created the Advanced Research Projects Agency (ARPA) to bolster technological innovation. One result of ARPA was the development in 1969 of ARPANET, a wide-area network (WAN) of computers at various research centers and universities around the country. The National Science Foundation (NSF) created a similar network in 1985, though this one was comprised of interconnected local area networks (LANs). The NSF network was meant to safeguard computer communication against nuclear war. These discrete networks created by the American science community were gradually joined together, eventually forming the comprehensive Internet as it is known today. At present, the Internet is believed to have over one billion users.

Basic infrastructure
The Internet arose as a series of smaller networks joined to a single spine, a T1 line created by the National Science Foundation in 1987 that linked 170 individual networks. The resulting NSFNET was the first main thoroughfare for data. Now, the Internet's backbone is composed of fiber-optic links connecting all of the routers on the network. The links between the routers are maintained by network service providers (NSPs) like SBC/AT&T. The networks administered by these companies are connected to one another by network access points (NAPs).

The network service providers make it possible for Internet service providers (ISPs) like America Online and Comcast to deliver web access to the general public.

Portable and mobile Internet access

When a computer has portable Internet access, it can get online from any number of different locations. Portable Internet access can include wireless Internet, Wi-Fi, or satellite access. A mobile Internet connection is slightly different, in that the user's access remains continuous even while the computer is in motion. In other words, the user does not have to connect to a different port or hub in each location. Mobile Internet connections can be through Wi-Fi, mobile WiMAX, and cellular broadband. This service, currently offered by many telephone service providers, is based on a network of satellites and broadcast towers that give the user web access so long as he or she is able to obtain a cellular phone signal.

Wi-Fi and Wi-Fi hotspots

Wi-Fi, short for "Wireless Fidelity," can be usefully thought of as a wireless network. In recent years, many businesses and public buildings have established themselves as Wi-Fi hotspots where people can access the Internet over a secure network. The newest versions of Windows automatically detect and connect with Wi-Fi networks. It may be necessary to obtain a password in order to have unfettered Internet access. Also, some businesses, like coffee shops and hotels, charge their customers for access to their Wi-Fi networks. These pay-for-access networks are run by telecommunications companies like Verizon and T-Mobile.

- 41 -

Portable WiMAX

Worldwide Interoperability for Microwave Access (WiMAX) is an Ethernet-compatible alternative to DSL or cable Internet connections. People who live in remote and rural areas can obtain WiMAX service even when cable coverage and the telephone services required for DSL are unavailable. WiMAX Internet access is distributed from a nearby tower and allows the recipient to move around and remain connected so long as he or she has a wireless modem and stays within range of the tower. Most WiMAX services require a subscription. Subscribers may be given access to the signal from towers other than the one closest to their home or office.

Modem connection through telephone line

One way to connect a modem to a computer is through a telephone line in what is called a dial-up connection. Dial-up connections have a low bandwidth, which means data cannot be transmitted very quickly. In order for an Internet connection to be effective, the computer's modem must be compatible with the modems used by the Internet access provider. Inferior phone lines and heavy Internet traffic may slow down online service. For instance, the Internet tends to run slower during normal business hours when many employees are accessing information on the Web. Also, dial-up connections travel over the same lines as telephone signals, so it is impossible to talk on the phone and use the phone line's dial-up connection at the same time.

Bandwidth and broadband

The bandwidth of an Internet connection is the amount of data that can be transmitted in a given amount of time. Baseband transmissions only allow one signal through at a time, while broadband transmissions allow the rapid passage of several signals at the same time. Broadband connections are required for cable television and high-speed Internet service. Broadband transmissions can be achieved with coaxial, fiber-optic, cable line, DSL, and wireless connections. The unit of measure for bandwidth is bits per second (bps) in terms of digital data, and hertz (Hz) in terms of analog data.

High-speed telephone line

For high-speed Internet access, the plain old telephone system (known informally as POTS in the world of telecommunications) found in most households and businesses can be improved by the addition of an Integrated Services Digital Network (ISDN) which permits the rapid transfer of video and voice data over copper telephone wires. A POTS can also be improved by adding a digital subscriber line (DSL) which, when accompanied by a DSL modem, accelerates the transfer of digital data. When a DSL system is installed, the user can use the Internet and talk on the phone at the same time. However, DSL connections are only available to those who live within 3.3 miles of the phone company's central switching office because the speed of the transmission depends on the distance it must travel. Another way to enhance a POTS is to add a T1 line, which is a traditional trunk line with 24 regular phone circuits capable of transmitting data at 1.5 Mbps.

Dial-up connection

In a dial-up Internet connection, a computer modem calls an Internet service provider (ISP) over the telephone line. The sounds of this procedure, a series of dialing tones, rings, and electronic beeps, are known as the handshake protocol. When the computer of the ISP answers the call, a dedicated circuit is formed between the ISP and the dialing computer. So long as this circuit exists, data can flow freely. Data from the user's computer is sent through the telephone wall jack and the telephone lines to the modem of the ISP, then to the router of the ISP, and then on to the Internet. Numerous handshake protocols must occur in order for this entire process to occur.

Voiceband modem

Voiceband modems convert digital data into analog signals that can be transmitted over telephone lines. For instance, a 0 bit is transmitted at 1070 Hz, while a 1 bit is transmitted at 1270 Hz. At the other end of the transmission, the receiving modem translates this analog signal back into a digital format that can be understood by a computer. At all times, the computers involved in such a transaction are communicating information related to the exchange, such as the size of the data packets, the speed at which data will be transmitted, and the general characteristics of the data.

ISDN

An Integrated Services Digital Network (ISDN) is a rapid, stable means of transmitting data over telephone lines. An ISDN connection does not require a modem, but instead relies on an ISDN terminal adapter, which transmits the digital signal over the phone lines. An ISDN usually transmits data at either 64 Kbps or 128 Kbps. This connection is only complete so long as the computer is performing an online task. In addition to its speed, one of the advantages of an ISDN is that telephone calls can be made while the computer is online.

DSL

A digital subscriber line (DSL) is another way to accelerate web access over telephone lines. It requires a DSL modem, which converts digital data into DSL-ready signals. A DSL connection stays open all the time, and it has a special filter that allows telephone calls to be made while it is in use. DSL connections are capable of speeds in the millions of bits per second (Mbps). One of the reasons for the speed of DSL technology is that it does not require the conversion of digital data into analog and back again. However, a DSL connection requires proximity to the telephone switching station.

Cable Internet service

Cable Internet service, in which digital data is transmitted over coaxial and fiber optic cables, is the fastest means of Internet access. A cable Internet connection is active at all times and can be delivered to remote areas via satellite dishes. The system of beaming signals to a satellite dish and then distributing them by cable to customers is known as community antenna television (CATV). Customers can obtain television as well as Internet access by this means. With CATV services, the speed of data from the Internet to the user's computer is about 6000 Kbps, while the speed of data transmission from the user's computer to the Internet is much slower, about 384 Kbps. Everyone on a cable network gets the same speed of service.

Cable modem

A cable modem enables the transmission of digital data over lines previously used exclusively for cable television. A cable modem is not actually a modem in a strict sense because it does not convert the digital signal into an analog signal. A cable modem requires alternating current. It is sometimes connected to a computer through either an Ethernet or

USB port, and connects to the wall via a coaxial cable. However, in many cases, the computer is attached to a router and the router is connected to the cable modem. In order to receive cable television and Internet service from a single outlet, the user may need to obtain a cable splitter. Also, the cable modem may require a coaxial cable-adaptable wall jack.

Satellite Internet service

A satellite Internet connection broadcasts signals from a satellite dish. These connections are capable of very high speeds, downloading between 400 and 500 Kbps and uploading between 100 and 256 Kbps. Also, satellite Internet connections provide service to very remote locations. These connections remain active at all times. The data is sent from the personal computer to the satellite modem, and from there to a satellite dish, a geostationary satellite, an Internet service provider, and finally to the Internet. When the user receives data this path is reversed. The satellite modem converts the signal into a frequency band that can be transmitted by the dish. In order to be effectively communicated, the signal must be converted and amplified. The satellites that provide satellite Internet access are orbiting about 22,200 miles above the planet and communicate with stations on earth via microwaves.

Fixed wireless Internet service

Fixed wireless Internet service, also called wireless broadband service, is the transmission of data signals over vast areas. For instance, many cities have wireless broadband for the entire metropolitan area, an arrangement known as a metropolitan area network (MAN). In the United States and United Kingdom, the Worldwide Interoperability for Microwave Access (WiMAX) ensures that wireless systems are compatible with Ethernet and other networks. The range of these networks is vast: one tower is capable of transmitting a WiMAX signal up to 3000 square miles. In order to access this service, users need to have a wireless modem or an antenna.

Protocols, UDP, and the TCP/IP protocol suite

The set of rules followed by computers when transmitting data is known as a protocol. In 1978, the Advanced Research Projects Agency (ARPA) developed the foundational set of protocols required for using the Internet; these protocols are known as the Transmission Control Protocol/Internet Protocol Suite, or TCP/IP. Some computers use the User Datagram Protocol (UDP) instead of TCP/IP for Voice over Internet Protocol (VoIP) and file-sharing. However, this system does not subdivide data into packets. The TCP breaks data down into packets, and gives them all the same IP address so that they will arrive at the correct destination; this same protocol is also used to reassemble packets of received data.

IP addresses

Every machine that is connected to the Internet has a unique Internet protocol (IP) address. An IP address consists of seven digits broken up into four groups (called octets) by decimal points, for example 426.6.35.4. There are both static and dynamic IP addresses: a static IP address remains the same for a machine, while a dynamic IP address changes every time the machine connects to the Internet. The data a computer receives over the Internet is sent to that computer's IP address. When the machine logs off, the Internet service provider (ISP) will assign the dynamic IP address to another computer. ISPs and

- 44 -

many websites have static IP addresses of their own.

Domain name and top-level domain

Because Internet protocol (IP) addresses are difficult to remember, locations on the Internet are given a domain name, more technically known as a fully qualified domain name (FQDN). For a website, the domain name includes the name of the web server, while for an email address it includes the name of the email server. For instance, the domain name in the website address www.fictional.com/made-up is fictional.com, and the domain name in the email address bsmith@fictional.com is fictional.com. A domain name must include at the end an extension, also known as a top-level domain. Some of the most common top-level domains are .com and .biz for businesses and other commercial ventures, .info, .int for international organizations, .mil for military organizations, .net for Internet organizations, .org for nonprofit organizations, and .edu for education-related institutions. Many countries have their own top-level domain; for example, the top-level domain for Italy is .it. Domain names are registered at the Internet Corporation for Assigned Names and Numbers (ICANN).

Netiquette

The general set of manners that a person should use when communicating on the Internet is known as netiquette. The foundation of netiquette is respect for the feelings of other people, even if they are anonymous. For instance, it is not considered polite to reply to all the recipients of an email when only one person needs to receive your message. Also, novice Internet users should be aware that writing in all capital letters is the Internet equivalent of screaming and is considered impolite. It is a good idea to

make sure the subject line of an email is appropriate to the body of the message, so that the recipient will know what to expect. Attachments can be infected with viruses, so it is a good idea to explicitly mention the contents of any attachments that are sent over the Internet.

Smartphones

A smartphone is similar to a cellular phone but also contains some computer features like a modem, memory chip, and microprocessor. A smartphone may be capable of playing music, taking photographs, accessing the Internet, and organizing personal information. Smartphones have high-resolution display screens, some of which are capable of showing movies and television. Also, the owner of a smartphone can download various ring tones so that a distinctive noise is made when the owner receives a phone call, text message, or email.

Text messaging

Text messaging, also known as texting, is the transmission of a short message over a smartphone, cellular phone, or other handheld device. Text messaging via computer is more commonly known as instant messaging. Many people use text messages to communicate short pieces of information that do not warrant an entire phone call. Text services for telephones are also known as short message services (SMS). This service was initially only available on GSM mobile phones, but is now available on all networks.

Wired network

A wired network is a system of computers and peripheral devices connected to each other by cables. Before the advent of wireless technology, all networks were wired. It is still common for local area networks and personal computing

Copyright © Mometrix Media. You have been licensed one copy of this document for personal use only. Any other reproduction or redistribution is strictly prohibited. All rights reserved.

stations to be wired. One of the benefits of a wired network is that it is easy to set up and take apart. Also, there is a very low amount of interference in network cables. In many cases, wired networks transfer data faster than wireless networks, which are susceptible to interference. It is also impossible for an outside computer to steal the signal from a wired network. However, there are some obvious physical limitations associated with wired networks. The wires themselves can be cumbersome, and are susceptible to physical damage which can impair the function of the system.

HomePNA technology

HomePNA is a system for utilizing the telephone wire infrastructure of a home or building to establish a computer network. The setup is similar to a system of Ethernet connections, except computers and modems are connected through telephone wall jacks and data is transmitted over the existing telephone wiring. This sort of system is slower than Ethernet, but in many cases is cheaper to install. Taking advantage of the network of cables that are already installed is convenient for many users. HomePNA systems are also very secure.

Ethernet system

In an Ethernet system, all of the devices on the network receive all sent packets of data simultaneously. However, only the device that requested the data will be able to access it. In other words, the data will only become visible to the user who needs it. Ethernet systems have what is called a carrier sense multiple access with collision detection (CSMA/CD) protocol, which moderates interference when two network devices attempt to broadcast packets simultaneously. The CSMA/CD protocol prevents this interference and

resends the data without requiring any input from the user.

Connection
An Ethernet connection is a type of network used to connect multiple computers to one another or to connect one or more computers to the Internet. An Ethernet connection requires all participating computers to have Ethernet ports and cables. Ethernet cables consist of four pairs of twisted wire with specific Ethernet jacks on each end. In many cases, Ethernet systems revolve around a central router, known as a hub, to which all the disparate computers are connected. This cuts down on the number of connections that need to be made between individual computers.

Networks

The various types of networks include:
- WAN (wide area network): a network covering a large area; typically composed of several smaller networks
- MAN (metropolitan area network): a network extended over up to 50 miles and capable of transmitting data and voice; one example is a cable television company
- LAN (local area network): a network restricted to a small area, as for instance a single building or home; primarily used for data
- HAN (home area network): a network restricted to a single home
- PAN (personal area network): a wireless network devoted to connecting a single person's electronic devices, such as his or her computer, phone, and personal digital assistant

Program Design and Development

Formal specification

A formal specification uses mathematical terms and logic to describe a hardware or software system. It is a very high-level description whose purpose is explaining what functions the software should perform rather than how the system should perform them. The programmer compares the formal specification against the proposed system design to determine whether the proposed system meets requirements or needs further revision. Consequently, the program's ultimate correctness depends upon the formal specification's ability to identify the problem accurately. Creating an accurate formal specification can be very difficult; however, a programmer can validate a specification by constantly comparing it against theorems that reflect qualities and characteristics the specification should possess. If the specification does not pass these theorems, it probably needs alteration. Formal specifications are written using specification languages, such as Z notation, VDM, LePUS3, Perfect, and CASL.

Assertions

An assertion is a statement used in testing the correctness of a program. It is a true-false statement (otherwise known as a predicate) that is placed at a point in the program where the programmer assumes the predicate will always hold true. Consider the following the assertions:

```
x = 7
// {x > 5}
x = x * 2
// {x >= 2}
```

The expressions set off in comments ($x < 0$ and $x >= 2$) are the assertions that programmer assumes will always be true. There are multiple types of assertions:

- Preconditions – are positioned at the beginning of a program section where they identify the conditions (i.e. states) under which the program will run.
- Postconditions – are positioned at the end of a program section where they identify the expected conditions after the program has executed.
- Loop invariant – are assertions that remain true at a certain point in a loop regardless of the number of times the loop has been executed.

Using assertions, the programmer can check the correctness of a program, or the program can terminate execution and avoid undesirable conditions.

Application of formal logic to software verification

When applying formal logic to software verification, developers use assertions (such as preconditions, postconditions, and invariants) to check the correctness of a program.

Preconditions establish the set of conditions that exist just prior to the program's execution. For instance, if a program is designed to sort customer names, we assume the input will be a list of customer names, which is the precondition. The programmer then monitors these conditions as the program executes and determines if the output results in the correct set of conditions, which are established by the postconditions. In this way, the programmer can assess the correctness of program execution by establishing assertions throughout it and then checking them. When checking the

- 47 -

correctness of a `while` loop, the programmer establishes a type of assertion known as a loop invariant, which is a value that remains true at certain point in the loop regardless of the number of times it executes. ———

Dynamic verification and static verification

Dynamic verification involves testing and experimentation. Its purpose is finding bugs in the system, and is carried out as a review process during software execution. There are three types of dynamic verification:

- Test in the small – evaluates one function or class.
- Test in the large – evaluates a group of classes using things such as module tests, integration tests, and system tests.
- Acceptance test – evaluates software acceptance criteria using functional tests and nonfunctional tests.

Static verification involves analysis through physical inspection. Its purpose is evaluating the correctness of the program; however, it can lead to false positives. Static verification includes the following tests: bad practices detection, software metric calculation, code conventions verification, and formal verification.

Waterfall model, incremental model, and iterative model

The waterfall model requires that every phase of software development (requirements specifications, design, implementation, and testing) must be completed before the next phase can start. Like a waterfall, the software development process can only flow in one direction.

The incremental model allows for a higher level of trial and error than the waterfall model, and makes use of prototyping methodologies. In the incremental model, developers first create a simplified version of the final product with limited functionality and test it. If it passes the test, more features are added. This cycle repeats until the software is fully functional.

The iterative model is very similar to the incremental model. However, rather than adding to each new version of the software product, each version is rebuilt. The iterative model serves as the basis for the *Rational Unified Process*, a software development paradigm that was developed by the Rational Software Corporate division of IBM. RUP changes the traditional software development phases, and includes new guidelines. RUP, which is marketed by IBM, led to the development of the noncommercial *Unified Process*.

Open-source development and agile methods

Open-source development pulls from both the incremental and iterative models. A programmer creates a software application, and places its source code and documentation on the Internet. Other programmers download the source code and documentation, add new features, and then send their revised version back to the original programmer, who updates the version stored on the Internet. The most famous example of open-source development is Linux.

Agile methods emphasize product implementation over requirements specification and design, making it far more responsive to changing requirements. One example of agile method is *extreme programming*, *XP*, in which a small group of developers work informally to create versions of the

- 48 -

software as quickly as possible. The developers work in a large group, exchanging ideas, and perform tasks such as analysis, design, implementation, and testing on a daily, informal basis. Stakeholders examine the many software versions and provide direction.

Data flow diagrams and data dictionary

A data flow diagram uses arrows and nodes to represent the path that data takes through a software system. Arrows illustrate the paths taken by the data between nodes; oval nodes illustrate the places where data is manipulated; and, rectangular nodes illustrate the places where data is stored within the system. Using data flow diagrams, developers can more easily understand the system, and identify the procedures upon which the system will be based.

A data dictionary contains information about the data that will be used by a system, such as the data identifier, restrictions on what constitutes a valid data entry, storage place of the data, and the references points of the data in the software. Data dictionaries facilitate communication between stakeholders and software engineers, and ensure uniformity throughout the system. A data dictionary can also be a software layer that enforces data entry and validation rules for databases.

Unified Modeling Language

Unified Modeling Language, or UML, is a software development tool designed specifically for object-oriented programming. It includes the following tools: use case diagrams, class diagrams, and interaction diagrams.

A use case diagram illustrates the proposed system from the user's perspective. It consists of a large rectangle that represents the entire system. Ovals within the rectangle represent the various features of the system. Stick figures outside the rectangle represent the groups of people (known as *actors*) who will be using the features, and are connected to those features via lines. The interactions between the features and system users are known as *use cases*.

An interaction diagram illustrates the events that actually take place as the program executes. A *sequence diagram* is one such example. Using rectangles and dashed lines (known as *life lines*), it represents the interactions between actors, objects, and software components. *Interaction fragments* within the diagram show alternative sequences.

Class diagrams

Class diagrams are one tool of Unified Modeling Language. They illustrate the relationships between classes in object-oriented systems. Each class is illustrated by a rectangular box, and arrows are drawn connecting the boxes in order to show the relationships (known as *associations*) between classes. Class diagrams are capable of showing three types of associations:

- *One-to-one relationship* – established when two classes associate with each other.
- *One-to-many relationship* – established when a single class associates with multiple classes.
- *Many-to-many relationship* – established when a group of classes associates with another group of classes.

In object-oriented programming, generalization applies to a class of objects whose features are the same as another class's but less specific. The generalized class will be identical to the other class

- 49 -

but will have fewer overall options. Programmers can implement generalization using inheritance; however, because inheritance causes coupling between two classes, it should be used sparingly.

Design patterns

Design patterns are readymade models that solve common problems arising during software development. Some of the more popular design patterns include the following:

- *Adapter pattern* – implemented when a software module fulfills the intended functions and goals of a program but cannot interface with the existing system. Using the adapter pattern, the software module can be *wrapped* in a second module that translates between the two interfaces.
- *Decorator pattern* – implemented when a system is at risk of becoming overly complex. It is designed specifically for systems that perform the same in a variety of ways contingent upon the situation. Using the decorator pattern, the programmer can better manage the system.
- *Templates* and *tool kits* – included with Java and .NET Framework.

When developing design patterns, programmers should seek to increase the efficiency and flexibility of the design. Coupling should be avoided, and cohesion should be maximized.

Operating system

An operating system, or OS, manages and controls all computer functions, such as calculations and the processing of data. It is the *master control system*, determining the manner in which data is sent to the hardware devices that make up the computer. It includes the following components:

- A *memory manager* determines and allocates the amount of RAM necessary to run a program. It can perform monoprogramming, which executes only one program at once, or multiprogramming, which executes multiple programs at once through techniques such as partitioning and paging.
- A *process manager* controls programs (also known as processes) as they are executing in memory.
- A *spooler* is a software application that regulates access to computer resources, such as printers.
- An *interrupt handler* is operating system software that examines and categorizes interrupt commands, which are signals that alert the CPU to stop a process so it can process a request, such as an I/O (input or output) or an error interrupt.

A *device manager*, also known as an *I/O supervisor*, regulates access to I/O (input or output) devices.

Semaphore

A **s**emaphore is a technique by which an operating system manages access to computer resources, such as printers, fax machines, CD players, etc. Using a flag system, a semaphore prevents two processes from accessing the same resource simultaneously. A *set flag*, which has a value of one, specifies the resource is being used. A *clear flag*, which has a value of zero, specifies the resource is available. However, if the flag process is interrupted during execution, it can still result in two processes accessing the same resource. To avoid interruption, a semaphore either temporarily disables the system's use of interrupt commands or uses a *test-and-set instruction*, which executes the entire flag sequence in one instruction, or executes none of it. Semaphores execute sets of instructions that establish *critical regions* in the computer system. Only one process can access these regions at a time—a requirement known as *mutual exclusion*.

Deadlock

Deadlock results in a computer system when multiple processes are blocking each other from using resources, or when multiple processes must create new processes to complete their function but the schedule table is full. Three conditions must be present for deadlock to occur:
1. Processes are competing for non-shareable resources.
2. Processes are requesting only part of a resource. As a result, the processes are using some of the resource and then returning to use more at a later time.
3. The processes cannot forcibly retrieve the resources they have been allocated.

Operating systems use a variety of techniques to overcome deadlock:
- *Kill* – forcibly removes the processes that are filling the scheduling table. This technique only treats the third condition; as such, it can only affect the system after the deadlock has occurred.
- *Spooling* – prevents deadlock from occurring. The process executes as if it has access to the resource, but in reality, its data is being stored for execution at a later, more convenient time.

Require each process to request all necessary resources at once. This prevents deadlock from occurring.

Network, internet, and distributed application architecture

A network is any system that links multiple computers either physically or wirelessly. It provides an effective means of sharing information and resources, such as data files, printers, and software applications. When a computer connects to the network, it becomes a *network node* and ceases to be considered a personal computer because its resources are shared. All networks have the following characteristics:
- Two or more linked computers.
- Network operating system that manages the sharing of peripheral devices (i.e. input and output media).
- Unique network address for each network node.

The Internet is a vast global system that connects computer networks. In essence, it is a network of networks linked through numerous electronic and optical devices. Using the Internet Protocol Suite (TCP/IP), a user can connect with literally millions of people, businesses, organizations, and governments across the world.

In a distributed application architecture, multiple independent computers exchange information over a computer network. Examples include client-server networks and peer-to-peer networks

Translator, compiler, and interpreter

A translator is a program capable of translating high-level primitives into machine language. In many cases, it must write (or compile) several short lines of machine instruction in order to translate one high-level primitive.

A compiler is essentially another name for a translator. It converts high-level language into machine language and, thereby, avoids the errors that normally occur when programmers translate by hand. Compilers are especially useful when using C++ and other high-level languages.

An interpreter is a program capable of executing a program as it is being translated from a high-level language into machine language. Interpreters differ from translators in that the latter must produce an entire machine-language copy of a program before it can be executed

Database management systems and data dictionaries

A database stores large quantities of information, all of which relate to a specific topic or subject. It also allows for easy retrieval and updating of stored information through software known as a *database management system*, or *DBMS*, which far exceeds the capacity and capabilities of other types of filing systems. It enables users to create, maintain, and use database contents and, in most cases, includes features for sorting information and the grouping of reports. A DBMS normally includes a *data dictionary*, which lists the names and descriptions of every data record type and the relationships between them. There are six primary types of database models: hierarchical, network, relational, distributed, object-oriented, and hypermedia. DBMSs are designed to work with each of these models.

Relational database model

A relational model is the basis for modern database design. It represents database information in two-dimensional tables, and shows the relationship between those tables. A relational database model consists of three basic parts: relations, attributes, and domains. *Relations* are represented by tables with columns and rows. Each column has a name, which is known as an *attribute*, and defines a unique data element. Columns contain a set of values of the same type. These values are known as *domains*. Each row (also known as a tuple) represents a specific entity and all the values that define it. Rows are often identified using keys.

Consider the following example:

Name of Person	Weight	Height
Paul	150	5'10"
Duncan	170	6'
Gurney	155	5'7"

In reality, the hard disk does not store information in the form of two-dimensional tables; rather, these merely provide a conceptual understanding of the operations of a relational database.

Distributed database model, object-oriented database model, and hypermedia database model

A distributed database model is a type of relational model. In a distributed database, information is spread out over multiple computers that are often separated by significant geographic distances.

The object-oriented database model derives from the object-oriented programming method and incorporates many of the same basic concepts, such as encapsulation and polymorphism. Object-oriented databases have five basic parts: objects, attributes, classes, methods, and messages.

A hypermedia database model (also known as a hypertext database model) contains data elements that define a wide variety of information, including text, graphics, sound, and video. Compared to more traditional databases, hypermedia databases possess far less structure between data elements.

- 52 -

Gantt chart, program evaluation and review techniques, and system flowchart

A Gantt chart illustrates the time requirements and tracking for every step in the systems development process. Each step is allocated a certain amount of time for completion. In most cases, each step is further divided into many different unique tasks (possibly hundreds), and each process will have a Gant chart.

A program evaluation and review techniques, or PERT, chart also shows time allocation and tracking. However, it provides a more complex illustration by showing every task and their dependence on each other. Each task is represented by a node, and the nodes are connected to each other in a network. Certain tasks cannot be started until the prior task has been completed.

A system flowchart shows the logical arrangement of the various components that make up a system—specifically the files, inputs, outputs, and processing— with an emphasis on the hardware devices that the system operates. Flowcharts are used most commonly during the systems design phase. For the sake of conformity and understanding, all flowcharts use the same symbols.

Security controls used by operating systems

Operating systems protect against outside attacks using the following controls:
- Login – requires the user to provide his name and password before accessing his account. Accounts are given by the *super user* or *administrator*, who controls settings and monitors the system.
- Auditing software – records and tracks activity within the computer in order to help the administrator detect malicious or destructive activity. Auditing software are capable of detecting *sniffing software*, which records and reports information to potential intruders.

Operating systems protect against internal attacks (i.e. unauthorized use) using the following controls:
- Privilege levels – protect multiprogramming systems by establishing two access modes: *privileged mode* and *nonprivileged mode*. In privileged mode, a user has access to *privileged instructions*, which include the ability to change memory limit registers. If a process tries to access privileged instructions in nonprivileged mode, control is transferred to an interrupt handler.

Pseudocode

Pseudocode is code that is described in general terms, avoiding the syntax of a particular language, but allowing programmers to analyze and understand the logic behind a system specification before converting it into actual programming language, which is more specific and complex. Pseudocode is written between the system specification phase and the coding phase and uses the same algebraic symbols that other computer languages use. These include the following:

- '+'means add.
- '-' means subtract.
- '*' means multiply.
- '/' means divide.
- '**' means exponentiation, or raising a value to a certain power. This symbol may vary depending on the language being used.

- 53 -

Using these algebraic symbols, computers can process expressions by computing their results. Pseudocode uses three types of simple statements: sequence, decision branching, and repetition.

Operator Precedence

In the absence of parentheses, operator precedence determines the order in which a computer evaluates program expressions. This order, from highest to lowest, goes as follows:

1. Exponentiation, or numbers that have been raised to a certain power.
2. Multiplication or division in the order they appear from left to right.
3. Addition or subtraction in the order they appear from left to right.

When parentheses are present, they are evaluated before any other expression. The innermost parentheses are worked before the outermost parentheses, and the expressions inside a parenthesis are worked in the order of operator precedence. For instance, consider the following expression:

A * (B - C)

First, the computer would calculate B - C because it is contained within parenthesis. Then, it would multiply the resulting value by A.

Statements Used In Pseudocode

Pseudocode is written in simple statements that fall under three basic categories:

- Sequence – arranges a group of computations into an ordered series of commands. Sequences

are established using the pseudocode statement SET.
- Decision branching – uses conditions, which are tests of the relationships between multiple variables. If the relationship is true, the computer will perform a certain sequence of events. If the relationship is false, the computer performs a difference sequence of events. Decision branching is a sequence using the pseudocode statement IF (followed by a condition)...THEN... ELSE...END IF.
- Repetition – instructs the computer to continue performing a certain action sequence as long as a condition is true, or sometimes for a pre-determined number of iterations. Once the condition is false, the computer moves to the next action sequence. Repetition is established using the pseudo code statement WHILE (followed by a condition)...END WHILE.

SET Statement

In pseudocode, the SET statement assigns values to variables. Consider the following examples:

SET X TO 5
SET Y TO 7
SET Z TO 9

X now equals 5; Y now equals 7; and, Z now equals 9. Assume the following statement is added after the above three:

SET Z TO Y – X

The value of Z now changes to 2. Assume the following statement is added to the above sequence:

SET Y TO Z ** 2

The value of Y is now 4 because Z was changed. The computer always executes the statement in the order they are written.

Comparisons And Logical Operators

In pseudocode, a condition statement will use symbols to instruct the computer to make certain comparisons. These symbols include the following:

- = prompts the computer to test if two values are equal.
- < prompts the computer to test if the left value is less than the right value.
- > prompts the computer to test if the left value is greater than the right value.
- >= prompts the computer to test if the left value is greater than or equal to the right value
- <= prompts the computer to test if the left value is less than or equal to the right value.
- <> prompts the computer to test if the left and right values are not equal

In addition to comparison symbols, condition statements often use the following logical operators:

- AND – indicates that both operators must be either true or false.
- OR – indicates that at least one operator must be either true or false.
- NOT – indicates that a true statement should be made false and a false statement should be made true

IF...THEN...ELSE...END IF Statement

IF...THEN...ELSE....END IF statements instruct the computer to engage in decision branching. A conditional statement will follow the initial IF clause. If the condition is true, the computer will carry out the statement sequence after the THEN clause. If the condition is false, the computer will skip the THEN clause and instead carry out the statement sequence after the ELSE clause. Once it has executed one of the clauses, the computer will move to the END IF statement. Consider the following example:

```
IF (X < Y) THEN
SET SMALLER TO X
ELSE
SET SMALLER TO Y
END IF
SET X TO 1
SET Y TO 2
```

If the X is less than Y, the computer will set the "smaller" variable to X. If X is not less than Y, the computer will set the "smaller" variable to Y. After one of the clauses is executed, the values of X and Y are set to 1 and 2, respectively.

WHILE Loop

WHILE...END WHILE statements instruct the computer to perform a repetitive function. A conditional statement will follow the WHILE clause, and the loop will repeat until the statement is false. Consequently, during the course of a WHILE loop, a value must change; otherwise, the loop will repeat into infinity. Consider the following example:

```
SET X to 100
WHILE X > 20
SET X TO X - 30
END WHILE
```

Before entering the WHILE loop, X is given a value of 100. Each time through the loop, the value of X is reduced by 30. Once it is less than 20, the loop will end.

The final value of X through this loop is 10.

Parallel Conversion and Pilot Conversion

Parallel conversion is a method of transferring data from an old, outdated system into a newer system. It involves using both systems, old and new, at the same time and then comparing their operation to find problems. Once the organization corrects any problems and determines that the new system meets all required specifications, the old system is deactivated. Parallel planning is very labor and time intensive, requiring extensive planning to execute properly. Pilot conversion is another method of transferring data between old and new systems. It is common in large organizations with multiple departments or locations that operate with a high level of independence. Only one location adopts the new system initially. If it is successful, other locations will follow suit.

Phased Conversion and Plunge

Phased conversion is a method of transferring data from an old, outdated system into a newer system. Only certain parts of the new system are implemented initially, and only specific departments can use them. If these parts fulfill their intended functions, additional parts of the new system are brought online, replacing those same parts in the old system, and more departments are brought into the mix. If the implementation is successful, the new system will eventually replace the old system. Phased conversion occurs along a detail schedule with specific milestones.

Plunge is another method of transferring data between old and new systems. It involves implementing the new system as quickly as possible. The changeover is immediate, using none of the precautions of the other conversion methods—parallel, pilot, or phased.

Programming Methodology

Programming methodology describes the method by which software is coded and put together. Software consists of three basic components:

- Units of code – are written by programmers. These units determine the interfaces, screens, processes, storage files, and outputs that a software application produces. Once a unit is completed, it is tested. If it fulfills all its requirements, it and other units are grouped together into a module.
- Modules – consist of units of code. Each module is tested to ensure that all of its units can work together to perform their intended functions. If it passes the test, it is connected to other modules to form a subsystem.
- Subsystems – consist of modules. Each time a new module is added, the system is tested to identify any errors in execution.

Designing Vs Programming Software

When designing software, programmers begin with a set of generalized, high-level concepts and work their way down to the algorithms that make up the program. In this way, software design is a top-down process. First, programmers determine the functional requirements of the software. Second, they define the relationships between modules. Lastly, they design the algorithms. By contrast, programming software is a bottom-up process. Programmers begin by coding and testing each algorithm. These algorithms are then combined into modules, which are tested and connected into groups known as subsystems. Programmers test each subsystem before combining them into the final program. In order to create a testing protocol for the final program, programmers must document and analyze each step in the programming process.

Algorithm

An algorithm instructs the computer to carry out an individual task or function. It is the most basic unit of a software program. When writing algorithms, programmers must be very precise; any ambiguity in the language could lead to errors and undesired results. These errors include endless loops (infinite repetitions in the performing of a certain task, and consuming an infinite amount of resources). To avoid these errors, the programmer must specify the exact amount of resources and the specific length of time the computer should spend to complete the task. Algorithms are essentially logical and mathematical solutions to particular problems, solved in the particular programming language being used.

Data Type

A data type describes a set of data values. Common data types include real numbers, Boolean variables, integers, characters, alphanumeric strings, and floating-point numbers. A data type also indicates all possible operations within a value set, all possible values within the set, and the storage method for the set. Data types also place constraints on the interpretation of data within a system and, thereby, enable the type system to evaluate the correctness of computer algorithms. All programming languages incorporate data types—though the terminology may differ between languages—and may permit

programmers to create new data types with their own operations. In most cases, new data types combine characteristics of existing data types.

Abstract Data Type

An abstract data type, or ADT, is a data type whose definition remains constant between different programs. In essence, when one or more programming languages use an ADT, they will have similar semantics for it. Common ADTs include stacks, queues, priority queues, strings, containers, lists, deques, maps, multimaps, multisets, trees, and sets. ADTs are used to describe abstract algorithms in simple terms, assess data structures, categorize data structures, and provide formal descriptions for programming languages. Although they are mostly theoretical and conceptual constructs, ADTs do appear in formal specification language. They can be implemented in the form of modules that include procedures for ADT operation. As conceptual tools, ADTs are important in object-oriented programming languages.

Stack

One of the most common and simple abstract data types is a stack. Its name derives from a stack of trays, which serves as a metaphor for data retrieval. Each tray represents a data element. The last data saved goes to the top of the stack and, as a consequence, becomes the first data returned when the computer retrieves information. A stack is known as a "last in, first out" (LIFO) structure. Stack abstract data types perform two primary operations:

- Push – occurs when a new data element is added to the stack.
- Pop – occurs when the computer retrieves the data that was saved most recently.

- 57 -

Stacks can include any data type, including stings, integers, real number, pointers, and even other stacks. Because the operations of a stack are the same regardless of the programming language being used, it is considered an abstract data type.

Queue

A queue is one of the most common abstract data types. It functions like a checkout line: The first person in the line will be the first person to leave the line. Similarly, in a queue retrieval system, the computer returns the first data element that was entered into the system; consequently, a queue is known as a "first in, first out" (FIFO) structure. A queue performs the same two operations (push and pop) as a stack abstract data type (the only difference is the pop operator):

- Push – occurs when a new data element is added to the stack.
- Pop – occurs when the computer returns the first data element that was saved.

The verb associated with entering data into a queue is "to enqueue." Similarly, that which pertains to the process of returning data is "to dequeue."

Array

An array is a type of data structure. It contains elements that are identified using two features: the name of the array, and the element's location within the array. Arrays can have any number of dimensions. The following example is a single dimension array:

$$ARY = [3,7,5,1]$$

The elements contained within this array are 3, 7, 4, and 1. If the system wanted to access one of them, it would identify both

the name of the array (ARY) and the single integer that corresponds to the element's location, which is usually zero-based (that is, the counting of positions begins at zero, instead of one). For instance, ARY(0) accesses the 3 element; consequently, ARY(0) = 3. The other elements are accessed as follows: ARY(1) = 7, ARY(2) = 5, and ARY(3) = 1.

Multidimensional Array

A multidimensional array is a type of data structure that is more complex than a single array. When a system accesses elements within multidimensional arrays, it identifies them using the array name and an integer set. Consider the following multidimensional array:

$$ARY = \begin{bmatrix} 1 & 4 & 8 \\ 3 & 7 & 5 \\ 2 & 9 & 0 \end{bmatrix}$$

The elements contained within the array are 1, 4, 8, 3, 7, 5, 2, 9, and 0. If the system wanted to access one of them, it would identify both the array name (ARY) and the two integers that correspond to the element's location. The first integer is the row of the data element, and the second integer is the column of data element. Once again, these tend to be zero-based. For instance, ARY(1,0) identifies the 3 data element; consequently, ARY (1,0) = 3. Other elements include ARY(0,0) = 1, ARY(2,1) = 9, and ARY(1,2) = 5.

Variables

A variable is a single location that stores one value within a computer's memory. It allows a computer to store various types of data, such as numbers and characters, on a temporary basis. The data contained within the variable is generally input into an algorithm, processed later in the algorithm, and used to generate output.

Variables are classified under two broad categories:

- Global – can be read and modified through any part of the program; as such, they are in scope throughout the entire program.
- Local – are in scope throughout only part of the program. This part usually encompasses a function or subroutine, over which the local variable can be read and modified. If a local variable is not in scope, it cannot be accessed without the part of the program which has it in scope passing it explicitly to another part of the program, where it is re-created as another local variable.

Loop and Condition Loop

A loop instructs the computer to carry out the same set of instructions more than once. There are three types of loops: conditional, counted, and infinite.

A conditional loop compares variables against a defined condition and, if the condition is true, carries out the instructions within the loop. The computer will continue to perform the instructions as long as the condition is true, and will only stop once it becomes false. Conditional loops use the terms WHILE or UNTIL. Consider the following example:

```
        A = 10
WHILE A < 100
LOOP
A = A * 2
END LOOP
```

The loop will repeat four times. The value of A at the beginning of the final loop will be 80. After that, the value of A will be 160, and it will fail the condition.

Counted Loop and Infinite Loop

A counted loop executes a set of instructions a certain number of times by defining a counting variable prior to entering the loop. The counting variable determines how many times the instructions will be carried out. Counted loops often use the terms FOR and NEXT. Consider the following example:

```
FOR A = 1 to 10
        X = X / 2
        Y = Y * 2
        Z = (Z + 1) / 2
NEXT
```

The above counted loop will be carried out ten times.

An infinite loop (also known as an endless loop) has no means of ending itself. It executes a set of instruction until the computer is shut down or an error occurs. Consider the following example:

```
        A = 5
WHILE A > 4
LOOP
A = A + 1
END LOOP
```

The above loop will never stop because the condition will always be true. Although infinite loops often occur due to error, they are sometimes intentional.

Logic Conditions

Computer algorithms perform tests on data, and then use the results of those tests to determine which instructions to perform. These tests are conducted using logic conditions, which compare the data to a constant or variable. Common logic conditions include the following:

- Equals is expressed as '=' or '= ='. This determines if the data is the

- 59 -

same value as the constant or variable.

- Less than is expressed as '<'. This determines if the data is of lower value than the constant or variable.
- Greater than is expressed as '>'. This determines if the data is of greater value than the constant or variable.
- Not equals is expressed as '!=' or '<>'. This determines if the data is not the same value as the constant or variable.

Boolean Operators and Limitations on Data Testing

In addition to the common logic conditions, computer algorithms use Boolean operators (also known as logical operators) to perform more complex tests on data. Boolean operators include the following:

- And is expressed as '&&'.
- Not is expresses a '!'.
- Or is expressed as 'II'.

When a computer tests data against a constant or variable, both the data and the variable must be of the same data type. For instance, an integer can only be tested against another integer, and a character can only be compared against another character. In some cases, if the data and variable do not match, the programming language will convert them into the same type, usually according to their ASCII value.

IF Statements

Using IF statements, computers perform logic tests on data. IF statements have three basic variations: ELSE, ELSE IF, and CASE. Although the syntax of an IF statement varies between programming languages, it generally follows the same

basic structure. Consider the following examples:

- IF X<Y, THEN A
Translation: If X is less than Y, perform action A.
- IF X!=Y, THEN A
Translation: If X does not equal Y, perform action A.
- IF X=Y && Y=Y, THEN A
Translation: If X equals Y and Y equals Y, perform action A.
- IF X<=Y, THEN A
Translation: If X is less than or equal to Y, perform action A.
- IF X=1 II Y=2, THEN A
Translation: If X equals 1 or Y equals 2, perform action A.

ELSE Statement and ELSE IF Statement

An ELSE statement is one variation on an IF statement. It instructs the computer to perform a secondary action if the logical test fails. Consider the following examples:

IF X<Y, THEN A ELSE B

Translation: If X is less than Y, perform function A. If X is not less than Y, perform action B.

An ELSE IF statement instructs the computer to perform a different logic test if the first logic test fails. Consider the following example:

IF X<Y, THEN A ELSE IF X=Y THEN B

Translation: If X is less than Y, perform action A. If X is not less than Y, determine if X equals Y (second logic test). If this is true, perform action B.

CASE Statement

A CASE statement (also known as a SELECT or SWITCH statement) is used

- 60 -

when a logic test could produce multiple outcomes. It instructs the computer to perform a different action for each outcome:

CASE 1: A
CASE 2: B
CASE 3: C

Translation: If logic test 1 is true, perform action A. If logic test 2 is true, perform action B. If logic test 3 is true, perform action C.

For statements, CASE statements provide a means of simplifying ELSE IF statements. For instance, the above CASE statement is the same as the following ELSE IF statement:

IF (logic test 1) THEN A ELSE IF (logic test 2) THEN B ELSE IF (logic test 3) THEN C.

Machine, Symbolic, and Assembly Languages

Machine language is the native language of a particular processor architecture. Almost no one can write directly in machine language, as it requires extensive knowledge of internal processor directives, and the ability to memorize commands as binary (zero and one) commands.

Symbolic language is the general name for the alternative to writing in machine code—namely, all languages which replace the sequences of zeroes and ones with symbols and acronyms; that is, words that describe what action the programmer wishes to perform using the processor's capabilities.

Assembly language was the first type of symbolic language, named such because it assembled the defined acronyms into sequences of binary code (0s and 1s). When writing in an assembly language,

the programmer must code every line of CPU instruction, meaning the ratio between a line of code in assembly language and a line of code in machine language is still one to one. Today, assembly language is used primarily for special purpose computer applications.

High Level Language

High level language has long replaced assembly language as the predominant programming language. High level languages possess a number of advantages over their forerunners:

- They do not require a one-to-one ratio between lines of programming code and lines of machine code.
- High level languages are separate from the instruction set of the CPU; consequently, they can be used on multiple types and models of CPU.
- A highly level language is similar to a natural language such as English, allowing the programmer to write code in a more intuitive way.

Once a program is coded in high level language, it must pass through a compiler, which translates into it machine language for the CPU. There are five categories of high level language: procedural, object-oriented, functional, declarative, and special.

<u>Procedural Category of High Level Language</u>
Procedural is a category of high level programming language. It instructs the computer to execute the code in the order it is written. There are several examples of procedural languages:

- FORTRAN or Formula Translation – was prominent in the late 1950s, and is still well-suited for programming applications in science and engineering.

- BASIC or Beginner's All-Purpose Symbolic Instruction Code – was available in 1964, and used mostly as a teaching tool. BASIC does not require a compiler; as a result; it saw a revival in the 1990s as a means of programming personal computers.
- COBOL or Common Business-Oriented Language – has been used since 1960s for business applications.
- Pascal – was a popular teaching language in the 1970s.
- C language – was created specifically for programming UNIX operating systems. It was developed in the early 1970s, and is still very popular as a general-purpose language.

Object-Oriented Category of High-Level Language

Object-oriented is a category of high-level programming language. In the object-oriented method, the programmer first defines objects and then assigns operations to those objects. Below are two examples of object-oriented languages:

- ◆ C++ – is derived from C language, and is used for a variety of applications. There are three principles to C++ language:
  1. Encapsulation – the process of hiding information inside an object.
  2. Inheritance – the process of transferring properties between related objects.
  3. Polymorphism – the process of giving the same name to different processes. This is allowed

as long as the processes exist in different classes of objects.

- Java – is derived from C and C++ languages. There are two types of Java programs:
  1. Applications
  2. Applets – mini-programs. For instance, a web document may embed an applet, and then a browser runs the applet after it has downloaded.

Special Category of High Level Language

Special is a category of high level programming language. It includes any languages that cannot be classified under the other categories, such as the following:

- PERL or Practical Extraction and Report Language – is capable of scanning text files, extracting information from text files, creating reports, and performing many of the same functions as the C language. Like JavaScript, PERL is known as a scripting language because it can be interpreted, or "read" (like a script) by the computer. For instance, the Common Gateway Interface (CGI) uses PERL to create scripts that manage HTML output.
- SQL or Structured Query Language – allows user to interrogate a database and, thereby, extract information.
- HTML or HyperText Markup Language.

HTML

HTML, or HyperText Markup Language, is classified under the special category of high level programming language even though it is not an actual programming language. Using HTML, programmers can embed formatting instructions into a file.

- 62 -

The browser then reads the instructions and uses them to display the file on a computer monitor. An HTML file generally begins with angle brackets (<>), which enclose the word HTML. This lets the browser know that it is an html document. The information enclosed within the angle brackets is known as a formatting tag. HTML files consist of a <head>, which identifies the title and browser parameters, and a <body>, which identifies the text and formatting tags. Between the <body>...</body> tags, the content of the document is laid out using the formatting capabilities of HTML.

Functional and Declarative
Functional is a category of high level programming language which includes a group of primitive functions. By combining these functions, a programmer can create new functions and programs. Functional languages are poorly suited for designing information systems, but have their benefits in the academic sphere. An example of a functional language is Lisp, which was made available in the early 1960s.

Declarative is another category of high level programming language. It uses formal logic to create new programs, and is also not suited to implementing information systems. Declarative languages differ from imperative languages in that declarative languages state known information and desired outcomes, and allow the machine to derive the process, whereas imperative languages describe explicitly how to solve a problem. Declarative languages are essential to artificial intelligence. An example of a declarative language is prolog, which was made available in the early 1970s.

Data Structure

A data structure contains a number of related variables. Using data structures, systems can process multiple variables at once. This ability is very useful when handling large amounts of data, such as customer lists, inventory lists, etc. Pseudocode allows the programmer to work with only one variable at a time, which has almost no practical value in modern information systems. Procedural programming languages can handle a limited number of advanced data structures, increasing their practicality. However, only database systems can support the most advanced data structures, which enable the real-time processing of information. A special type of data structure is an array. It stores data in a list where it can be accessed easily. All data in the array must be of the same type. Procedural languages such as C, C++, Java, FORTRAN and COBOL make extensive use of arrays.

Array, One-Dimensional Array, Two-Dimensional Array
An array stores data in a fixed-size sequence. Every element within the sequence must be of the same data type—i.e., an array must contain all integers or all characters or all alphanumeric strings. Using a subscript (also, index), the computer selects data from the array for processing. In most cases, the subscript uses a zero-based set of enumerated integers (i.e., 0, 1, 2, ... n) and moves through the array by addressing the desired index value of the array. For instance, in C:

    float accounts[10];

...would create a 10-element array of floating-point (decimal) numbers called 'accounts', which could then be modified using the index values 0-9 (10 total).

Therefore, if we wished to store the value 15.9 in the first index of the 'accounts' array:

accounts[0] = 15.9;

Like all variables, the computer's memory stores the array only as long as the program is running.

A one-dimensional array is an array with data aligned in a single row, like a list.

A two-dimensional array arranges data in multiple rows and columns.

Record
A record is one of the simplest data structures. It contains one or more data elements, and stores them in sequential positions in the computer's memory. In many cases, these elements are of completely different data types (i.e. integers, text, alphanumeric strings, or any other type of value).

A record consists of a name and different fields. Each field holds a data element. For example, a record might store information on a house. Each field within the record would contain a different characteristic of the house—square footage, dimensions, lot size, cost, street address, construction, names of owners, and any other pertinent information. Expressing these elements requires different data types, both numeric and textual. A computer stores records within files on the hard drive, and cannot process them without accessing and reading them.

Files Processed By Procedural Languages

There are two types of files that procedural programming languages are capable of processing. Both are featured prominently in mainframes that perform batch processing:

- Sequential files – are best suited for storing information that is processed routinely. The computer must access the entire file before it can process any of the records contained therein.
- Random files (also known as direct access file) – allows the computer to process any individual record without accessing the entire file. In order to access the record, the user must have a record key, which is normally a unique number or designation. An example is an invoice number or a shipping number.

Database

A database stores large quantities of information, all of which relate to a specific topic or subject. It also allows for easy retrieval and updating of stored information through software known as a database management system, or DBMS, which far exceeds the capacity and capabilities of other types of filing systems. It enables users to create, maintain, and use database contents and, in most cases, includes features for sorting information and the grouping of reports. A DBMS normally includes a data dictionary, which lists the names and descriptions of every data record type and the relationships between them. There are six primary types of database models: hierarchical, network, relational, distributed, object-oriented, and hypermedia. DBMSs are designed to work with each of these models.

Hierarchical Database Model
A hierarchical database model arranges information in the form of an upside down tree-like structure, much like a

- 64 -

family tree (i.e. the lineage of many children can be traced back to a single parent). At the top of the hierarchy sits a general subject, such as the United States of America. This subject is then divided into a group of related topics, such as the individual states that comprise the USA. These topics can be further divided into even smaller topics, such as the counties in every state.

Subjuect ->topic->subtopic, etc

Hierarchical databases are often described as a one-to-many relationship because every data element can be traced back to a single, overarching topic. Additionally, all related data elements reside on the same level in the hierarchy. The hierarchical model is very useful for nesting information, and was used prominently in early databases; however, since then, it has become obsolete.

Network Database Model
A network database model is similar to the hierarchical model because the nodes at the top of the model branch out into multiple nodes at the bottom. However, unlike a hierarchical model, nodes at the bottom can connect to multiple nodes at the top. This allows the model to display many-to-many relationships, which are the redundant relationships between information.

A network model consists of two main parts: records and sets. Records contain fields of information related to a specific topic, and sets display the one-to-many (hierarchical) relationships between records. Although network models can handle more complex information than hierarchical models, they are still obsolete.

Relational Database Model
A relational model is the basis for modern database design. It represents database

information in two-dimensional tables, and shows the relationship between those tables. A relational database model consists of three basic parts: relations, attributes, and domains. Relations are represented by tables with columns and rows. Each column has a name, which is known as an attribute, and defines a unique data element. Columns contain a set of values of the same type. These values are known as domains. Each row (also known as a tuple) represents a specific entity and all the values that define it. Rows are often identified using keys. Consider the following example:

Name of Person	Weight	Height
Paul	150	5'10"
Duncan	170	6'
Gurney	155	5'7"

In reality, the hard disk does not store information in the form of two-dimensional tables; rather, these merely provide a conceptual understanding of the operations of a relational database.

Distributed Database Model, Object-Oriented Database Model, And Hypermedia Database Model
Distributed database models are a type of relational model. In a distributed database, information is spread out over multiple computers that are often separated by significant geographic distances.

The object-oriented database model derives from the object-oriented programming method and incorporates many of the same basic concepts, such as encapsulation and polymorphism. Object-oriented databases have five basic parts: objects, attributes, classes, methods, and messages.

A hypermedia database model (also known as a hypertext database model) contains data elements that define a wide variety of information, including text, graphics, sound, and video. Compared to more traditional databases, hypermedia databases possess far less structure between data elements.

Object-Oriented Programming Method

In the object-oriented programming (or OOP) method, programmers use objects as the basis for designing software applications. Objects are defined by both the data they contain and the relationships between them. There are ten basic concepts in OOP:

1. Class – describes the characteristics (attributes, fields, behaviors, etc.) of an object.
2. Object – an instance of the class. Whereas the class is a blueprint, the object is the created output of that blueprint, inheriting the qualities of the class, but can be further modified.
3. Instance – is one copy of an object. For example, if the office of U.S. President were a class, then Ronald Reagan would be an instance (object) of the President class.
4. Method – a routine which belongs to an object or class. If Ronald Reagan cut taxes more thoroughly than many other presidents, then perhaps "CutTaxes" could be a method that belongs to the Ronald Reagan object.
5. Message passing – describes the methods by which objects communicate to other objects.
6. Inheritance – is the process by which classes impart their attributes to subclasses and objects. For instance, if Ronald Reagan (object instance) is a President (class), and all presidents can veto, then the "Veto" method is available to the Ronald Reagan object. This reduces redundancy.
7. Abstraction – is method simplifying and modeling programming problems.
8. Encapsulation – hides the functional details of a class. The "Veto" method might be complex, but only the person who writes it in the class needs to know exactly how it works. Others can use the method whenever they invoke the class, without having to understand how the class works, internally.
9. Polymorphism – allows classes and their subclasses to be handled in the same manner.
10. Decoupling – separates object interaction from its class.

Structured Query Language

Structured query language, or SQL (pronounced "sequel"), helps manage information within relational databases. Based on relational algebra, SQL allows the user to interrogate databases and extract information in the form of records. Additionally, it facilitates the process of updating information, changing schemas, and controlling access to data. SQL consists of the following elements:

- Clauses – the optional parts of statements.
- Expressions – generate values or tables containing information.
- Predicates – define the conditions that SQL will use when finding data.
- Queries – retrieve specific information from the database.
- Statements – influence schemas and information, and manage other aspects of database information retrieval.

- 66 -

- Insignificant white space – part of statements and queries, but is largely ignored by SQL.

Data Warehouse

A data warehouse facilitates the reporting and analysis of information and, thereby, aids the process of management decision making. Data warehouses use a relational database management system, but tend to store data differently than operational databases. Most data warehouses include tools for managing data dictionaries; retrieving, changing, and loading information into a repository; business intelligence; and managing metadata. There are three primary design methodologies in data warehousing:

- Bottom-up – initially creates data marts to analyze and report on business processes. The data marts are then connected to create the warehouse.
- Top-down – stores all organizational information in a centralized data warehouse. Data marts are then created to process information specific to a department.
- Hybrid – combines the speed advantage of a bottom-up design with the consistency advantage of the top-down design.

Data Mart

A data mart is similar to a data warehouse but has a much narrower focus, concentrating on only one function or subject area. It analyzes information for the benefit of a specific department or group within an organization. Although data marts are generally used in concert with data warehouses, they are not the same. Data marts provide information that fulfills user needs. Conversely, data warehouses focus on information that already exists and the methods for storing and retrieving that information. In a bottom-up warehousing methodology, data marts are created and then connected to create a data warehouse. In top-down warehousing methodology, all organizational information is first stored within a central warehouse and then data marts are created to extract and analyze information.

Data Mining

Data mining is a method of examining information and extracting trends or forecasts that had gone unnoticed beforehand. Data mining uses data warehouses and data marts as sources. It is very useful in marketing, scientific research, and surveillance. In most cases, data mining is not performed on all available data but, rather, a sampling of that data; consequently, the accuracy of the trend or forecast depends entirely on how well the sample represents the population as a whole. Data mining consists of four basic tasks:

- Classification – arranges data elements into groups that the user defines.
- Clustering – arranges data elements according similarity rather than predefined groups.
- Regression – models the data according to the function that is least error-prone.
- Association rule learning – examines different variables for any relationships between them.

XML

XML, or Extensible Markup Language, provides a set of rules and specifications for the electronic encoding of documents, using open standards produced by W3C. XML is specifically designed to be used over the Internet in order to simplify, generalize, and increase the usability of web documents and services. RSS, Atom, SOAP, and XHTML are examples of XML-based formats, which have become the default language for most office productivity software, including Microsoft Office, iWork, and OpenOffice.org. XML uses the following constructs:

- Characters – comprise XML documents. All characters are taken from Unicode.
- Processor and application – The processor examines the markup, converts it into structured information, and then sends it to the applications.
- Markup and content – the two categories of characters that comprise an XML document. Markup is offset using chevrons ("<" and ">").
- Tags – surrounded by the aforementioned chevrons, tags identify the beginning, end, and empty-element elements in a document.
- Element – a logical component of the XML document that begins with a start-tag and ends with an end-tag.
- Attribute – a special type of markup containing a name/value pair.
- XML declaration – the information that precedes an XML document.

Electronic Document Management

An electronic document management (or EDM) system helps manage, track, and store electronic documents and images of paper documents. Like most document management systems, EDM has tools for storing data and metadata (e.g., the date when the data element was stored and the person who stored it); integrating data with other applications; filing, retrieving, indexing and distributing in certain formats; providing document

security, workflow and versioning (i.e. checking the information in and out to users); collaboration between users and searching for specific files and folders. As part of enterprise content management, EDM has applications for digital asset management, document imaging, and records management.
Image processing occurs when a document image is captured, stored, processed, or retrieved. These images can contain numbers, text, graphics, photographs and even handwriting.

Web Design

The purpose of web design is creating a web site, which uses the Internet to deliver content to a user. This content is created in hypertext or hypermedia, and is accessed using a web browser. Web sites usually contain text and images. Using HTML/XHTML/XML tags, programmers can imbed various types of media—such as pictures, videos, and plug-ins—into web pages. There are four basic considerations when designing web pages:

- Content – the information contained in the page. It should relate to other information on the site, and fulfill the needs of the users.
- Usability – refers to the ease with which the site can be navigated and interfaced.
- Appearance – refers to the graphics and text layout of the page. It should be uniform throughout the site.
- Visibility – describes the ease with which the site can be found. Does it appear in search engines?

Hypertext

Hypertext describes text, images, and other types of media that are viewed on an electronic device, such as a computer monitor. Hypertext can be static (meaning the information contained in the document does not change) or dynamic (meaning the information changes in response to the user). Static hypertext is especially important in the realm of electronic books; however, it also applies to software and documents used to cross-reference data. Dynamic hypertext usually includes user interfaces, such as pull-down menus. In most cases, hypertext documents contain hyperlinks, which allow the user to access related information by pointing and clicking. Because hypertext is capable of interacting with and reading documents, it also provides a structure for extracting information from databases and, most famously, the World Wide Web. Using various software packages, users can create hypertext documents, but these are limited to containing text and only few types of graphics.

Hypermedia

Hypermedia simply expands the concept of hypertext. It uses hyperlinks to arrange multiple types of media (text, graphics, video, audio, etc.) into a non-linear presentation. In this way, hypermedia differs from multimedia, which arranges multiple types of media into a linear presentation. The most well-known example of hypermedia is the World Wide Web, which includes hyperlinks, text, images, and videos that can be navigated in any order. Electronic documents are the most common method of displaying hypermedia, usually though applications such as Web browsers, media players, and voice command browsers. Users can create hypermedia documents using Adobe Flash, Adobe Director and Macromedia Authorware. Databases can make use of hypermedia through applications such as Visual FoxPro and FilmMaker Developer.

Systems analysis

Systems analysis and design is a model for observing and improving systems, and consists of six phases. The first phase is investigation and planning. The second is analysis, in which required improvements are outlined. Next is design, in which a plan for making the improvements is created. The fourth phase is development, in which the new software is created and tested. Phase five is implementation, in which the new software is put into action. The sixth and final phase is maintenance, in which bugs are diagnosed and corrected. This six-phase process is known as the systems development life cycle, or SDLC.

Testing new software

Before a piece of software is introduced to the public, it goes through what is called alpha testing, which is performed by the employees of the software publisher. After all of the problems discovered during alpha testing are resolved, the software program undergoes beta testing, which is performed by sophisticated computer users not employed by the software publisher. In some cases, beta testing is performed by unpaid volunteers on the Internet. Many computer hobbyists enjoy performing beta testing for new programs. After problems discovered during beta testing are resolved, the software will be released to the general public. Following the release, it is still likely that bugs will be discovered, so the software publisher will usually continue to work on patches and new versions of the program.

Software version and software release

When a piece of software receives a major upgrade, a new version of the software is released. New versions are typically designated by numbers, such as 1.0 or 2.0, placed after the name of the program.

One notable exception to this format is Windows, which has new versions like Windows XP and Windows Vista. A software release, on the other hand, represents only a minor change to the program. The standard format for indicating a release is adjusting the number in the tenth decimal place of the version number: changing from 2.0 to 2.1, for instance. Releases, which are also known as additions, typically feature more subtle changes to the original program.

Software copyrights

A software copyright safeguards ownership of a program and restricts the rights of non-owners to alter and distribute the program. A consumer who purchases a piece of software does not have the right to sell copies, but is permitted to install the program and make a back-up copy. Moreover, purchasers are allowed to copy sections of software for use in a teaching situation. For instance, computer science professors can use sections of software to illustrate principles of programming. The copyright notice on a piece of software typically appears in the form of the copyright symbol followed by the year (e.g., ©2010), though the absence of this notice does not preclude copyright protection.

Data

In computing, data can be described as any symbols that are used to represent numbers and letters. The format in which data is stored is known as data representation. On modern computers, data can be represented by numbers, text, images, music, and more. Data is either analog or digital: analog data is exemplified by music or color, while digital data is exemplified by binary code made entirely of zeros and ones.

Algorithms

An algorithm may be expressed as a formula or as a sequence of instructions that will accomplish a specific task. In computer programming, professionals use algorithms to circumvent the need for long sequences of code. Instead of telling the computer program what to do in every conceivable circumstance, the programmer can write an algorithm that tells the program to do a certain thing if one variable is true, and to do something else if that variable is false. In other words, an algorithm can reduce a near-infinite range of possibilities to a simple "yes or no" choice. Algorithms are also capable of many other functions in computer programming.

Stages in hardware development

A new piece of hardware goes through the following five stages:
- Product development: specifications are determined and a manufacturer creates prototypes of the new device
- Product announcement: production of the new device is announced to the public; interestingly, many of the products that are announced are never actually produced
- Product introduction: the product is made available on a limited basis, and typically at a high price
- Product maintenance: the demand for the product is assessed and a price is set
- Product retirement: the project has become outdated and production is discontinued; at this point, the manufacturer usually ceases to offer technical support

VDE

A visual development environment (VDE) enables a computer programmer to use the shortcut of point-and-click technology instead of laboriously typing out an entire code. Sometimes, computer programs contain repetitions of vast code strings which can be extremely tedious to retype; a VDE eliminates that tedium. A VDE also often contains a form design grid within which the programmer can make changes to the design of the user interface. Most VDEs also allow customization by the user. For instance, the programmer can choose from a range of background colors for the program.

Digital circuit theory and combinational logic

In digital circuit theory, information is encoded as a series of digits—1s and 0s—that are stored in numerous devices. Each device stores one of the digits. This method of storing information differs from the analogue method, in which information is stored in only one device that can display any value within a range of values.

Combinational logic is part of digital circuit theory and a type of digital logic. When implementing combinational logic circuits, developers use boolean circuits in which output is a pure function of present input. Consequently, combination circuits do not have memory. In computer circuitry, combinational logic is used in the ALU (Arithmetic Logic Unit) to perform mathematical calculation and in other systems to perform Boolean algebra on input signals and data stored in memory. Combinational logic serves as the basis for many other computer circuits as well, such as encoders, decoders, half adders, full adders, multiplexers, demultiplexers, half subtractors, and full subtractors.

Sequential logic

Sequential logic is part of digital circuit theory and a type of digital logic. In sequential circuits, the output is contingent on both present input and input history, meaning sequential circuits have memory. Consequently, they are often used in creating a computer's memory and can be designed as finite state machines, such as Moore Machines and a Mealy Machines. Using finite state machines, developers can test the system even without understanding all of its base logic functions. The simplest component of a sequential system is a *flip flop*, which is an electronic circuit with two stable states. Because a flip flop has two stable states, it is capable of representing one bit of data. Flip flops are manipulated using control signals and gate/clock signals. There are two primary types of sequential logic circuits: synchronous and asynchronous.

Synchronous and asynchronous sequential systems

Synchronous sequential systems use digital circuits that are synchronized by clock signals, which are governed by a specific timing margin. When the clock signal is sent, the entire system changes state. A sequential system consists of a combinational logic device and a *state register*, which is a pair of flip flops that represents a binary number. When the state changes, the state register sends the previous combinational logic state as an input through the combinational logic device. The clock should only move as quickly as time required to calculate the most time-intensive calculation.

Asynchronous systems are not governed by a clock; rather, they have a modular design consisting of numerous concurrent hardware devices that achieve synchronization through communication interfaces. Asynchronous systems are much more difficult to design because they must account for all possible states in all possible timings. If they fail to account for this, the logic will be unstable. However, stable asynchronous systems are considered superior because they run as fast as their gates allow.

Number representation within computers

Computers represent numeric values using binary notation, which can store any integer value between 0 and 65536 in 16 bits. Binary notation is a base two system, meaning it consists of only two digits, 1 and 0. For instance, the binary representation for the number fourteen is 1110. It consists of four position holders. The position holder farthest to the right is the one position. Each subsequent position is twice the quantity of the previous one.

1	1	1	0
eight	four	two	one

The occupied spaces are eight, four, and two: 8 + 4 + 2 = 14. By using a radix point, binary notation can represent fractional values in the same way a decimal does. The first position immediately following the decimal point has a value of one-half. Each subse-quent position is twice the quantity of the previous one.

The above notation represents the number 14 5/8. There are several forms of the binary notation, including two's complement notation and floating point notation.

Arithmetic in binary notation

Binary notation consists of only two digits, 1 and 0. Adding these digits produces the following values:
$0 + 0 = 0$
$0 + 1 = 1$
$1 + 1 = 10$ (which is expressed as 2 in base ten notation)

When adding together larger binary values, we can add by columns, much like we do when adding together numbers in a base ten system.

If a column has a sum total value greater than 1, we drop the smaller position and raise the larger one. For instance, in the second column from the right in the above example, the sum total was 10 (two in base ten); therefore, we dropped the 0 beneath the column, and brought the 1 to top of the next column. In the fifth column, the sum total was 11 (three in base ten); therefore, we dropped the 1 and raised the 1. Performing addition in two's complement notation is similar to the algorithm with one exception: Every number, even the answer, must be truncated to the same length.

Two's complement notation

Two's complement notation is the most popular method of binary notation and is capable of representing both positive and negative integers. Each value in the system is represented by a pattern of bits—a many as 32 bits, in some cases. Consider the example below, which uses a 3 bit pattern:

Bit Pattern	Corresponding Value
011	3
001	1
111	-1
101	-3
010	2
000	0
110	-2
100	-4

Regardless of the length of the bit pattern, the value 0 will always consist of all zeros in the pattern, and the value -1 consists of all ones in the pattern. The leftmost bit is known as the *sign bit*, which determines whether the corresponding value is positive or negative—0 means positive while 1 means negative. Also, the bit patterns are *complementary*, meaning the negative patterns are always the opposite of the positive patterns of the same magnitude. This allows the machine to simply invert the pattern to provide the positive decimal value, leading to faster handling of negative numbers. Performing addition on these numbers can lead to the problem of *overflow*, which occurs when the sum total falls outside the range of values the bit pattern is capable of representing. In 32 bits, that value is 2,147,483, 647.

Excess notation

Excess notation is a method of storing positive or negative integers using binary notation. Each value is represented by a bit pattern of the same length, and pattern length determines the type of excess notation. For instance, a pattern with a length of three bits is known as excess 4 notation, and a four bit length pattern is known as excess 8 notation. Consider the following example of excess 4 notation:

Three-Bit Pattern	Corresponding Value
111	3
110	2
101	1
100	0
011	-1
010	-2
001	-3
000	-4

In excess notation, the leftmost digit is the *sign bit*, which determines whether the corresponding value is positive negate—1 means positive while 0 means negative.

(This is opposite from two's complement notation.) The bit patterns are complementary, meaning the negative patterns are always opposite the positive patterns of the same magnitude. The bit pattern representing the positive number of the greatest magnitude will always consists of all ones, and the bit pattern representing the negative number of the greatest magnitude will always consist of all zeros. The bit pattern representing 0 will always have a one in the leftmost bit followed by all zeros.

Floating-point notation

Floating point notation is a method of storing fractional values using binary notation. Consider the following example:

01011110

To determine the value represented by the above floating point notation, we divide its bit into three section:

♦ *Sign bit* – is the leftmost digit: 0.
♦ *Exponent field* – consists of three digits following the sign bit: 101.
♦ *Mantissa field* – consists of final four digits: 1110.

First, we extract the mantissa field and place a radix point in front of it:
.1110
Second, we examine the exponent field, and determine the type of excess notation: 101
In this case, it is three-bit excess notation, and the represented value is 1. Consequently, we move radix point in the mantissa one digit to the right. (If the value had been negative, the point would have been moved to the left.)   1.110

The above binary notation corresponds to a base-ten value of 1¾. This value is positive because the sign bit is 0. Floating point notation can be represented using multiple bit lengths. Most computers use

- 73 -

a length of 32 bits (as opposed to 8 bits in the above example). Using the appropriate bit length is important in avoiding truncation errors and round-off errors.

Instruction set

An instruction set, also known as an instruction set architecture or ISA, includes machine language specifications and sets of native commands carried out by processors. It can be implemented in both hardware and software. An instruction set resides within the section of computer architecture associated with programming, where it handles components such as native data types, instructions, interrupt and exception handling, external I/O, memory architecture, addressing modes, and registers. The microarchitecture of a computer decodes and sequences ISA instructions using transfer language; however, computers with completely different microarchitectures are capable of implementing the same instruction set. There are multiple types of ISAs, including the *complex instruction set computer* (*CISC*), *reduced instruction set computing* (*RISC*), and the *minimal instruction set computer* (*MISC*). Each type has the same three grouping of instructions:
- Data transfer group.
- Arithmetic/logic group.
- Control group.

Instruction set architectures

Instruction sets come in multiple types of architectures:
- *Reduced instruction set computing* or *RISC* – is designed so that the CPU can execute as few instructions as possible. It reduces the number of operations that instructions perform and, in doing so, increases speed and efficiency. It can use both 2-operand and 3-operand instructions. Examples include PowerPC processors and SPARC.
- *Complex instruction set computer* or *CISC* – is designed so that the CPU can execute numerous complex and redundant instructions. A single instruction can carry out a task that would require several instructions in RISC. Consequently, CISC architecture facilitates programming. It can use both 2-operand and 3-operand instructions. Examples include the Pentium processors.
- *Minimal instruction set computer* or *MISC* – are type of stack machine. It contains very few basic operations and operands. Less time is required to decode but the dependency between instructions is increased. Use 0 or 1 operands.

CPU and the arithmetic logic unit

The central processing unit, or CPU, manages data manipulation within the computer. It consists of three parts:
- Arithmetic/logic unit – carries out operations (addition, subtraction, multiplication, etc.) on data.
- Control unit – manages machine activities.
- Register unit – consists of registers, which are data storage cells that provide temporary information storage within the CPU. There are two types of registers: special-purpose and general-purpose.

General-purpose registers provide temporary storage for data the CPU is using. Specifically, it contains the inputs to the arithmetic/logic unit and the outputs it produces. Before the CPU can

- 74 -

perform operations on data contained in main memory, the control unit must retrieve the data and send it to the general purpose registers. Then, the control unit informs and turns on the required circuitry within the arithmetic/logic unit and identifies the registers to which the output should be sent.

Instruction register and program counter

When the CPU executes a program, it uses two special-purpose registers: the instruction register and program counter. The instruction register provides temporary storage for instructions that are being executed. The program counter provides temporary storage for the address of the next instruction that will be executed, keeping track of the computer's place in the program. These registers play a large role in the *machine cycle*—the three-step process by which the CPU executes a program. These steps include fetch, decode, and execute. During fetch, the CPU retrieves information from two memory cells in main memory, and deposits it into the instruction register. The CPU then moves the program counter up two spaces so that it points to the address of the next instruction set. At this point, the CPU decodes the information in the instruction register using op-code and then executes it.

Data path and control sequencing

Data path is the array of functional units that carry out data processing operations. These units include arithmetic logic units and multipliers. In most cases, the central processing unit is comprised of a data path and a control unit, which manages the interaction between the data path and the main memory. Early computers suffered from a lack of flexibility because the program that each device followed

was wired directly into the control unit. However, when developers learned that a program could be stored as data in main memory, they developed the *stored-program concept*. As a result, the control unit could extract a program from memory, and deliver it to the data path.

Control sequencing manages the execution order of a set of instructions intended to carry out a certain operation.

Data transfer group of the instruction set

Using instructions contained within the data transfer group, the CPU can request the movement of data between two locations, such as the CPU and the main memory. However, more accurate descriptions of this process are "copy" or "clone" because the data is seldom erased from the first location. The data transfer group uses terms such as LOAD, which requests that data stored in memory be moved to a general-purpose register, and STORE, which requests that data be stored in a memory cell. The data transfer group also includes the *I/O instructions*, which manage the computer's input/output activities and enable communication with peripherals and other devices that are not part of the CPU-main memory. Examples include keyboards, monitors, and printers.

Arithmetic/logic group and the control group of the instruction set

Using instructions contained within the arithmetic/logic group, the CPU can instruct the arithmetic/logic unit to perform a certain task. Along with basic addition and subtraction, this unit can also perform tasks using Boolean operators (such as AND, OR, and XOR), and move contents from left to right (or right to left) in the registers using SHIFT or ROTATE procedures. When performing SHIFT commands, the information at the end of the register row will simply fall off and be discarded. When performing ROTATE commands, the information at the end of the row will be placed in the empty registers at the beginning.

Using instructions contained within the control group, the CPU can manage program execution. One example of a control instruction is a JUMP, also known as a BRANCH procedure, which falls under two categories:

- Unconditional jumps – instruct the computer to skip to a specific step during program execution.
- Conditional jumps – instruct the computer to skip to a specific step only if a certain condition is present.

Memory manager

A memory manager is part of the operating system. It manages the usage of main memory within the computer by determining and allocating the amount of RAM necessary to run a program. In an operating system, memory managers can function in one of two possible ways:

- Monoprogramming – RAM can contain and execute only one program at once.
- Multiprogramming – RAM can contain and execute more than one program at once.

Although multiprogramming can involve running multiple programs simultaneously, it can also involve running the programs concurrently. In concurrent operation, the operating system holds multiple programs in RAM but only executes one at any given time. After a certain duration has passed, the operating system then moves to another program. Multiprogramming can be

executed using a variety of techniques, including partitioning and paging.

Virtual memory, partitioning, and paging

Virtual memory is created when the memory required to run a program is greater than the computer's actual main memory capacity. In essence, virtual memory is the false impression of additional memory. This can be done using a technique known as paging.

Paging creates virtual memory by dividing the program into separate units called page segments, each of which contains only a few kilobytes of information. The memory manager then alternates these pages between main memory and mass storage, ensuring that the required pages are stored in main memory. In certain cases, paging can lead to *thrashing*, in which the operating system has difficulty transitioning between pages.

Partitioning is a concurrent multiprogramming technique. The operating system sets aside an area in RAM known as a partition, which is capable of holding multiple programs. The system then executes each program one at time. Partitioning requires more memory than paging because it stores the program in its entirety.

Cache memory

Cache memory is a special memory area located within the CPU. It possesses several hundred kilobytes of high-speed memory, and contains information that is needed immediately. Cache memory saves the registers from constantly having to extract data from main memory, speeding up program execution because the machine cycle is not hampered by having to communicate with main memory. If information is changed within cache memory, it is later saved to main memory.

The components within a computer's memory serve the following functions:

- *Registers* – contain information that is needed to perform the current operation.
- *Main memory* – stores information that will be needed soon.
- *Mass storage* – stores information that will not be needed for some time.

Main memory

Main memory is the area in which a computer stores information. It consists of numerous circuits, each of which holds one *bit*. From an organizational standpoint, main memory is divided into units known as *cells*. Each cell holds one *byte* (eight bits) of information. Programmers conceive of a cell as consisting of a row of bits. The leftmost bit is regarded as the *high-order end* because it contains the *most significant bit*. The rightmost bit is regarded as the *low-order end* because it contains the *least significant bit*. Cells are identified by an *addressing system* that starts with zero. Multiple cells can combine to store long strings of information that may exceed eight bits. In addition to storage circuitry, main memory also includes circuitry that enables other circuits to store and retrieve information. The process of retrieving data from main memory is known as a *read operation*, which requests the address of the desired data. The process of storing information to main memory is known as a *write operation*, which requests that information be placed at a specific address.

Random-access memory, dynamic memory

Random-access memory, or RAM, is another name for the computer's main memory. Random-access implies that stored data can be accessed in any order independent of physical location, unlike mass storage, magnetic disks, or optical disks. This is because RAM consists of addressable cells.

Dynamic memory is one method of implementing RAM. Rather than using flip-flops to store bits of information, *dynamic RAM* (or *DRAM*) uses small electric charges that fade out very quickly. As a consequence, the computer must use refresh circuits that replenish the electric charges multiple times per second. This storage method allows for quicker response time and a greater level of miniaturization. By using *synchronous dynamic RAM* (or *SDRAM*), a computer can achieve ever faster response and retrieval times.

Measuring memory capacity

For the sake of convenience, main memory systems are designed such that the total number of cells equals a power of two. For instance, early computers had 2^{10}, or 1024, cells. Consequently, one *kilobyte* is equal to 1024 bits, two kilobytes is equal to 2048 bits, and so on. Later computers would use the prefixes *mega* and *giga*. One megabyte is 1,048,576 (1024^2) byes, and one gigabyte is 1,073,741,824 (1024^3) bytes. There is a problem with these prefixes, however. Outside the computer industry, they only apply to powers of ten, not powers of two; consequently, they become quite cumbersome and confusing when dealing with large amount of memory. To remediate this problem, industry experts have suggested that the prefixes kilo, mega, and giga refer only to power of ten, and have proposed a new system of prefixes for powers of two: *kibi* (kilobinary), *megi* (megabinary), and *gibi* (gigabinary). This can cause problems for users in buying mass storage, as hard disk vendors might advertise a particular drive at 500 gigabytes (500 billion bytes), while operating systems such as Windows will measure that size in traditional binary units, thus resulting in a drive that has a different vendor-reported capacity than its operating system-reported capacity of 465 actual gigabytes.

Mass storage

Mass storage, also known as secondary storage, includes any devices that provide additional memory storage, such as flash drives, compact disks, DVDs, magnetic tapes, and magnetic disks. There are two types of mass storage devices:

- *On-line* – The device can operate without human intervention because it is attached to the machine.
- *Off-line* – The device only operates after some type of human intervention, such as turning on the power or plugging the device into the correct port.

Mass storage devices offer advantages such as low cost, less instability than main memory, substantial storage capacity, and archival storage. A disadvantage is that they require substantially more time than main memory to access and retrieve data. Disks usually have to be formatted according to a particular file system, so that the operating system has a database of the physical disk locations of various files for access purposes. At the physical level, a mass-storage device simply writes to the storage addresses specified by the operating system.

Network topology

Network topology describes the arrangement of nodes within a network.

It can be either centralized or decentralized. There are three basic arrangements:

- Bus network – links each node in the network sequentially using a single cable.
- Star network – a centralized topography in which a central computer (also known as a switch or hub) connects all nodes and regulates network access.
- Ring network – a type of decentralized network topography in which each node links to two other nodes and the final node connects to the first node, making a ring configuration. As long as the network incorporates two-way communication, a node failure or cable break will not bring down the entire system.

Repeater, bridge, and switch

The following devices are used when connecting multiple bus networks to create a single extended communication system:

- Repeater – passes signals between two bus networks, but has no ability to read the signals. This is the simplest method of connecting networks.
- Bridge – first reads the destination address of the signal, and only forwards it to the other network if the signal is intended for a computer on the opposite side of the bridge. This is a more efficient method because two computers on the same side of the bridge can communicate without hampering communication on the other side.
- Switch – is similar to a bridge, but is capable of connecting more than two bus networks. It is also an intelligent device that only

forwards traffic to its destination, instead of blindly passing it out to everyone on the network and relying on the machines to interpret whether it's for them or not.

Routers

Routers allow multiple networks to be linked across an *internet* (which is defined simply as network of networks) by forwarding messages. Routers are unique from other network devices because they enable each network to retain its own individual characteristics. Each device in an internet has two addresses: the first identifies its location in the original network, and the second identifies its location in the internet. Assume, for instance, that a device in Network A wants to communicate with a device in Network B. The device in Network A sends the message to its access point, which then sends the message to the router for Network A. Each router has a *forwarding table*, which is used to send messages in the appropriate direction and to the appropriate address. Upon receiving this message, the router for Network A consults the forwarding table, and then forwards the message to the router for Network B. Finally, this router sends the message to its network access point, which contacts the appropriate device.

Protocol, Carrier Sense, and Multiple Access with Collision Detection

A network protocol regulates communication across a network. It prevents collisions, which occur when network devices try to transmit simultaneously, and the hoarding of network resources.

Carrier Sense, Multiple Access with Collision Detection, or CSMA/CD, is a type of protocol designed for bus networks on the Ethernet standard, and is most effective for networks that are medium-sized and smaller. It is not compatible with wireless star networks because devices on these networks cannot always detect collisions (i.e. the hidden terminal problem.) CSMA/CD relies on a method known as carrier sensing, which is capable of detecting collisions. Once a collision is detected, the CSMA/CD transmits a jam signal that stops both devices from sending. Then, in order to determine which node is allowed first access to data, the network operating system generates a random number. This number represents the length of a time a device must wait before resending its request. CSMA/CD ensures that all computers have equal and fair access to network resources.

Carrier Sense, Multiple Access with Collision Avoidance

Carrier Sense, Multiple Access with Collision Avoidance, or CSMA/CA, is a type of WiFi network protocol that tries to avoid collisions rather than detect them. In doing so, it addresses the *hidden terminal problem* inherent to some wireless networks. Even though all devices on a wireless network communicate with a central access point, a single device cannot always detect collision with another device because some blockage (such as an object or distance) may exist between them. When implementing CSMA/CA, a network device locates a silent channel and waits a moment to ensure that no signals are broadcast over the channel. If the channel remains silent over the period of time, the device will send. If the channel does not remain silent, the device will wait a random duration before trying again. Once this duration passes, the device can send down the first available silent channel without waiting. In this way, precedence is given to devices that have been waiting the longest, and there

- 79 -

can be no collision between transmitting devices and devices waiting to transmit. Because this method does not solve completely the hidden terminal problem, some WiFi networks require devices to send request signals to the access point before transmitting their messages.

Pipelining and out-of-order execution

Pipelining is a technique by which a computer can increase its throughput without modifying its execution speed (i.e. the time required to fetch and execute a single instruction). Pipelining involves overlapping the execution of the steps in the machine cycle. For instance, the computer can simultaneously execute one instruction while fetching the next instruction in the sequence. In essence, multiple instructions are in the pipe at the same time. JUMP commands negate the effectiveness of pipelining because the instruction in the pipe is not ultimately required.

Out-of-order execution, or OOE, is a type of high-performance processing in which the microprocessor follows an instruction set that allows it to avoid certain delays inherent to in-order execution, such as the stalls associated when the necessary operands are unavailable. When a stall occurs, the computer instead executes instructions for which the operands are ready and then reorders the instruction set. The original order is known as *program order*. The new order is known as *data order*, and requires complex circuitry to run.

Order of instructions

In-order execution:
1. Fetch instruction.
2. Send instruction to the correct functional unit if input operands are available. If operands are not available, stall processor until they are.

3. Send instruction to correct functional unit for execution.
4. Have the functional unit write the results back to the register file.

Out-of-order execution:
1. Fetch instruction
2. Send instruction to queue, also known as instruction buffer or reservation status.
3. Remove instruction from queue and execute it when the necessary input operands come available, regardless of the length of time it has been waiting relative to other instructions.
4. Send instruction to correct function unit for execution.
5. Send results of execution to queue.
6. Record the results back to register file only after earlier, older instructions are executed and written back. This process is known as the graduation or retire stage.

Parallel processing

Parallel processing occurs when a computer performs several tasks or actions simultaneously. It requires multiple processing units, and has given rise to *multiprocessor machines*. There are a number of architectures for executing parallel processing:

- MIMD or multiple-instruction stream, multiple-data stream – involves connecting multiple processing units (i.e. CPUs) to the same main memory. In this way, each processor can function independently while synchronizing its work with other processor by leaving messages in common memory cells. This architecture allows different instruction sets to be performed on different data sets.

- SIMD or single-instruction stream, multiple-data stream – involves linking several processors together so they can execute simultaneously the same instruction on different sets of data. This architecture is best-suited when the same tasks must be performed on a large block of data
- Build a large computer that consists of numerous smaller computers, each of which has an independent memory and central processor. In this architecture, large tasks are broken down into subtasks, and assigned to each smaller computer.

Distributed systems

A distributed system is a group of software units that are processed on different computers via networking technology. Common types of distributed systems include global information retrieval systems, computer games, network infrastructure software, and company accounting systems. At one point, distributed systems were created from the ground up; however, by understanding the common systems (security, communication, etc.) that all distributed infrastructures share, developers have been able to create standardized infrastructures that can be installed on any network and that enable the creation of a distributed system simply by developing a single, unique application to be run by that system. One example is Enterprise JavaBeans, which facilitates the development of new distributed systems through units known as *beans*. These beans inherit an enterprise infrastructure, and develop only the application that is unique to the system. Another example is the .NET framework, which uses units called *assemblies*.

Asymptotic analysis

Asymptotic analysis is a method of analyzing algorithms by describing their limiting behaviors. Asymptotic analysis is often used to assess the performance of algorithms when handling very large quantities of input data. Consider, for instance, the following example that uses the function f(x):
$$f(x) = x^2 + 2x$$

If x is very large, the value of 2x becomes insignificant compared to x^2; therefore, f(x) is asymptotically equivalent to x^2 as x approaches infinity. This is expressed as follows:
$$f(x) \sim x^2$$

In computer science, asymptotic analysis is often used to describe resource usage as the size of a computational problem increases. This increase is described as *order of growth*. It can be understood as a mathematical function and expressed using *Big O notation*, which is capable of showing limiting factors.

Exact analysis

Exact analysis provides a more specific measure of algorithm efficiency than asymptotic analysis, which focuses on limiting behaviors and order of growth. To perform an exact analysis, developers must make assumptions about algorithm implementation. These assumptions are known as the *model of computation*. A model of computation defines the allowable operations in computation and their costs per unit. In many cases, these operations are the primitive operations. When defining the model of computation, developers may use an abstract computer, such as a Turing machine or a recursive function, or they may assume a unit time for the execution of a certain operation. In order for these time assumptions to be accurate, they must be bound by constraints.

ithm design

Algorithms are usually created using certain design techniques, or paradigms, which including the following: divide and conquer, greedy, dynamic programming, backtracking, and branch and bound. Paradigms offer a number of advantages:

- They can address a wide variety of problems by offering different templates specifically suited for solving the problem
- Most high-level languages can translate these paradigms into common controls and data structures.
- They allow for precise analysis of the temporal and spatial requirements of the algorithm.

When analyzing whether or not an algorithm is best-suited for handling the problem at hand, developers usually consider the running time of the algorithm, the optimal performance of the algorithm, and comparisons between the algorithm and another one under consideration.

Calculating the running time of an algorithm

When determining the running time of an algorithm, we must first count the number of basic operations the algorithm performs under a *worst-case input*. Examples of basic operations include assignments, variable comparisons, and arithmetic operations. Consider the following example:

        x = 2
        loop
            get (y);
            x = x * 2;
        until (y = 16 or x = 16)

The worst-case input for the above algorithm is x iterations, meaning four iterations. The worst-case input varies according to the type of algorithm, the basic operations it performs, and the input size:

- *Sorting algorithm* – performs the basic operation of *comparison*. x = number of items to be sorted (x is the worst case input)
- Multiplication algorithm – performs the basic operation of single-digit arithmetic. x = the total number of digits in both variables being multiplied.
- Graph searching algorithm. x = number of graph edges or number of graph nodes

Best-case scenario, average-case scenario, and worst-case scenario

Best-case scenario, average-case scenario, and worst-case scenario are the minimum, average, and maximum lengths of time an algorithm requires to perform a function respectively. Consider, for instance, the issue of sorting a list with 10 entries using an insertion sort algorithm. The analysis for the insertion sort search would go as follows:

- Best-case scenario – is calculated using the formula $n - 1$ where n is the length of the list. This assumes that, each time the computer selects a new entry as the pivot entry, it is already in the correct place.
- Worst-case scenario – is calculated using the formula $(\frac{1}{2})(n^2 - n)$. This assumes that the list is arranged in reverse order, and each pivot entry must be compared to all previous entries.
- Average-case scenario – is calculated using the formula $(\frac{1}{4})(n^2 - n)$. This assumes that that each pivot entry must be compared to half of the previous entries.

Comparing two different algorithms

When analyzing two different algorithms in order to determine the one that best addresses the problem, we compare their best-case scenarios, average-case scenarios, and worst-case scenarios. We often create graphs based on the worst-case analysis for an algorithm.

The worst-case graph for the insertion sort algorithm indicates that, as the length of the list increases incrementally, the time required for algorithm completion also increases incrementally; consequently, insertion sort algorithms are less efficient for longer lists. Conversely, the worst-case graph for the binary search algorithm indicates that, as the length of the list increases incrementally, the time required for algorithm completion decreases incrementally; consequently, binary search algorithms are more efficient for longer lists.

Big-theta notation

Big-theta (Θ) notation is a method of classifying the time complexity of algorithms according when a realistic set of bounding criteria can be provided to determine best and worst case scenarios. This allows one to evaluate and compare algorithms by their performance under a variety of realistic inputs. Closely related to O ("Big O") notation, Big Theta notation deals with algorithms whose formulae can be tightly bounded, and Θ notation is thus preferred in many scientific and mathematical circles due to its increased precision (*n* is not necessarily assumed to tend towards infinity).

Divide and conquer algorithm design paradigm

Divide and conquer is an algorithm design paradigm that utilizes multi-branch recursion. In essence, an algorithm designed using divide and conquer methodology functions by taking the main problem and using a recursive process to break it down into progressively smaller sub-problems. Once the sub-problems are small enough to be solved directly (these states are known as *base cases*), their solutions are combined to provide an answer for the original main problem. Popular examples of divide and conquer algorithms include syntactic analysis, sorting programs such as quick-sort and merge sort, programs that multiply large numbers, and programs that calculate discrete Fourier transforms. A special type of divide and conquer algorithm is capable of condensing a main problem into a single sub-problem, often by using techniques such as *tail recursion*, which uses simple loops. An example is a binary search algorithm.

Implementation method for divide and conquer algorithms

Divide and conquer algorithms are normally implemented as recursive programs that store sub-problems in a procedure call stack. When using this method, programmers must be wary of allocating sufficient memory to the procedure call stack; otherwise, stack overflow may cause the program to fail. To avoid this problem, programmers should reduce the number of parameters and variables used in the recursive procedure, and/or employ an explicit stack structure. In most cases, divide and conquer algorithms reduce the problem to the simplest and smallest base cases possible. These cases need no processing to solve. However, in some cases, the efficiency of the program may be improved if recursion is stopped at a relatively large base case, and the bases cases are then solved by non-recursive processes. If a programming language does not support recursive procedures, divide and conquer algorithms can be implemented as non-recursive programs,

- 83 -

which hold sub-problems within stacks, queues, and similar data structures. Such programs have more freedom when determining the order of problem solving.

Divide and conquer algorithms offer several advantages:

- Problem solving and efficiency: Divide and conquer algorithms improve the asymptotic cost of solving problems; their big-theta notation is expressed as $\Theta(log\ n)$, meaning they require incrementally less time to solve a problem as its size increases. Also, because they divide main problems into smaller sub-problems, they excel at solving complex issues.
- Parallel processing: Divide and conquer algorithms are ideally suited for multiprocessor machines because each processor can handle a separate sub-problem.
- Rounded arithmetic: Divide and conquer algorithms produce more accurate results when performing arithmetic that requires rounding, such as floating point numbers.
- Memory usage: Divide and conquer algorithms are cache-oblivious, meaning cache size is not an explicit parameter in the problem. Problems are simply divided into sub-problems until the can be solved solely within the cache.

Greedy algorithm design paradigm

Under the greedy algorithm paradigm, programs always select the *locally optimal solution*, i.e., the solution that best fits only the current stage of the problem rather than the overall problem. Greedy algorithms hope this method will find the best solution to the overall problem, also known as the *globally optimal solution*.

Greedy algorithms have five basic components:

1. Candidate set – contains the data used to devise a solution.
2. Selection function – chooses the best candidate and adds it to the solution.
3. Feasibility function – examines the candidate in order to determine whether or not it can be used to solve the problem.
4. Objective function – gives a value to the solution.
5. Solution functions – determine if the complete solution has been found yet.

In most cases, greedy algorithms are too short-sighted to find the globally optimal solution; they commit to solutions too early because they do not operate on all data at once. Greedy algorithms are only effective if a problem has the *greedy choice property* and an *optimal substructure*.

Greedy choice property and optimal substructure

Greedy choice property implies that, no matter which decision a computer makes at the current stage of a problem, it can solve any sub-problems that might arise later on the process. A greedy algorithm will not be effective unless the problem has the greedy choice property because such algorithms are incapable of reconsidering or changing past decisions. They can only make choices that reduce the current problem into a smaller one.

Optimal substructure is present only if the optimal solution in any current stage always eventually leads to the optimal global solution. Essentially, the locally optimal solution must also hold the optimal solutions to any sub-problems that arise. Greedy algorithms and dynamic programming algorithms will

- 84 -

not be successful unless an optimal substructure is present.

Practical applications of greedy algorithms

Because greedy algorithms are *short-sighted* and *non-recoverable*, they are poorly suited to solving complex problems. However, they do have certain useful applications:

- Handling simple problems.
- Prioritizing options with a search.
- Providing quick approximations of the optimal solution.

There are a few variations on the greedy algorithm, such as pure greedy algorithms, orthogonal greedy algorithms, and relaxed greedy algorithms. Some common practical applications of the greedy algorithm include selection algorithms, branch and bound algorithms, and network routing in which a message is forwarded to the device nearest the target destination. Also, if a greedy algorithm does prove capable of finding the globally optimal solution for a particular class of problem, it will become the preferred algorithm for that problem due to its fast execution speed. Examples include Kruskal's algorithm, Prim's algorithm, and Dijkstra's algorithm.

Dynamic programming design paradigm

Under the dynamic programming algorithm paradigm, programs solve problems by using recursive processes designed to divide the problem into simpler steps. A dynamic programming algorithm is not likely to be successful unless the problem has the following properties: *optimal substructure* and *overlapping sub-problems* that are only slightly smaller than the problem. If the sub-problems are too much smaller, the

algorithm is instead relying on a divide and conquer design paradigm. The term overlapping sub-problem implies that the spaces for solving sub-problems are small: In effect, when solving a problem, a recursive algorithm should be solving the same problems repeatedly rather than generating new sub-problems. In dynamic programming, the recursive algorithm avoids solving the same problem repeatedly and, instead, solves it only once. There are two methods of carrying out dynamic programming in computer programming: *top-down approach*, and *bottom-up approach*.

Top-down and bottom-up approaches as they relate to dynamic programming

The dynamic programming paradigm can be implemented using one of the following methods:

- *Top-down approach* – the most direct method using recursive procedures. Assuming the main problem can be divided into overlapping sub-problems using recursion, the solutions to the sub-problems are stored in a table. Before solving a new sub-problem, the computer will check the table to determine if it has already been solved. If so, the solution in the table is used. If not, a new solution is added to the table.
- *Bottom-up approach* – carried out after a problem has been solved using recursion. The sub-problems are then solved from the bottom-up and their solutions are reconstructed into larger sub-problems. Eventually, these are built upon iteratively to reconstruct the main problem. This method is usually carried out in tabular form.

Practical applications of the dynamic programming design paradigm

Dynamic design algorithms include the following:

- String algorithms such as Levenshtien distance, longest common subsequence, longest increasing subsequence, and longest common substring.
- Approximate methods for solving the linear search problem.
- Artificial neural network, specifically the adaptive Critic training strategy.
- Interval schedule problem solving methods.
- Word-wrap problem solving methods.
- Solutions to the Markov decision process using the Value Iteration method.
- Determining global distance between two time series using the dynamic time warping algorithm.
- Methods for solving recursive least squares.
- Methods for solving problems on bounded tree width or bounded clique-width graphs, usually through tree decomposition.
- Transposition tables and refutation tables in chess.
- Methods for order optimization in chain matrix multiplication.
- Optimization of relationship database queries using the Selinger algorithm.

Backtracking design paradigm

Under the backtracking paradigm, a program solves problems by choosing candidates that build towards the overall solution and discarding partial candidates once it is apparent they can no longer contribute to the solution. Backtracking is only effective for problems that possess partial candidates, which are known as *backtracks* and are expressed as *c*; however, where backtracking is applicable, it is certain to find all possible solutions to a finite problem in a bounded amount of time. The pseudocode for a backtracking algorithm includes six procedural parameters (P represents the data for problem to be solved):

1. root (P) – Partial candidate is returned to the root of the search tree.
2. reject (P,c) – If the partial candidate does not contribute to the solution, reject returns *true*.
3. accept (P,c) – If the partial solution does contribute, accept returns *true*. Otherwise, it returns *false*.
4. first (P,c) – The first extension of the partial candidate is generated.
5. next (P,s) – The alternative extension of the partial candidate following extension s is generated.
6. output (P,c) – The solution c of P is applied where appropriate.

Implementation method for backtracking algorithms

When implementing the backtracking design paradigm, the algorithm first identifies a set of partial candidates that could provide all possible solutions once completed. To complete the partial candidates, the algorithm follows *candidate extension steps*. The partial candidates are represented conceptually as nodes on a tree structure (known as a *potential search tree*), and are parents to the partial candidates that are extended from them by one step. If a partial candidate cannot be extended any further, it is represented as a leaf. The backtracking algorithm starts at the root of the tree, and goes through it recursively in depth-first order. Each partial solution, or *c*, is checked to determine if it can contribute to the overall solution. If it cannot, the subtree that stems from the solution is skipped (i.e. pruned). If it can, the algorithm reports the solution to the user, and continues going through the solution's subtree recursively. The *actual search tree* is the part of the tree that is actually searched. When calculating the total cost of a backtracking algorithm, we multiply the number of nodes by the cost of acquiring and processing each node.

When writing a backtracking algorithm, the programmer should use boolean-valued (true or false) functions:

- Reject procedures should return *true* only if there is no possible way the extensions of the solution candidate can contribute to the solution. If it returns true in any other instance, the algorithm may miss certain valid solutions.
- Accept procedures should only return *true* if the candidate provides a valid solution to the problem. This indicates that the all extensions of the candidate have passed the reject test.
- First and next procedures identify the children of the solution candidate that extend from it by one step. First(P,c) produces the first child of the candidate, and next(P,s) generates the next sibling in the extension. If no additional children exist, both procedures should return a *null* candidate.
- Root, first, and next procedures identify all partial candidates and the potential search tree. They should include every possible solution while ensuring that no partial candidate appears more than once in the tree.

Branch and bound algorithm design paradigm

Under the branch and bound design paradigm, algorithms find the optimal solution to a problem by systematically identifying all solution candidates and then eliminating large subsets of those candidates by estimating lower and upper bounds for the problem. Branch and bound algorithms are reserved for optimization problems, specifically discrete and combinational optimization. *Optimization* describes a problem solving technique in which the best possible solutions are chosen from a set of real or integer variables. In *discrete optimization*, the variable set is confined to discrete values, such as graphs or integers. *Combination optimization* is a branch of discrete optimization whose goal is finding the least-cost solution to a problem. Each solution has a specific numerical cost, and by reducing these solutions to discrete values, the algorithm can find the best possible one.

Implementation method for branch and bound paradigms

To implement a branch and bound algorithm, we need two types of procedures:

- *Splitting procedure* – uses a recursive application to divide the total set of solution candidates (represented as *S*) into multiple smaller subsets. This procedure is known as *branching* because it defines *S* as a tree structure. Each node on the tree represents a subset of the solution candidates.
- *Upper and lower bound computation procedure* – also known as bounding, it uses a function to determine the upper and lower bounds for a subset of *S*.

Using these two procedures, the algorithm is able to *prune* branches (i.e. eliminate subsets). As the program records the upper and lower bound of each subset, it stores the minimum observed upper bound as global variable m. The program discards any subset whose lower bound is greater than m. The best possible solution is found once the upper bound for S matches the lower bound for S. This means S has been reduced to a single candidate.

The success and efficiency of a branch and bound algorithm is predicated largely on the procedures for splitting and for computing upper and lower bounds. In most cases, programmers should only use splitting procedures that generate non-overlapping subsets. There are two circumstances in which the branch and bound algorithms will terminate:

- The only remaining subsets have upper and lower bounds that equal the global variable m. This is the ideal termination point.
- A certain amount of time passes. All remaining subsets represent a range of values that include the global variable m. This can be expressed an error criterion.

If a branch and bound algorithm is poorly defined, it may result in repeated branching. This creates extremely small subsets, which makes the solution domain too cumbersome and impractical to be useful. Branch and bound algorithms are similar to backtracking but possess certain differences; namely, they can move through the tree in any direction, and they are used exclusively for optimization problems.

Practical applications of branch and bound algorithms

Branch and bound algorithms are ideal for heuristics and problem-solving methods that seek practical solutions rather than mathematically precise solutions. Under such methods, the algorithm ceases to split or branch the total solution set once the upper and lower bounds reach a specific threshold. This approach greatly reduces the number of mathematical computations that must be performed, and works well for statistical estimates, noisy cost functions, and probability studies. The branch and bound paradigm is popular when designing game tree search algorithms and alpha-beta pruning. It is popular for solving NP-hard problems, including integer programming. In integer programming, all problems are mathematical optimizations or feasibility programs with variables that are restricted to being integers.

Glass-box testing

Glass-box testing assesses the effectiveness of software based on its internal composition. Two popular methods of glass-box testing include the Pareto principle and basis path testing. According to the Pareto principle, most problems within large software systems are due to just a few modules; therefore, test methodologies that adhere to the Pareto principle seek to identify only the problematic modules and focus their attention in that direction. This approach is more likely to solve problems than one that performs less comprehensive tests on all software modules. Basis path testing is based on a branch of mathematics known as *graph theory*. Basis path techniques test software by executing every instruction in the software at least once. Even though these techniques are incapable of testing all possible paths through a software system, they can still ensure that each instruction is tested.

Black-box testing

Black-box testing assesses the effectiveness of software based on the user's perspective. It is not concerned with the internal composition of the software or the method by which it carries out a task, instead focusing solely on timely and accurate performance. Popular methods of black-box testing include boundary value analysis, beta testing, and alpha testing. Beta testing involves distributing an early version of the software to a test group consisting of target users. By observing these users, testers can assess software performance under actual conditions and make appropriate revisions to the final product. When this type of testing occurs at the developer's site, it is known as alpha testing. Beta testing also allows developers to gather customer feedback that can be used for marketing purposes and the development of companion software.

Boundary value analysis

Boundary value analysis is a form of black-box testing that identifies an *equivalence class*, which is a range of values, for a particular software application. When receiving data within this range, the software should always perform in the same way. If testers can determine the correct class, they can validate the software using very few examples. This minimizes the total number of test cases. Once the equivalence class is determined, the software is tested using the extreme values within the range. Consider, for instance, a program designed to accept input values within a specified range. When performing a boundary analysis on this software, testers would input the highest and lowest value within the range. Now, consider a program designed to manage multiple functions. It would be tested using the largest number of functions.

Upper and lower bounds on the complexity of a problem

The upper and lower bounds on the complexity of a problem are used to classify computation time. In essence, we take the most efficient algorithm for solving a problem, and then determine the upper and lower bounds on the minimum amount of time the algorithm will need to solve the problem. The upper bound on the time complexity of a problem $T(n)$ is simply the longest time a particular algorithm requires to find a solution. The lower bound of $T(n)$ is the more difficult determination. It is the shortest time any algorithm (out of all possible algorithms) requires to find a solution. All possible algorithms include those that have yet to be discovered, and cannot have a time complexity lower than $T(n)$. The complexity of an algorithm is generally its worst-case complexity—though not necessarily. Upper and lower bounds are expressed in big O notation.

Deterministic and nondeterministic algorithms

Nondeterministic algorithms require a device to exercise some type of creative ability. Deterministic algorithms have no such requirement. Consider, for instance, the following instructions:

Deterministic: Perform function A if X > Y or function B if X<=Y.

Nondeterministic: Perform function A or function B.

Although there is no set course of action prior to executing the instructions, they take far different approaches in their implementation. The first instruction provides a specific set of directions. The second instructions require the device to exercise its own judgment. From a purely functional standpoint, a deterministic algorithm will always produce the same results if it receives the same input data. A nondeterministic algorithm, on the other hand, could very well produce different results even when receiving the same input data. From a purely technical standpoint, nondeterministic algorithms are not true algorithms.

Time complexity

The time complexity of a problem is determined by the time required to execute its solutions. We should note that in computer science, algorithms are used to formulate solutions to problems; therefore, when determining a problem's complexity, we examine the simplest possible algorithm that can be used to solve the problem. From the machine's perspective, complexity is not a function of the number instructions an algorithm must run. Rather, complexity is function of the number of times an algorithm must execute instructions. Consequently, an algorithm with 30 instructions, each of which is executed only once, is considered to be less complex than an algorithm with only one instruction that is executed 200 times. This is because the latter algorithm requires longer execution time. The time complexity of an algorithm is inversely proportion to its efficiency. Time complexity is expressed in big O notation.

Big O notation

Big O notation is used to express our current understanding of a problem's time complexity, and is a variation on big-theta notation. This variation is due to the problem that we often have difficulty being certain that we have an accurate set of bounds for n. Consequently, we use big O (pronounced "big-oh") notation, which looks at the worst case scenario given n inputs. One compares the graphs of competing algorithms *f(n)* and *g(n)* as n approaches infinity, and chooses the algorithm with better worst-case per-formance. There are two broad classifications of worst-case graphs.

Parabolic and exponential formulae tend towards an asymptote parallel with the time axis, thus tending towards rapid, exponential increases in time cost as n increases. Logarithmic and square root formulae, however, tend towards an asymptote parallel with the dependent variable n, resulting in a decreasing growth of time cost as n tends toward infinity. Therefore, in a worst-case scenario, time complexities in the format $O(log\ n)$ are superior to those of $O(n^2)$. This is inferior to big-theta notation; however, it is often difficult to determine adequate bounds, making this a popular fast litmus test.

Space complexity

Space complexity measures the complexity of a problem according to its storage space requirements rather than its time requirements. The storage space requirement is simply the total amount of storage space necessary to solve the problem. Consider, for instance, that the problem of sorting a list with n entries has a time complexity of $O(n\ log\ n)$. This identical problem has a maximum space complexity of $O(n + 1) = O(n)$; the computer must store the list itself (length n) and one additional entry for temporary storage. A problem's space complexity never grows faster than its time complexity because, as the list grows, the time complexity increases more rapidly than the space complexity. If a program solves problems using information stored in a table, space complexity is a better measure than time complexity. However, if program relies on data compression, time complexity is the better measure because the problem requires additional time to compress and decompress information.

Polynomial problems

A polynomial problem is any problem in $O(f(n))$ where $f(n)$ is a polynomial or is bounded by a polynomial. The expression P represents the entire population of polynomial problems, which include the problems of sorting lists and searching lists. If a problem falls within class P, it can be solved in polynomial time using a deterministic algorithm. This is an important distinction in computer science. Problems that do not fall within P often have excessive execution times for only moderately sized inputs; therefore, if a problem cannot be solved in polynomial time, it may not even have a practical solution. Even if a problem does not fall within P but is theoretically solvable, it may have such a large time complexity that it is practically unsolvable. These types of problems are described as *intractable*. Class P establishes a boundary between practical and intractable problems.

Exponential problems

Exponential problems are any problems that are not bounded by a polynomial; therefore, they are not included in class P and tend to have very long execution times. Consider the polynomial expression $f(n)$ and the exponential expression 2^n. As n increases, the values of 2^n will become much larger than the values $f(n)$. Consequently, algorithms that have complexities $\Theta(f(n))$ are usually much more efficient than algorithms that have complexities $\Theta(2^n)$. This is because the latter is not bounded by any polynomial and solving it becomes exponentially more time-consuming as n increases. Problems often become exponential due to the size of their output. However, problems can be exponential even if their output is merely a yes or no answer. One such example is truth statements regarding the addition of real numbers.

Traveling salesman problem

The traveling salesman problem is one of the most famous unsolved problems in computer science. A traveling salesman must visit clients in several different cities while staying within his travel budget (i.e. not exceeding a certain mileage total). In solving this problem, we must systematically examine all possible paths through the cities, and find one that does not exceed the mileage total. This method poses difficulty because it is not bound by a polynomial. As a consequence, the solution cannot be found in polynomial time, and solving the problem using this method becomes impractical as the number of the cities increases. Therefore, in order to reach a viable solution, we need a more efficient solution, which can be found using a *nondeterministic algorithm*:

(Select one possible path through the cities and calculate its total distance.)
if (total distance <= allowable mileage total)
then (declare success)
else (declare nothing)

In the above algorithm, computer must rely on its creative capacity when deciding on a path because it receives no addition instruction on how to do so. The traveling salesmen problem is one of many nondeterministic polynomial problems that have no deterministic solution. It can only run in polynomial time using nondeterministic algorithms.

Nondeterministic polynomial problem

A nondeterministic polynomial problem, also known as an NP problem, includes any problem that has a polynomial time solution when executed by a nondeterministic algorithm. Consider, for instance, the traveling salesman problem, which is an NP problem because it currently can be solved only by a nondeterministic algorithm. Even as the number of cities the salesman must visit increases, the solution time required by a nondeterministic algorithm increases at a relatively slow rate. Both the time necessary to choose a path through the cities and the time necessary to compute the distances of those paths are proportional to the total number of cities. Because the time necessary to compare those distances to the salesman's maximum allowable mileage total does not depend on the number of cities, the problem is bound by a polynomial. The drawback of the nondeterministic algorithm is its reliance on guessing. All problems in class P also fall under class NP.

NP-complete problems

NP-complete problems are a special class of problems within class NP. Their purpose is resolving the longstanding issue of whether or not all class NP problems are also class P problems. We already know that all class P problems fall under class NP, but we do not know if the inverse is true. However, if just one NP-complete problem could be solved in polynomial time using a deterministic algorithm, we can conclude that class NP is the same as class P because the same algorithm would be capable of solving all NP problems. The traveling salesman problem is an example of an NP-complete problem. If a deterministic solution were discovered for class NP, the consequences could be dire because many encryption systems rely on the current inefficiency of solving such problems. An efficient solution would compromise their integrity.

Classes of computer science problems

Computer science problems can be divided into two broad classes: solvable, which can be solved algorithmically, and unsolvable, which cannot be solved

algorithmically. Solvable problems can be divided further into two subclasses:
- Polynomial problems – are bound by polynomials and can produce practical solutions in polynomial time using deterministic algorithms.
- Nonpolynomial problems – are not bound by polynomials but can be solved in polynomial times using nondeterministic algorithms. These can produce practical solutions only when the inputs are carefully selected or small.

The NP-class problems include polynomial problems and some nonpolynomial problems; however, they defy exact classification.

Consider the mathematical functions $f(n)$ and $g(n)$. If $g(n)$ is bounded to $f(n)$, the values of $f(n)$ will become increasingly larger than the values of $g(n)$ as the value of n increases.

Turing Machine

Developed by Alan Turing in 1937, a Turing machine is a theoretical device that is studied by computer scientists so they can better understand the limits of mechanical computation, CPU function, and complexity theory. A Turing is not a practical piece of technology; rather, it is only a thought experiment that can replicate CPU functions and the logic of any algorithm no matter how complex, and whose abstract properties aid the understanding of computer science. According to the Church-Turing thesis developed by Turing and Alonzo Church, Turing machines are capable of giving exact definitions for algorithmic processes or mechanical procedures and informally expressing effective methods in logic and mathematics. There are numerous variations on the Turing machine. A *universal Turing machine*, or *UTM*, can replicate the function of any other Turing machine.

Turing machines are theoretical devices that consist of the following components:

- A single strip of infinite tape that gives the machine limitless memory capacity. The tape consists of sequential cells, and extends into infinity at both ends. Each cell contains a symbol that can be altered.
- Control unit with a read/write head. The unit is capable of scanning a symbol stored in a cell and making changes to it.

As the machine performs computation, it will move through a finite number of states. It begins in the *start state* and ends in the *halt state*. During computation, the machine executes a program that gives instruction according to the machine's state and information contained in the current tape cell. Each step in the program involves scanning a symbol in a tape cell using the read/write head, writing a new symbol in the cell, shifting the head one cell to the left or right, and finally, changing states.

Executing the successor function

The successor function is the process by which a Turing machine increases a nonnegative integer value by one. Consider, for instance, that the following section of tape on a Turing machine:

The current value is one. The machine will increase the value to binary two by going through the following states:

- START – The read/write head starts in the cell farthest to the right, which contains an *. It rewrites the *, moves one cell to

the left, and then changes to the ADD state.
- ADD – The read/write head changes the 1 value to a 0 value, moves one cell to the left, and then transitions to the CARRY state.
- CARRY – The read/write head changes the 1 value to a 0 value, moves one cell to the right, and then transitions to the RETURN state.
- RETURN – The read/write head changes the 0 value to another 0 value, moves one cell to the right, and then transitions to the RETURN state.
- RETURN – The read/write head rewrites the * value and then transitions to the HALT state.
- HALT – The machine ceases computation. The revised section of tape looks like this:

Church-Turing thesis

The Church-Turing thesis is related to the concept of *Turing-computable functions*, which include any computations that can be performed using the successor function (i.e. a nonnegative integer input value n is given an output value of $n + 1$). According to the Church-Turing thesis, all computable functions are also Turing-computable functions; consequently, Turing machines possess a computational power capable of handling any algorithmic system and, therefore, can express solutions to any computable function. Because all research to date has validated this thesis, Turing machines are regarded as a standard of comparison for computers and computational systems. The power of a computational system is directly related to the number of Turing-computable functions it can perform, and

Turing machines show the limitations on computers.

Turing machine

A Turing machine has the following components:

- Tape: broken up into ordered cells, each of which contains a symbol or is blank; a Turing machine will contain enough information to perform its intended function.
- Head: able to read and write the symbols on the cells; for each state, the head may only move one cell to the left or right.
- Finite table: commands the machine to perform a particular instruction sequence; this sequence depends on the symbol being read and the state of the machine at the time. Turing machines may have a 4-tuple or 5-tuple finite table. The 4-tuple model instruction sequence is to erase or write a symbol; *or* move the head one cell to either side; *and then*, maintain the current state or recommend a new state. The instructional sequence for the 5-tuple finite table is erase or write a symbol; *and then* move the head one cell to either side; *and then* to maintain that state or recommend a new state.
- State register: maintains a copy of one of the Turing machine's start states, which is set into motion when the machine starts

Finite-state machine

A finite-state machine (often referred to as a finite-state automaton or state machine) is a theoretical machine consisting of a set of states, actions, and transitions between states. Finite-state machines are used to create models of computer behavior. These models are useful in the design of computer programs. A finite-state machine has a finite internal memory, a sequential reading apparatus, and an output apparatus (e.g., a user interface). The machine begins in its start state and then changes state in response to input. The operation is complete when the machine has passed through all of the accept states. These machines are used in engineering, artificial intelligence, and linguistics programs, in part because they are able to handle multiple problems simultaneously.

Finite-state machines include the following:

- Current states: the products of the past states. The current state indicates all the past states since the initialization of the machine. The identity of the state and of the past states is based on the total possible number of states for the memory of the machine.
- Transition: change of state; the fulfillment of a condition must precede every transition
- Action: the activity to be performed, as for instance input action (depends on present state and input), transition action (takes place during change of state), entry action (takes place when a state is entered), and exit action (takes place when a state is exited).
- Finite state-machines may be described with state transition diagrams, like this one:

Current State Condition	State 1	State 2	State 3
Condition A	...	...	...
Condition B	...	...	...
Condition C	...	State 3	...

Acceptors/Recognizers class of finite-state machines

One class of finite-machines is acceptors and recognizers. In response to an input, these machines issue a binary "yes or no" output. Every state in such a machine constitutes either an acceptance or a rejection. Inputs, which are expressed as symbols, are accepted when the current state indicates as much, following the processing of all input. The diagram for acceptors and recognizers includes a start state, represented as an arrow pointing to the diagram. The successful completion of a procedure, represented on the diagram as a double circle, is known as the accept state.

Transducer class of finite-state machines

The finite-state machines known as transducers are divided into two types: Moore machines and Mealy machines. The output of a Moore machine depends on the state, which means in turn that it is based on entry action. One example could be a thermostat set to seventy degrees. If the room is colder than seventy degrees, the command *Heat* would lead to the entry action of the furnace running. If the room is warmer than seventy degrees, the command *Cool* would initiate the entry action of the air conditioner running. If the room is exactly seventy degrees, the thermostat will not initiate any actions.

Mealy machines

The output of a Mealy machine totally depends on input actions and the current state. Mealy machines reduce the total number of states. Imagine the scenario of a thermostat set to seventy degrees. In a machine, there are only two possible input actions: the heat turns on when the thermostat is below seventy, and the heat turns off when the temperature is seventy or above. Whereas the Moore machine thermostat had intermediate stages, in which the temperature was either rising or falling toward seventy, the Mealy machine does not.

Mathematical terms used in describing finite-state machines

If a finite state machine is deterministic or can be classified as acceptor deterministic, it is a quintuple with the symbols Σ, S, s_0, δ, and F, where Σ is the input alphabet (finite set of non-empty symbols); S is the set of states; s_0 is the initial state (a component of S); δ is the state-transition function ($\delta: S \times \Sigma \to S$); and F is the set of final states (a component of S). If a finite-state machine is classified as a transducer, it is a sextuple with the symbols Σ, Γ, S, s_0, δ, and ω, where Σ is the input alphabet (a finite set of non-empty symbols); Γ is the output alphabet (a finite set of non-empty symbols); S is the finite set of non-empty states; s_0 is the initial state; δ is the state-transition function ($\delta: S \times \Sigma \to S$); and ω is the output function.

Context-free language

A context-free language is any language that is generated with *context-free grammar*. A language based on a context-free grammar has the ability to nest clauses to an indeterminate depth but forbids grammatical structures from overlapping. All context-free programming languages can be understood by *pushdown automata*, or finite state machines with a single infinite stack. When nesting units, the beginning of the unit is pushed in at the top of the stack and then recovered at the very end. All context-free languages have certain qualities:

- Can be described by a regular grammar; therefore, all regular languages are context-free.

- Do not necessarily include all context-sensitive languages.
- Include the intersections of context-free and regular languages.

Pushdown automata

Pushdown automata are a type of finite-state machine that utilizes a stack data structure. They select transitions by following a transition table, which is indexed according to the following parameters: input signal, current state, and the symbol at the top of the stack. Additionally, while performing the transition, pushdown automata use the table to determine whether to manipulate or ignore the data stack. In nondeterministic pushdown automata, the transition table offers a variety of transitions from which to choose. In deterministic pushdown automaton (a less powerful machine), the transition table offers only one possible transition based on the input signal, current state, and top of stack symbol. In order to have a computation power equal to a Turing machine, a finite automaton must utilize two stacks. All context-free grammars have an equivalent pushdown automaton; therefore, every language generated by a context-free grammar has an identical language generated by a pushdown automaton. The inverse is also true.

Pushdown automata are 7-tuples with the symbols Q, Σ, Γ, δ, q_0, Z, and F, where Q is a finite set of states; Σ is the input alphabet (a finite set); Γ is the stack alphabet (a finite set); δ is the transition relation; Γ^* is a finite, even empty, set of the elements in Γ; ε is an empty string; q_0 is the start state; Z is the initial state; and F, a subset of Q, is the set of accepting states. In computer science, the formal definition of a pushdown automaton is M = (Q, Σ, Γ, δ, q_0, Z, F).

Linear bounded automata

A restricted nondeterministic Turing machine that is classified as an acceptor and is represented by context-sensitive language is known as a linear bounded automaton. These machines have an input alphabet with two unique symbols, one that furnishes left and right end markers, and one that creates a boundary for the header. The distinguishing feature of these machines is that even though the tape is technically infinite, the header only reads part of it. The initial input length restricts the length of the tape, so the machine's computational ability is limited as well. This makes the linear bounded automaton a more realistic Turing machine. Linear bounded automata are represented with context-sensitive language, so it is impossible for the sequential form of the derivation string to be longer than the original string.

Regular language

A formal language is defined as regular if it has the following characteristics:
- It can be accepted by deterministic and nondeterministic finite state machines alike.
- It can be accepted by alternating finite automata.
- It can be accepted by read-only Turing machines.
- It can be described by formal regular expression, though regular expression in many programming languages can be adjusted to describe languages that are not regular.
- It can be generated by both regular and prefix grammars.
- It can be defined by monadic second-order logic.
- It can be recognized by a finite monoid, and is the preimage of a

- 96 -

finite monoid subset, designated under the homomorphism of the free monoid in the alphabet.

Regular languages are context-free, and may have an infinite number of finite sequences taken from a finite alphabet.

Context-sensitive language

A formal language that is created with a context-sensitive grammar is known as a context-sensitive language. Context-sensitive languages consist of all the unions, concatenations, and intersections of two context-sensitive languages. Also, every context-sensitive language has a context-sensitive complement. All context-free languages are context-sensitive languages. When these languages are part of a language string generated by an arbitrary deterministic context-sensitive grammar or an arbitrary context-sensitive grammar, they may become a PSPACE-complete problem. Context-sensitive languages may be described by a linear bounded automaton (nondeterministic Turing machine), meaning that the same type of machine can describe every context-free language and context-sensitive language. Finally, context-sensitive languages can be accepted by a nondeterministic Turing machine that uses linear space, so these languages are placed in the NLIN-SPACE class.

Context-free grammar

Context-free grammars, used to create programming languages and compilers, create context-free formal languages, so grammatical structures do not overlap despite the fact that clauses can be nested to an arbitrary depth. These grammars can be parsed by nondeterministic Turing machines (linear bounded automata) and express themselves in Backus-Naur Form. The production rules (also known as rewrite rules) for these grammars require that the grammar be expressed in the form $V \rightarrow w$, where V is a single nonterminal symbol and w is a string of terminal and/or nonterminal symbols or is empty. The leftmost side of a production of context-free grammar must be a single nonterminal symbol. Parse trees, on which nonterminal symbols are represented as nodes and terminal symbols are represented as leaves, are used to describe the nesting structures of various expressions of context-free grammar.

A context-free grammar is a 4-tuple with the symbols V, Σ, R, and S, where V is a finite set of non-terminal symbols (variables, also known as syntactic categories, stand for different phrases or clauses); Σ is a finite set of terminal symbols that define the alphabet, make up the whole sentence, and are disconnected from V; R is the finite set of rewrite or production rules correspondences of V and Σ); and S, which represents the entire sentence, is the start symbol (part of V). Context-free grammars are formally defined $G = (V, \Sigma, R, S)$.

Context-sensitive grammar

A context-sensitive grammar generates formal languages that are also context-sensitive. Although it less stringent than a context-free grammar, it can still be parsed by a linear bounded automata. According to the production rules for context-sensitive grammar, both sides of a production rule may have a context of terminal and nonterminal symbols. In some definitions of context grammar, the production rules have the form u $\rightarrow$ v, in which both |u| and |v| indicate string length and |u|<=|v|. In other definitions of context grammar, the production rules have the form S $\rightarrow$ λ:

- S can never appear on the right side of the rule.
- λ is an empty string, which indicates that the context-sensitive language that has been generated is a proper superset of the context-free language.

Context-sensitive grammars are 4-tuples that use the symbols N, Σ, P, and S. The formal definition of a context-sensitive grammar is $G = (N, \Sigma, P, S)$ in which all P rules are expressed in the form $\alpha A \beta \rightarrow \alpha \gamma \beta$:

- A is a single nonterminal symbol.
- α is a string consisting of nonterminal and terminal symbols.
- β is a string consisting of nonterminal and terminal symbols.
- γ is a nonempty string consisting of nonterminal and terminal symbols.

The α and β create the context of A and determine if γ is capable of replacing A. This quality makes the grammar context-sensitive. By contrast, in context-free grammar, the single nonterminal symbol has no surrounding context.

Operational semantics

Operational semantics are one of the three major classes of formal semantics in computer science, concerned primarily with interpretation of language phrases into mathematical formalisms. Using a rigorous mathematical approach, operational semantics describe the method by which a computer interprets a valid computer program as a sequence of computational steps. The program is then defined by these steps. The final step should return the value of the program. A single program may have many possible final return values. This is especially true of nondeterministic programs, and may

also be true of deterministic programs with many computational steps; the semantics cannot always identify the sequence of steps that brought about the return value. Operational semantics can define an abstract machine, such as an SECD machine, by defining phrases in terms of the transitions between machine states. Operational semantics can also provide definitions in terms of syntactic transformations on the actual language phrases. Lambda calculus is one of the earliest forms of operational semantics.

Axiomatic semantics

Axiomatic semantics are one of the three major classes of formal semantics in computer science. Using mathematical logic, axiomatic semantics define program command phrases in terms of their impact on the assertions of the program state. These phrases are described using logical axioms, which are statements that do not distinguish between the meaning of a phrase and the logical formula that represents it. They are one and the same because the axiom states the precise findings of the logic. Logical statements are written in the form of predicates with variables that define the program statement. Axiomatic semantics are tied closely to *Hoare logic*, which is a formal set of logical rules used to determine the correctness of a computer program.

Denotational semantics

Denotational semantics are one of the three major classes of formal semantics in computer science, focused primarily on translation. Denotational semantics translate each phrase of the program language into a mathematical object known as a denotation, which defines the meaning of each phrase. This process is similar to compilation except that the denotation is a mathematical formalism, not a different computer language. When translating functional languages, denotational semantics produce domain theory. Domains are mathematical objects that express the purpose and functions of a computer program. Examples of domains include partial functions, actor event diagrams, environment and system games, etc. Denotational semantics should always be compositional. This means that the denotation of a program phrase should consist of the denotation of the program subphrases.

Formal semantics

Formal semantics has several common variations:

- Attribute grammars: denotation semantics that adds attribute notation to the original language; these are used in code-generating compilers, formal semantics, and context-sensitive enhancement of regular or context-free grammars.
- Game semantics: derived from game theory.
- Concurrency semantics: includes the Actor model and process calculi; used to describe computations occurring at the same time.
- Action semantics: breaks denotational semantics into separate modules, namely three semantic entities (actions, data, and yielders) and two formalization layers (macro-semantics layer and micro-semantics layers).
- Algebraic semantics: describes semantics with algebra.
- Categorical semantics: derived from category theory.
- Predicate transformer semantics: describes program fragments with a post-condition and precondition function.

Decidable language

A decidable language, also known as a recursive language or a Turing-decidable language, is type of a formal language. The entire class of decidable (or recursive) languages is referred to as R, and encompasses all regular, context-free, and context-sensitive languages. In essence, a decidable language is a simply a formal language that can be represented using a Turing machine that accepts strings of input. If the string is part of the language, the Turing machine will halt and accept it. If the string is not part of the language, the Turing machine will reject it. Consequently, the machine is known as a *decider* because it decides the recursive language. If a decision problem has an algorithm that terminates on all inputs, it is considered decidable; otherwise, it is not decidable. All computable functions fall under R.

Discrete structures

A mathematical structure in which each constituent value is distinct from all others is known as a discrete structure. In a continuous structure, on the other hand, there is no strict division between values. The set of real numbers is an example of a continuous structure. Calculus and analysis are both confined to continuous mathematics. Discrete mathematics includes rational numbers, countable sets, integers, graphs, and mathematical logic. Computers store information in discrete units and follow discrete steps in their operations, so they may be usefully approached with discrete mathematics. Discrete math has proven especially useful in the development of algorithms, programming languages, and software.

Application of discrete structures in theoretical computer science

Discrete mathematics continues to influence computer science theory, particular in the areas of logic and graph theory. Computer scientists use discrete mathematics to develop mathematical computing algorithms and formal languages. They also use it to perform computability studies, which consider the limits of computation, and complexity studies, which consider the length of time required to complete a set of operations. Discrete mathematics is used in the examination of VLSI electronic circuits and in computer system models that use Petri nets and process algebras. Computer scientists also use discrete mathematics in automata theory. Finally, discrete mathematics is useful when applying computational geometry algorithms to geometrical problems or when applying computer image analysis to image representations. There are some applications for continuous mathematics in computer science, most notably in analog computation, computability analysis, analog models of computation, and information-based complexity.

Mathematical logic

Mathematical logic is part of discrete mathematics and tied closely to computer science. It studies the expressive ability of formal systems and deduction through formal proof systems. Mathematical logic focuses on examining logic mathematically and applying formal logic to other mathematical fields, and can be divided into the subfields of set theory, model theory, recursion theory, and proof theory. In computer science, mathematical logic aids in the following:

- Computability studies, which are used to determine feasible computability and concrete programming languages.
- Semantics of programming languages, which are connected to model theory and program verification.
- Curry-Howard isomorphism and proof theory, such as intuitionistic logic.
- Lambda calculus and combinatory logic, which are viewed as idealized programming languages.
- Computational complexity theory, which result in Fagin's theorem and its assertions about NP problems.

In computer science, mathematical logic forms the basis for the following formal methods:

- Specification languages, which determine the correctness of program behavior. These include Z specification language, automated theorem provers, minimalist specification logics, etc.
- Boolean logic, which helps design computer circuits.
- Predicate logic and logical frameworks, both of which help determine program correctness.
- Formal semantics of programming languages, logic programming, temporal logic, and other fundamental logic concepts in computer science. These can be expressed using formal logic.
- Notion of institution, which provides an abstract method of formalizing logical systems in order to facilitate the classification of any logics that come about.

Applications of mathematical logic to computer science

Computer scientists use mathematical logic in computation theory, as for instance Curry-Howard correspondence and game semantics. Mathematical logic is also useful when using algorithms to solve equations, or when testing programs with automated theorem proving or model checking. Computer scientists use mathematical logic in programming language theory, abstract interpretation (used to prove the properties of program), computational complexity, and descriptive complexity theory. They also find it useful when dealing with process calculi and program logics, both of which test the correctness of programs. Finally, mathematical logic is useful in Hoare logic, dynamic logic, and Hennessy-Milner logic, all of which are used to determined program correctness.

Graph theory

Graph theory is the study of networks and graphs—which are mathematical structures that model data elements from the same data group—and is connected to combinatronics. Specifically, graphs show the pairwise relations between data elements, and consist of nodes (also known as vertices) and edges that connect the nodes. There are two types of graphs:

- Undirected – does not distinguish between the nodes at the end of each edge.
- Directed – clearly distinguishes the nodes at each end of an edge.

Computer science is especially concerned with developing algorithms to manage and control graphs. For instance, graph rewrite systems help to formalize the transformation of graphs, which describes the process of using automatically creating a new graph out of an existing graph. In higher-level operations, graph algorithms are often responsible for identifying paths between two nodes (depth-first search and breadth-first algorithms) and identifying the shortest part between nodes (e.g., Dijkstra's algorithm and the Floyd-Warshall algorithm). There are also directed graph algorithms that find flow rates. Graph theory is also used in network analysis.

Graph data structure

A graph data structure consists of a limited set of ordered pairs. These pairs are connected by an edge (arc). The two members of the pair are known as nodes, or vertexes. Nodes are typically assigned letters (e.g., *a* and *b*), and edges are identified by placing the related nodes in parentheses, as in (*a*, *b*). Nodes may also be assigned an integer or symbol in accordance with some value external to the graph. If a value of this type is assigned to an edge, it is known as an edge structure. One data structure that computers use to display information is an adjacency list, which is a collection of lists of destination and source nodes. Another graph structure is the incidence list, which catalogues the various edges. One problem with the incidence list is that it cannot account for new edges. An adjacency matrix is a two-dimensional Boolean matrix, in which rows and columns depict destination and source vertexes, and matrix entries indicate where the nodes are connected by edges. An incidence matrix is also a two-dimensional Boolean matrix. In it, rows identify vertexes and columns identify edges. The array of data indicates the incidences of vertexes and edges.

Combinatorics

Combinatorics is the study of countable discrete structures, and includes many branches, including the following:

- *Enumerative combinatorics*, which involves counting structures that fall under a certain class and size.
- *Matroid theory*, which analyzes a set of criteria, determining when

it can be met, and then creating objects that fulfill the criteria.

- *Combinatorial optimization*, which involves identifying the largest, smallest, and optimal objects. It aids in the study of algorithm theory and computation complexity theory.
- *Probabilistic combinatorics*, which determines the probability of finding a certain property in a random discrete object. Probabilistic combinatorics provides the basis for many formulae and estimates used in the analysis of algorithms.
- *Combinatorics on word*, which studies formal languages and has applications to theoretical computer science and automata theory.

Randomized rounding

Randomized rounding, which is derived from probabilistic combinatorics, is a technique for creating and studying approximation algorithms. These algorithms allow a computer to solve intractable problems, or problems that cannot be optimally solved within a particular interval. An approximation algorithm comes up with a rough estimate of the answer. By using probability theory and linear relaxation, computer scientists have come up with the three-step system of randomized rounding. First, the problem is formulated with the integer linear program (ILP). Then, an optimal fractional solution is calculated using the ILP's linear programming relaxation. This solution can be calculated in polynomial time, thanks to the linear programming algorithm. Finally, the fractional solution is rounded off to an integer solution, with a cost close but just a bit higher than the fractional solution. The increase in cost is bound using probabilistic combinatorics.

Combinatorial optimization

Combinatorial optimization involves studying discrete optimization problems—i.e., problems that have discrete solution sets or solutions sets that can be reduced to discrete, such as the traveling salesman problem. Combinatorial optimization assigns each possible solution a certain numerical cost, and then identifies the least-cost solution. This has important applications to computer science, especially in the fields of algorithm theory, computational complexity theory, software engineering, and artificial intelligence. Although any search algorithm should be capable of solving combinatorial optimization problems by selecting the best solution from a discrete data set, there is no guarantee the algorithm will find the optimal solution or run in polynomial time. Some common combinatorial optimization problems include shortest paths, shortest path trees, flow and circulations, spanning trees, matching, and matroid—all of these fall under the class of polynomial-time algorithms and the theory of linear programming.

Discrete probability theory

In discrete probability theory, the probability distribution of a random variable x (called the discrete random variable) is calculated with a probability mass function. The probability mass function is expressed as

$$\sum_{u} P(x = u) = 1$$

where u includes all possible values of x. This set of possible values is either finite or countably finite (i.e., values can be counted even though the list may be infinite). As an example, consider the number of mailboxes on a stretch of road. In discrete probability theory, each of these mailboxes is treated as a discrete event in a finite sample space. The total mailboxes will always be a natural number. Discrete probability theory is used in computer science to create discrete uniform distributions, which enable equal-probability random selections.

Discrete uniform distribution

Discrete uniform distribution is a probability distribution that enables a computer program to make an equal-probability random selection between multiple options. In essence, the distribution is discrete and uniform if it contains a finite number (n) of equally spaced values, each of which has an equal probability ($1/n$) of being selected. Each one of n values represents a possible option expressed as:

$$k_1, k_2, \ldots k_n$$

The probability that the computer will select any option k is $1/n$. Consider, for instance, the colors of a rainbow: red, orange, yellow, green, blue, indigo, and violet. Each represents a possible value of k; therefore, the probability that a computer will select any one color is $1/7$.

Number theory

Number theory concerns the properties and problems of numbers, especially integers. Computer scientists who focus on computational number theory spend most of their time performing integer factorization and prime testing functions with fast algorithms. Integer factorization is the process of breaking an integer down into a set of prime numbers which, when multiplied together, produce the integer. For instance, the factors of 8 are 2, 2, and 2. It is common for a cryptography protocol to require the factorization of large integers. Prime testing is a system for determining whether an input number is prime. This process is also useful in cryptography.

Recursion

In computer science, recursion involves solving a larger problem by finding solutions to smaller versions of the same problem. The universality of the recursion method makes it an integral part of computer science, and the vast majority of high-level programming languages support recursive procedures. In these languages, the program text enables functions to call themselves. For instance, imperative languages use while and for loops to create looping structure that perform repetitive actions. Functional programming languages perform recursion by calling code repetitively. According to computability theory, any recursive-only language is mathematically identical to imperative language and, therefore, can solve similar types of problems even in the absence of looping structures. Recursion is so effective because it is capable of using a finite set to express an infinite set of data. This means a finite recursive program can describe an infinite number of calculations.

Recurrence relation

A recurrence relation is an equation in which each element in a sequence of terms is a function of the previous term. Recurrence relations are considered a part of nonlinear analysis and can behave quite unpredictably. The solution to a recurrence relation should be closed-form, or non-recursive. These relations are used in digital signal processing because they can model system feedback, or the transition of an output into an input at some future point. One particular application is in infinite impulse response (IIR) digital filters, as in the following equation for a feedforward IIR comb filter: $Y(t) = (1 - \alpha)X(t\text{-}T)$, where T is the delay; $X(t)$ is the input at time t; $Y(t)$ is the output at time t; and α is the level of delayed signal that is fed back into the output.

Important terms

- Computer: a mechanical device for converting data arranged as programs into comprehensible information
- Information technology: equipment designed to arrange, organize, and display data
- Communications technology: electronic equipment designed to communicate vocal, visual, and textual information over long distances; also known as telecommunications technology
- Online: being connected to the Internet; capable of accessing information through a computer network
- Network: a link between multiple computers or electronic devices; may be arranged hierarchically or with a flat organizational structure
- Email: a method of communicating across a computer network; short for "electronic mail"
- Bit (b): a single binary digit, a zero or one
- Byte (B): a combination of eight bits representing a single character, such as a letter or number
- Kilobyte (KB): 1024 bytes, the size of a small computer file
- Megabyte (MB): 1,048,576 bytes, the size of a large computer file
- Gigabyte (GB): 1 billion bytes, typically used when describing the total storage capacity of a computer system
- Terabyte: one trillion bytes
- Petabyte: one quadrillion bytes
- Connectivity: the degree to which computers in a network are connected to one another; increased connectivity in computing is indicated by the ubiquity of email, social networking, and e-commerce
- Interactivity: the degree to which a computer user can tailor the operations of the computer to his or her specifications; software programs are increasingly interactive, which enables novice users to navigate new applications easily
- Multimedia: the set of technologies that enable information to be presented in a variety of ways; examples include sound, video, images, and text
- Integrated circuit: an electronic circuit, usually placed on a tiny piece of silicon or some other special material, capable of containing a variety of electronic components
- Solid-state device: any device in which electrons pass through a solid material rather than a vacuum; in many solid-state devices, electrons pass through silicon
- Silicon: an element frequently used as a semiconductor in integrated circuits; abundant in clay and sand, and therefore cheap to obtain and use
- Semiconductor: designation for any material which is a moderately good conductor of electricity; e.g., silicon
- Chip: a piece of silicon containing potentially millions of integrated circuits; also known as a microchip
- Computer professional: any person whose employment has to do with computers; includes computer designers, testers, and analysts, as well as software and security professionals

- Information systems department: the members of an organization who handle computer systems and data; these people are responsible for software installation and computer maintenance
- Chief information officer: the individual in charge of a company's information systems department; typically heads up a team of programmers, web designers, network administrators, systems analysts, and technical support employees
- Systems analyst: the person who examines the strengths and weaknesses of a business' computer system and recommends solutions to observed problems
- Computer programmer: an individual who writes the computer code for software applications
- Security specialist: a professional whose job is to examine computer systems and ensure that they are defended against security threats; security specialists install antivirus programs, firewalls, and malware detectors. In addition, security specialists are trained to respond to breaches of security.
- Database administrator: an employee who keeps track of data and comes up with effective ways to store and distribute it; database administrators are responsible for maintaining and disseminating the information that is most valuable to the business
- Computer operator: anyone responsible for the setup and maintenance of mainframes and supercomputers; these employees are highly trained on specialty machines and are capable of installing upgrades or patches whenever necessary
- Technical support specialist: any person responsible for diagnosing and solving hardware and software problems
- Website designer: someone responsible for creating and maintaining the website for a business; modern web designers need to be fluent in the programming languages HTML, XML, and JavaScript at the very least
- Technical writer: an individual responsible for producing all the text that accompanies computer products; for instance, technical writers are responsible for composing the documentation and user manuals for new pieces of hardware or software; a technical writer must have both a high degree of technical knowledge and fluency in English
- Computer salesperson: anyone responsible for helping customers find computers that are appropriate for their needs; most salespeople work on commission, which means that they earn more money by selling more computers; quality salespeople also strive to satisfy customers
- Quality assurance specialist: individual responsible for diagnosing and fixing problems with new software; a quality assurance specialist may be charged with spotting physical defects on the assembly line, or may be responsible for testing the operation of software
- Computer engineer: someone responsible for designing and testing new hardware products, for instance circuit boards, microchips, and peripherals

- Manufacturing technician: anyone responsible for the physical construction of computer hardware, including peripherals, circuit boards, and microchips
- Esc: also known as the Escape key; can be used to cancel the last action, or to exit the open application
- Function: labeled F1 through F12 and positioned along the top of the keyboard; used to initiate special commands in the open application
- Print Screen: automatically prints the screen that is currently visible on the monitor; in some configurations, this button will merely send the screen to the system clipboard instead of actually printing it
- Backspace: erases the character directly to the left of the cursor or, on a web browser, goes back to the previous page
- Home: moves the cursor to the beginning of a line or the beginning of the document
- End: moves the cursor to the end of the line or to the end of the document
- Enter: either completes an ongoing function or moves the cursor to the next line
- Control and Alt: used in combination with other keys to perform special functions; for instance, Alt+X exits the program, and Ctrl+S saves an open document
- Tab: moves the cursor one tab stop to the right; can also move the cursor from one field to another on a spreadsheet or form
- Page Up and Page Down: shifts the cursor either one page up or one page down; a faster method of scrolling than the up and down arrows

- Cyberspace: a common name for the online world originating in the work of the science fiction novelist William Gibson; cyberspace does not have physical dimensions, but rather includes all of the chat rooms, blogs, websites, and other "virtual realities" of the Internet
- Internet: the worldwide network of computers which combines governmental, commercial, private, and public networks
- World Wide Web (WWW): the network, or web, of servers that support documents written in Hyper Text Markup Language (HTML), a language created specifically for the Internet; the pages on the web can link to other documents and graphics. The WWW is also the venue for the use of the hypertext transfer protocol (HTTP)
- HTTP (Hypertext Transfer Protocol): used to transfer information over the Internet; capable of transmitting files that contain audio, text, and video
- FTP (File Transfer Protocol): used to transmit information between two computers on the Internet; in this arrangement, one computer is the host and the other is the client
- POP (Post Office Protocol): transfers email from the email server to the client's inbox
- SMTP (Simple Mail Transfer Protocol): transfers email from the client computer to the email server
- VoIP (Voice over Internet Protocol): allows users to converse over the Internet by converting audio into transferable digital packets
- IRC (Internet Relay Chat): transfers text between multiple users on the Internet

- BitTorrent: a system for rapidly transferring files by dividing them into many small parts; a downloading computer receives bits of the file from many different uploading computers

Programming, Language Topics

Programming

In computing, a program is a set of instructions that convert data into information. Programming is a five-step process. The first step is identifying the problem, or determining the function that the computer program is to perform. The second step is inventing a solution to the problem, and the third step is composing program code in the appropriate syntax. The fourth step is program testing and troubleshooting. The fifth and final step is the comprehensive and detailed documentation of the programming work that was done. This documentation is meant to be read by users and other programmers.

Problem clarification

Problem clarification, the first step in computer programming, is the process of establishing the problem to be solved or the function to be performed by the program. One of the issues that must be determined is the form that the data output shall take. It can then be decided what the appropriate input will be, as well as how it will be processed by the computer. Commercial computer programmers have to make sure that their plans fit within the budget of the project and that the tasks can be accomplished with the available manpower. Also, programmers need to keep extensive documentation during the problem clarification stage so that the process can be duplicated and improved in the future, as well as so that potential user questions can be answered.

Program design

The design of a program begins with the development of an algorithm or formula. This is essentially an outline of the sequential steps that need to be taken in order to accomplish the goal of the program. Software is typically designed according to a hierarchy chart, in which the broad tasks are listed first and more specific tasks are listed below. The programmer will then begin to add detail to these tasks by writing pseudocode (an informal description of the algorithm for the programmers) or creating flowchart representations of program processes. At this point, the programmer can begin to use pre-made forms and logic tools to create program structures. This careful approach to programming makes it possible for others to go back and determine how a program was created, which makes it easier to resolve problems with the final product.

Program coding

The actual writing of a computer program is called coding. There are different programming languages in which coding can be performed. Advanced programs are composed in high-level coding languages like C, C++, or Java. Each of these languages is appropriate for certain types of programs and each has a different syntax. In computer programming, syntax is the unique order in which a programming language must be written. Just as the words in an English sentence must be placed in a certain order to make sense, so must the terms in program code.

Program testing

Before they can be used, much less released to the general public, computer programs have to be tested. Early stages of testing involve programmers entering various sets of data into the program to see if the desired results are achieved. Also, programmers will perform disk-checking, which is a process of checking the program for textual or logical errors. Sometimes, a programmer accidentally makes syntax errors, which can be easily corrected. A logic error, on the other hand, is a control structure error that may be more difficult to fix. There are various diagnostic programs available to help programmers locate problems.

Documentation and maintenance step of programming

After a computer program has been written and tested, the programmers need to compile a set of documents explaining how the program is to be used. Most programmers find it useful to take notes for this documentation during program development so that they do not forget details. The final version of the documentation, called the user manual, is typically posted online or distributed to customers in a print version. Program documentation should be accompanied by operator documentation and any text necessary to help programmers fine-tune already existing systems.

Program flowchart

A program flowchart displays the steps of the program in picture form using symbols created by the American National Standards Institute (ANSI). The terminal symbol indicates the beginning and the end of a program. The process symbol, a rectangular box surrounding a calculation, indicates a formula that must be applied at a particular point in the program. A large process is indicated by the predefined process symbol. The input/output symbol indicates a point at which data must be imported from an external source or exported to an output device like a printer. A decision symbol marks the point at which the program must make a binary decision based on

current status. The direction in which the program is proceeding is indicated by arrowheads or flowlines. In some cases, connectors substitute for flowlines.

Data type

A data type describes a memory location, specifically the proper method for encoding and performing operations on a variable stored within the location. Variables allow high-level programming languages to store data using descriptive names instead of numeric addresses. When the variable is changed, the value related to the descriptive name also changes while the program is being executed. In most programming languages, programmers must identify variables using descriptive statements, which include the data type. Programming languages include a number of primitive data types, such as Boolean, character, real or float, and integer. Less common examples that are growing in popularity are hypertext (such as HTML), images (such as JPEG and GIF), audio, and video. Certain program languages, especially some object-oriented languages, allow the user to add data types that were not included as primitives.

Variable

A variable is a single location in the computer's memory capable of storing one value. Such locations provide temporary storage for multiple types of data (see data types), including numbers and characters. Program algorithms will later input, process, and generate output based on this data. There are two broad classifications for variables:
- *Global variables* – are considered "in scope" through the entire program, meaning they can be

read and changed through any part of the program.

Local variables – are considered "in scope" throughout only part of the program, such as a specific function or subroutine, which can read and modify the variable. For instance, if an integer variable were declared in both an object and a function which is defined inside of the object, and the programmer referenced the variable from within the function, the local copy of the variable (that is, the copy within function) would be that which is resolved, as it shares a scope (one might think of the word "visibility") with the code being executed. Variables belonging to objects can be referenced outside of those objects by specifically naming the object to which they belong, as long as they are not defined as private. Variables defined inside of functions or subroutines only exist while the method is executing, and are thus always inaccessible from outside of the method.

Integer data type

Integer data types contain whole number numeric data, and allow a program to perform traditional arithmetic operations, such as addition and subtraction, and comparisons, such as less than, greater than, or equal to. In most cases, integer data is stored in a two's complement notation, which allows efficient math on signed values (that is, being able to differentiate between positive and negative). Consider the following example:

```
int MaxOccupancy = 300;
```

`int` – assigns integer data type to variable.

`MaxOccupancy` - the name of the variable.

`300` - the value assigned to the variable.

Real data type

Real data types, also known as float (short for floating point) data types, may contain numeric data other than whole numbers stored in a floating-point notation. Real data types can perform the same operations as integer data types even though the method adding two numbers together will differ. Consider the following example:

```
float Length, Width, SquFeet;

Length = 27.5;
Width = 18.3;
SquFeet = Length * Width;
```

`float` - assigns float data type to variable.

`Length`, `Width` and `SquFeet` - are the variables. Multiple variables can be assigned to the same data type.

Character and Boolean data types

Character data types store symbols using Unicode or ASCII, and can perform the following operations, among others: comparing symbols to determine their correct alphabetical sequence; creating one long string symbols by combining multiple, shorter strings of symbols; and, determining the presence of one string of symbols inside another string. Consider the following example:

```
char Vowel, Consonant;

Vowel = 'a';
Consonant = 't';
```
`char` – assigns character data type to variable.

`Vowel` and `Consonant` – are the variables.

Boolean data types only store data that can be assigned a value of true or false, and can perform operations that will determine whether a stored value is true or false. Boolean data types use IF...THEN...ELSE statements, and operators such as AND, NOT, and OR, ELSE.

Data structure

A data structure stores multiple related variables using some type of conceptual shape or arrangement. Consider, for example, a daily planner, which arranges information in a conceptual way. It consists of tables with rows and columns. Each column on each page may represent a calendar date, and each row may represent an hour of each day. The entries in each table would list the activities planned for a specific date at a specific time. Another conceptual arrangement of data is a technical manual, which is divided into chapters, headings, subheadings, paragraphs, and sentences. Using data structures, systems can process many variables at once—a useful ability when handling large amounts of data, such as customer lists, inventory lists, etc. Types of data structures include lists, stacks, queues, trees, and arrays. Procedural languages such as FORTRAN and COBOL make frequent use of arrays, and can handle a limited number of advanced data structures. Modern, object-oriented languages such as C# can handle a vast assortment of data structures, including lists and custom classes and objects that describe a specific concept.

Homogenous array

A homogenous array is a common type of abstract data structure in which all data must be the same type (integer, real, character etc.). It can store a block of variables in either a one-dimensional list

or multi-dimensional array consisting of rows and columns. The program must declare the dimensions of the array. Consider the following example:

```
char Letters [4][5]
```
The above array is identified by the variable Letters. It will have four rows and five columns, and contain character data types. Any time during the program's execution, it can refer to the array using its name or to a specific data element using indices. An *index* is an integer value that identifies a single entry by listing its column and row number. For instance, in FORTRAN language, the indice Letter [1][1] would identify the entry that corresponded to the first row, first column. In C, the same entry would be identified as Letter [0][0] because numbering in C begins with 0 rather than 1.

Heterogeneous array

A heterogeneous array is a common type of abstract data structure capable of storing different data types. Consider, for instance, a set of information containing the name of a product, its price, and the number of product units sold. This information could be stored in the following array, using C#:

```
String ProductName = "Book IV";
Float Price = 29.95F;
Int UnitsSold = 2318;
Object[] Params;
Params[0] = ProductName;
Params[1] = Price;
Params[2] = UnitsSold;
```

Object [] declares a dynamic array named Params. In this case, it consists of three components: ProductName, which is character data type; Price, which is a float data type; and, UnitsSold, which is an integer data type. The program can refer to the entire array using its name, or to parts of the array using the array name

and the components name, e.g.:
`Product.UnitsSold` (which would evaluate to 2318).

List and queue

A list is a basic abstract data structure that arranges data entries sequentially. Entries at the beginning are called the *head*, and entries at the end are called the *tail*. Data can be searched, rearranged, and changed. There are two basic types of lists: queues and stacks.

A queue receives new entries at the tail and removes old entries at the head, much like a checkout line: The people at the head of the line have been their longest and are served first. New people go to the end of the line and work their way forward. A queue is known as a "first in, first out" (FIFO) structure, and performs the following functions:

- *Pushing* – occurs when a new data element is added to the stack.
- *Popping* – occurs when the computer returns the first data element that was saved.

The process of entering data into a queue is known as *enqueue*. The process of returning data is known as *dequeue*. In many cases, queues provide the underlying structures for *buffers*, which store data temporarily for transfer between two locations.

Stack

A stack is a common type of list data structure. It receives and removes new entries at the head, also known as the *top*. The tail is known as the *base* or *bottom*. The data saved most recently always goes to the top of the stack and will always be the first data returned when the computer retrieves information;

consequently, a stack is a "last in, first out" (LIFO) structure. It performs the following functions:

- *Pushing* – occurs when a new data element is added to the stack.
- *Popping* – occurs when the computer retrieves the data that was saved most recently.

In many cases, stacks provide the underlying structure for *backtracking* programs, which retrieve instructions in an order that is reverse from which they were entered. An example of backtracking is a recursive process, in which instructions are discarded as they are used, such as "undo" operations or an algorithm to reach the end of a maze.

Tree

A tree is a hierarchical abstract data structure that consists of *nodes*. The top node is known as the *root node* while bottom nodes are known as *terminal*, or *leaf*, nodes. Consider the following example:

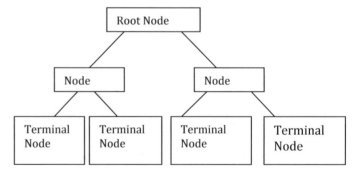

Lower level nodes cannot be connected to any more than one higher level node, and the *depth* of a tree is its total number of horizontal layers. In a *binary tree*, no node will have more than two descendants. A node's descendents are known as *children* while the ancestral nodes are known as *parents*. If we isolate one parent and its children, we have a *subtree* from the main tree.

Abstract data type

Abstract data types, or ADTs, present information in such a way that users can more easily understand and access it. In essence, an ADT takes an abstract algorithm stored in the computer's memory, and converts it into a simpler form, such as stacks, queues, priority queues, strings, containers, lists, deques, maps, multimaps, multisets, trees, and sets. All of these must be simulated but will remain constant between different programs because all programming languages will have similar semantics for them. ADTs facilitate processes such as categorization, formal description in programming languages, assessing data structures, etc. They can be implemented in the form of modules that include procedures for ADT operation. As conceptual tools, ADTs are important in object-oriented programming language.

Static and dynamic abstract data structures

Abstract data structures fall under two main categories:
- Static structures – do not change their size or shape over time. Consider, for instance, a list of people born in a specific year. If the list is complete, it will neither increase nor decrease. The number will remain constant. Static structures are easier to maintain than dynamic structures because they only require a method of accessing data and changing data at a set location.
- Dynamic structures – change their size and shape over time. Consider a list of names of people who belong to a certain organization. As its membership increases or decreases, the list must change sizes. Dynamic structures can be difficult to

maintain because they require a method of adding or removing entries and acquiring more memory space as the structure grows.

Pointers

Pointers are memory cells containing the encoded numeric addresses that a program uses to identify a specific data entry in the computer's memory. In data structures, pointers store the location of a data entry. As information is moved around within the structure, the pointer will update to reflect the new location of the information. Consider, for example, a subroutine that performs an action, such as spell check, upon a large block of text. One could pass the entire block of text as a parameter to the subroutine, and thus provide it its own copy with which to work, which it would then have to return at completion, or one could simply pass a pointer to the text variable—that is, a reference to it—so that the huge amount of data contained in it does not have to be needlessly moved. The speed increase of using a pointer in this manner is proportional to the size of the data being referenced. As a further example, CPUs use pointers known as *instruction pointers*, which hold the next instruction to be carried out in a list. Many programming languages include pointers as a primitive data type.

One-dimensional, homogenous array

One-dimensional homogenous arrays are ideal for storing sequences of data because they store data elements in consecutive memory cells. Consider the following example, which stores weekly weight measurements:

```
int Weight [15];
```

The above declaration statement establishes a one-dimensional homogenous array referred to as

- *113* -

`Weight`. It contains integer data types and consists of 15 consecutive memory cells. The address of the first entry in the array is x. To locate other entries in the array, the program must subtract one from the desired entry and add x. For instance, the fifth entry in the array `Weight` would be located at the following address:

$$x + (5 - 1)$$

That is to say (providing that each array value occupies one word-sized chunk of memory—say, 32 bits or 4 bytes), that one could find the location of any array element by adding its zero-based index (hence the subtraction of one) to the address of the beginning of the array.

If the programmer wanted to enter a value of 150 into the fifth memory cell of the array, he would use the following assignment statement in C++:

```
Weight [4] = 150;
```

Two-dimensional homogenous array

Two-dimensional homogenous arrays are ideal for tables of information. They come in two varieties: *row major order*, which stores data row by row in the computer's memory, and *column major order*, which stores data column by column in the computer's memory. Consider the following example—a two-dimensional array that contains the weekly weight measurements of multiple people:

```
int Weight [5][10];
```

The above declaration statement establishes a two-dimensional homogenous array referred to as `Weight`. It contains integer data types and consists of 5 rows and 10 columns. The entry in which the first row intersects the first column has the address of x. To locate a specific entry in the array, the

program must use the following address polynomial:

$$x + (c * (i - 1)) + (j - 1), \text{ where:}$$

- c is the number of columns in the array.
- i is the row containing the desired entry.
- j is the column containing the desired entry.

If the programmer wanted to enter a value of 140 in the entry where the fourth row and fifth column intersect, he would use the following assignment statement in C++:

```
Weight [3][4] = 140;
```

Implementation strategies for heterogeneous arrays

Consider the following fixed heterogeneous array, which contains the name of each product, its price, and the number sold:

```
struct Product
    {char ProductName[8]};
    float Price;
    int UnitsSold;
    } product[5];
```

The array consists of five sets of ten contiguous memory cells. For each set, the first eight cells contain character data types that identify the product's name; the ninth cell contains a float data type identifying the product's price, and the tenth cell contains an integer data type identifying the number sold. Counting memory addresses here is more difficult than in homogeneous arrays, as each data type may occupy different amounts of memory. For instance, the char data type usually uses one byte, the float data type usually uses four, and the int data type usually uses 4. Thus, each element of struct type Product will use (8*1)+4+4 = 16 bytes, and the entire array will therefore use 16*5 = 80 bytes.

To change the entry in the `Price` cell, the user would input the following statement:

```
product.Price = 5.50;
```

Note that we are using the object product, not the struct type Product. In this C++ example, the code is case-sensitive, and it is important to remember to use the instance of a class or type and not the class itself, unless it is defined as static.

In non-managed languages, dynamic heterogeneous arrays are best created using *pointers*, which allow for memory management methods to be performed.

Implementation strategies for lists

A contiguous list is the best technique for storing static lists of names. It consists of a large block of memory cells, which are divided into groups to form subblocks. Each subblock stores a name on the list. For instance, 200 consecutive memory cells would be allocated for a contiguous list to accommodate 20 subblocks of 10 cells apiece. If a name on this list does not use the entire 10 cell allotment, the empty cells are filled with ASCII spaces.

A linked list is the best technique for storing dynamic lists. It relies on *pointers*, which enable the information to be stored in separate linked locations rather than in one large block of memory cells. A program can add information to the list without the risk of exceeding the capacity of a single, large block. Different languages handle the structure of these differently, but a common set of characteristics includes each element in the list containing both a data field and a pointer field, where the pointer fields include pointers to the next (and sometimes previous) element. Linked lists often contain sentinel nodes demarcating the first and last elements in a list, but sometimes simply include null

pointers to indicate that no node succeeds or precedes the current one.

Implementation strategies for stacks

When creating a stack, a programmer must allocate a memory block with sufficient space to hold the stack at its largest size. The first entry in the stack will go into the base end. Additional entries are inserted in sequence starting from the base entry. The top of the stack will change locations as the program pushes and pops entries; consequently, the address of the top must be marked by a stack pointer, which is stored in an additional memory cell. When a new entry is pushed onto the stack, the pointer will point up to the vacant location and then the new entry will be placed on this location. When an entry is popped out of the stack, the pointer will point to the entry that was beneath the removed entry.

Implementation strategies for queues

When creating a queue, a programmer must allocate a memory block with sufficient space to hold the queue at its largest size. Information is pushed into the queue at the tail, and popped out at the head. Consequently, there must be two pointers—a head pointer and a tail pointer—to track activity at both ends. The tail pointer always points to the first vacant entry at the tail, and the head pointer always points to the first entry that can be removed at the head. When the head and tail pointers are pointing at the same location, the queue is empty. In order to prevent the queue from crawling through the computer's memory, the programmer may implement a circular queue, which inserts entries in the vacated spaces at the head and, thereby, allows the queue to move around in a loop.

Implementation strategies for binary trees

In a binary tree, a parent node cannot have in excess of two child nodes. When stored in the computer's memory, binary trees usually rely on a linked structure with pointers. Each node counts as a single entry, and consists of three parts:

- Data contained in a node.
- Left child pointer that links to the node's first child.
- Right child pointer that links to the node's second child.

The nodes at the bottom of the tree must use NIL pointers to indicate there are no additional nodes, and the node at the very top is identified by a root pointer.

Binary trees are sometimes stored as a single block of contiguous memory cells in an Ahnentafel list—a method borrowed from genealogy—rather than a linked structure. In such, a root node is followed by both its children—left then right—after which the left child's two children are followed by the right child's two children. This pattern continues until the tree is finished. As one might notice, this is most efficient for complete trees.

Iterative structure and sequential search algorithm

An iterative structure is a programming algorithm that repeats a set of instructions through a loop. There are several types of algorithms capable of creating iterative structures, such as sequential search and insertion sort.

A sequential search algorithm is designed to scan a list of values and find a specific entry. It searches the values in sequential order, making it ideal for shorter lists. In pseudocode, the sequential search algorithm is expressed thusly:

```
    bool Search (NumberList,
SearchValue)
if (NumberList is empty)
        return false
    else
        for CurPos from 0
to (Size(NumberList) – 1)
            if
NumberList[CurPos] =
SearchValue
                return
true
    return false

Search(List,10)
```

This sequential search algorithm will search NumberList for the value of SearchValue. If it finds it, the search is considered a success. If it does not find it, the search is considered a failure.

Loops

A loop is an iterative structure in which the program executes the same set of instructions until a certain *termination condition* has been met. Following are two primary loop structures:
while (termination condition) do (set of instructions)

repeat (set of instructions) until (termination condition)

While statements are considered *pretest loops* because the condition is executed before the set of instructions. Repeat statements are considered posttest loops because the set of instructions is executed before the condition. Controlling a loop involves three steps:

- Initialize – creates an initial value to send through the loop.
- Test – determines whether the current value fulfills the termination conditions.
- Modify – alters the current values to bring it nearer the termination condition.

Consider the following while statement:

```
Value = 2

while (Value < 20) do (Value
= Value * 2)
```

This loop will execute four times. Then, Value will no longer be less than 20. Consider the following repeat statement:

```
Value = 2

repeat (Value = Value + 2)
until (Value = 9)
```

The loop will never end because Value will never equal nine.

There is also a third primary loop structure, known as the for loop:

```
for (variable) from (starting value) to
(finishing value) [loop (increment)]
```

This is a controlled loop in which the developer knows exactly how many times the loop will iterate. Consider the following pseudocode:

```
for Value from 2 to 5
loop 1 (print Value)
```

The loop will run four times, printing the numbers two through five to the user.

Insertion sort algorithm

An insertion sort algorithm is an iterative structure capable of sorting a list. For instance, consider the following list of numbers: 9, 3, 5, 1, and 7. Using an insertion sort algorithm, a computer can sort this list from lowest to highest. An insertion sort program will make use of a *pivot entry*, which is a temporary storage space that is separate from the list. As the program runs, list values take turns being moved into the pivot entry in order to create a blank entry (or hole) in the list. This hole allows the values within the list

to be moved around. Consider the following pseudocode:

```
procedure Sort
(NumberList)
    n = Size(NumberList)
    for Pivot from 1 to (n -
1)
        x = Pivot
        while x > 0 and
Value(x) < Value(x - 1)
            swap (Values
of x and x - 1)
            x = x - 1
```

The above algorithm is essentially a loop within loop. The outer loop maintains the pivot location in the overall list, while the inner loop does the work of moving the pivot location's value into the correct location. Pivot and x are variables denoting the array position in the list, while the pseudocode's Value method returns that array position's value. This algorithm will eventually sort the aforementioned list into numeric order.

Recursive structures

A recursive structure is a programming algorithm that repeats a set of instructions until a certain task has been completed. Unlike iterative structures (which rely on loops that complete the entire instruction set and then repeat it), recursive structures repeat the instructions as subtasks of themselves, interrupting their execution to begin a new subtask. In this way, all subtasks are left unfinished until the task has been completed. For example, consider a person conducting research on house construction. As he reads one article, he notices that it makes a distinction between homes with cement foundations and homes with peer and beam foundation. Because he doesn't understand the difference between the two, he must find and read a new article on foundation before he can finish reading his original article. This is an example of a recursive process. One instruction set cannot be finished until its subtask is finished. A binary search algorithm is a type of recursive structure.

Control of recursive processes

Recursive processes use the same types of controls as loops:

- Initialize – gives the algorithm an initial list and a target value. This is not always necessary, depending on the recursive process.
- Modify – divides the list into smaller and smaller portions.
- Test for termination – ends the algorithm once the *base* or *degenerative case* has been fulfilled. The base case is fulfilled once the target entry is found, the most basic number has been reached, or the list is empty.

Common examples of recursive procedures include computing a factorial, the Fibonacci sequence, a greatest common divisor, and binary searching of sorted data. For instance, the Fibonacci sequence can be computed by pseudocode as such:

```
Given n >= 0:
int factorial (n)
1. if n = 0, return 1
2. else, return [ n ×
factorial(n-1) ]
```

Note that the program will execute the method inside of itself continually until n = 0, and then the return values will be supplied iteration by iteration up the chain of execution until the final number is returned to where the factorial method was initially called.

Binary search algorithm

A binary search algorithm is a type of recursive structure. For example,

consider the following list of numbers: 1, 3, 5, 7, 9, 11, 13, and 15. If we wanted to determine if the value of 11 was present on the list, we it might use the following algorithm:

```
bool Exists(n,List)
int TestValue
if (List is empty)
    return false
else
    (Assign the middle entry
    in the sorted List as
TestValue)
    case (TestValue = n)
        return true
    case (TestValue < n)
        (Assign left half
    of List to List and call
Exists(n,List)
    Case (TestValue > n)
        (Assign right half
    of List to List and call
Exists(n,List)
List = 1, 3, 5, 7, 9, 11,
    13, 15
Exists(11,List)
```

The TargetValue is 11, and the program will begin searching the list at the middle value: 9, which becomes the TestValue (Technically, because there's an even number of values on the list, there is no middle value, meaning the computer will select the first value in the second half.). Then, once the program has run through the appropriate case for 9 and established it is less than the 11, it will move to the second half of the list and make 13 the TestValue. Finally, in performing the third and last set of subtasks, the program will find the TargetValue.

Procedures

A procedure is a set of instructions that carry out a certain function. This allows developers to repeat common tasks with a single line instead of having to re-enter the logic in place after place. This allows changes to a certain task to be made to

- 118 -

one piece of code, rather than everywhere that task is performed. For instance, if a program needed to set a piece of data from a data source, the developer could connect to the database manually each time the connection was to be made, set that data, and close the connection, but what would happen were the data source's name or connection information to change? The developer would have to search through the code for all the places (potentially thousands of places) which contain said code, and make the changes. A procedure would solve this problem by allowing the developer to change the information in one place and invoke this process from multiple places, thus saving countless hours of time and many potential errors. Procedures have names by which they are "called", and often sets of parameters which allow custom information to affect the process in question.

To illustrate our data source example in pseudocode:

```
Procedure SetData(DB,
FieldName, FieldData)
  (Open and configure DB)
  Set Value of FieldName
to FieldData
  (Close DB)
```

In this example, SetData is the procedure's name, and DB, FieldName, and FieldData are parameters which are set when the procedure is called, allowing this code to be reused dynamically. Anywhere in the code, a developer could set the Customer database's CustomerCount field to the integer 15000 by simply writing:

```
SetData(Customer,
CustomerCount, 15000)
```

If the information needed to connect to DB should ever change, this now only has to be modified in one location, instead of many. The main benefit to procedures is reusability.

Parameters

Parameters are generic terms used by procedures, and fall under two categories:

- *Formal parameters* – are the formal terms used by the procedure. They must be listed in the procedure's header
- *Actual parameters* – are the specific terms that are inserted into the formal parameters once the procedure starts executing. For example, a procedure could have a formal parameter named `country`. However, once the procedure is applied, `Israel` could be inserted in place of `country`.

Consider the following procedure's header:

procedure ListCountrybyPopulation (country, population)

The name of the procedure is ListCountryByPopulation, and it includes two formal variables named country and population. Now, consider the method by which formal parameters are assigned actual parameters.

ListCountrybyPopulation (Israel, 7,500,000)

The above statement transfers the actual values of Israel and 7.5 million (actual parameters) into the formal parameters of country and population. Formal parameters are those used when defining a procedure and actual parameters are those values which are assigned to the formal parameters' variables when the procedure is being called.

Transferring parameters

Programming languages use one of two possible methods for transferring actual parameters into formal parameters:

- *Passing by value* – When the routine (procedure or function) is called, the program makes a copy of the data passed into the routine's parameters rather than allowing the method direct access to that data. The procedure can only change data within the copy, never within the calling code. This method ensures that data can never be altered mistakenly, but is inefficient when dealing with large amounts of data.
- *Passing by reference* – gives the procedure direct access to the location of the actual parameters within the calling code. This allows the procedure to change information within the calling computer. This method is more efficient but less safe.

The developer can usually define within the procedure's definition whether it is expecting a value or reference parameter.

Functions

A function is similar to a procedure; however, rather than only performing an action, a function generates a value for the calling code, and then sends the value back to the program where it can be stored as a variable for later retrieval or applied immediately. Consider the following example:

```
float SquareFootage
(float Length, float Width)
    {float SquareFeet;
    SquareFeet = Length *
Width;
    return Square Feet;}
```

The first line is function's header, which declares the data type (float), the name of the function (SquareFootage), and the formal parameters. The second line declares a local variable named SquareFeet. The third line specifies the calculation method. If the program wanted to use the above function elsewhere, it could do so as follows:

- Price = 100 * SquareFootage (100, 200)

The above statement calls upon the SquareFootage function and applies actual parameters (100, 200) to the formal parameters.

Methods

Method is a term used in object-oriented programming. It simply describes a procedure or function as a member of an object, and helps to determine how an object will respond to a wide range of events. In the object-oriented paradigm, every system consists of objects. Each object performs a specific set of functions, and contacts and interacts with other objects to solve problems. Consider, for instance, an object-oriented program that makes uses of spreadsheets. A particular spreadsheet might be an object, and it may have a method to open it, one to save it, one to insert rows and columns, etc. In C++ programming, methods are known as *member functions*.

Exception handling

Exception handling is the process by which a program manages special conditions (known as exceptions) that change the normal function of program execution. Put simply, exception handling signals that a program could not execute properly. It can be carried out by a computer language construct or a hardware device. When the program recognizes an exception, it will save the current state of execution in a certain location, and then transfer program execution to an exception handler, which is a specially designed subroutine. In some situations, such as a page fault, a program will use the saved data to resume normal execution. In other situations, the exception cannot be handled transparently. Run-time engine environments use *automated exception handlers*, which attach to the engine and identify the root-cause of the exception by recording all debugging information within the computer's memory when the exception was thrown. Exception handling is often difficult to carry out in modern Enterprise-level applications.

Exception handling syntax

Most programming languages use the same basic types of exception handling syntax. For instance, the most popular syntax initiates an exception program using a special statement, such as throw or raise, followed by an object or a special type. When defining their scope, exception handlers begin with a marker clause, such as try or begin, and conclude with a first handler clause, such as catch, except, or rescue. After the scope has been defined, the exception often includes several handler clauses that identify the types of exceptions it handles as well as the name of the exception object. In some programming languages, exceptions can use an else statement in the event that an exception is not found by the time the handler's scope is finished. The end of the exception uses clauses such as finally and ensure, which allows code to execute at the end of an exception handling routine and frees computer resources used by the exception.

Concurrent processing

Concurrent processing is the term used to describe the ability of a program or operating system to keep a number of processes logically active concurrently even though only one operation can take place at a time. The operating system creates this illusion of concurrently active processes by interleaving the execution order of their commands, thus juggling the execution of many processes at once. Problems arise when the processes must communicate between themselves and/or access the same resources.

Communication in concurrent processing

In concurrent processing, a main program simultaneously opens and operates multiple other programs. In many cases, one program may need to reach a certain point before another can continue running; consequently, they must communicate between themselves as they execute. Consider, for instance, two programs that must update a list. If they access the list at the same time, it may result in only one update going through and the second update being lost. To avoid this problem, programmers must design the system such that certain data items are given *mutually exclusive access*, meaning only one application can access them at any given time. There are two methods for achieving mutually exclusive access:

- Program each application so that it is capable of identifying all applications and blocking their access when it is accessing the data. This method can be problematic because one segment error can bring down the entire system.
- Program the data item itself with a *monitor*, which prevents other applications from accessing it when it is already being accessed.

Scope

The scope of a variable defines sections of a program in which the variable exists, can be used or even known to exist.

Scopes can nest programming elements or be nested within programming elements, and contain various types of information, such as:

- Declarations. Definitions of identifiers. Statements and expressions that define executable algorithms.

The type of scope dictates program semantics, and varies between programming languages. Scope also determines *information hiding*, which is the program's ability to access and see variables. Consider, for instance, a *namespace*, which is a type of scope that uses a single identifier to group several related identifiers logically. A variable declared within a procedure only exists within that proce-dure and its scope is thus that procedure. Once the procedure has completed, the variable is destroyed. A variable that is a member of an object can share the same name as a variable that is a member of another object, as their scopes are different. For example, if ObjectA and ObjectB each have a variable named ObjName, from within ObjectA, ObjName will resolve only to ObjectA's version, and likewise for ObjectB. However, if outside the scope of either of these objects, one has to reference the object in order to reference the variable, e.g., ObjectA.ObjName. ObjName is thus a member of ObjectA, and is limited by its parent's scope. This allows a program to be organized logically and for common names to be reused without conflict.

Name binding

Name binding is the process of associating a programming object, such as data or code, with an identifier. Programming language performs name binding as an aid to programmers. Once an identifier is associated with an object, the identifier is described as *referencing* that object. Binding and scoping are related because the scope dictates which objects are referenced by which identifiers, both lexically and at execution time. If binding occurs before the program runs, it is described as *static*. If binding occurs while the program is running, it is described as *dynamic*. In dynamic binding, the program receives both the request for the object and the object itself at runtime. Dynamic Dispatch is a type of dynamic name binding used by several languages, including C++.

Imperative programming and declarative programming

The imperative paradigm, or procedural paradigm, views programming as sequence of commands that control data in order to solve a particular program. This represents the more traditional approach, and serves as the basis for machine language and pseudocode. The programmer first develops an algorithm to generate a specific result, and creates a sequence of commands to carry out the algorithm.

In the declarative paradigm, the programmer provides a description of the problem to the programming system, and the system solves the problem using a series of general-purpose, problem-solving algorithms. Consequently, the focus is creating a detailed description of the problem rather than writing algorithms. The declarative paradigm was given a boon by with the creation of *logic programming*, which relies on formal mathematical logic.

Functional programming paradigm

The functional paradigm views programming in terms of a mathematical function with an input-to-output relationship. In essence, the program is series of functions that accept input and generate output. The output of one

- 122 -

function becomes input for another function, and so on. In this way, predefined functions (also known as predefined programming units) can be nested inside one another with simpler functions going inside the more complex functions. Consider, for instance, a program designed to determine the total difference in rainfall between Spring 2009 and Spring 2010:

(Find_diff (Find_sum
Rainfall_Spring2009)   (Find_sum
Rainfall_Spring2010))

The above program uses a common functional programming language known as LISP. It uses output from two simpler functions (Find_diff and Find_sum), and finds their difference to produce new output.

Object-oriented programming paradigm

The object-oriented paradigm views software systems as collections of objects. It led to the emergence of *object-oriented programming*, or *OOP*. Each object consists of data and a set of procedures (known as methods) for interacting with that data. Objects can work with other objects in order to solve programs and generate certain outcomes. Consider, for instance, a text document that contains sales data. Under the object-oriented paradigm, the document is created as an object containing information (i.e. sales data) and methods for changing that data (i.e. adding data, deleting data, sorting, etc.). Assume the program wants to extrapolate sales projections. By having the sales data object interact with an object containing mathematical functions, the program could generate the desired projections. There are a few key terms associated with the object-oriented paradigm:

- *Object* – a programming unit consisting of data and methods for interacting with that data.
- *Class* – type of object. Multiple objects may be based on the same lines of written code. All objects based on this code are in the same class.
- *Instance* – a single object from a particular class. An object is an "instance of a class." Where the class is a blueprint, the object is the result.

Program statements

The statements that comprise a program fall under three categories:
- Declarative statements – define the terminology that is unique to the program so that the terms may be used later in the program. Examples include names that refer to data items.
- Imperative statements – lay out the programming steps that carry out the algorithm.
- Comments – explains the various steps of the program in language that humans can more easily understand. These are used for particularly confusions portions of the program.

Most programs follow the same basic structure: a series of declarative statements followed by imperative statements. This includes objected-oriented programs; the methods that govern objects are, for all intents and purposes, small strings of imperative statements.

Literal

A literal is a preset, unchanging value used by programs. It can be changed, but it is set to a value directly instead of being assigned to anything dynamic. Consider, for instance, writing an error message in an application. Should a user, for example, attempt to enter into a locked field, the developer might write a method with the following code to account for this circumstance:

MessageBox("Entry is not allowed into field " + sField);

In this example, the literal is enclosed within quotation marks (the common method for denoting a string literal) and a variable is appended to the end. There would be no reason to assign the literal value to a variable, as it is just used in this one location, while the information that changes is derived from the value of sField.

Literals are problematic in programming for two reasons:
- They are essentially scalar quantities. They can be difficult to interpret and troubleshoot at a later date, especially with numeric values.
- They can be difficult to locate and alter in the program.

Constant

A constant is a name that describes a present, unchanging value. It remedies the problems associated with literals, such as their ambiguity of meaning and difficulty to alter in the program. Consider the following declarative statements that established a constant in C#:

```
const string
C_COMPANYNAME = "Davis
Company";
```

This statement assigns the name C_COMPANYNAME to the value "Davis Company," which is the name of the company (it is assumed that this information will never change at runtime). In C#, the value might be used thusly:

```
string sGreeting = "Welcome
to " + C_COMPANYNAME +_"!";
```

As the company's name is a constant value that is never expected to change at runtime, and is something that might be referenced in many places, this constant would most likely be placed in a global utility namespace for easy use throughout the program, so that if the company's name were to change, it could be altered in one place and be reflected everywhere C_COMPANYNAME is used. Note that the main difference between a constant and a variable is that the constant, once initialized and assigned a value, cannot be changed.

Assignment statements

An assignment statement is a type of imperative statement that assigns a value to a variable (i.e. a specific location in the computer's memory). Like most imperative statements, assignment statements describe the algorithms involved in the program and come after all variables have been assigned. Consider the following example:

```
A = B + C;
A := B + C;
A = B + C;
```

The above statement is written in three different languages—C, Ada, and APL respectively. The variable A is assigned the value of the sum of B and C. Many assignment statements will involve mathematical expressions of greater complexity than above, such as the following:

```
x = 2 * (7 + 3) - 4
```

In calculating the above statement, the program will follow the rules of *operator precedence*: parenthesis, exponents, multiplication, division, addition, and subtraction. In the above statement, x equals 16. Some programming languages are capable of *overloading*, which is putting a mathematical expression to multiple uses. For instance, the '+' symbol is also used to combine words and phrases in several languages, as string concatenation.

Control statement

A control statement is a type of imperative statement that manages the sequence of program execution. An example is the `goto` statement, which directs program execution to a different location marked by a name or number. Control statements are often misused, resulting in branching structures that are overly complex, poorly written, and unreadable by other people. To avoid this problem, programmers rely on a method known as *structured programming*, which seeks to make the most efficient, accurate, and readable use of control statements. Most modern programming languages use control statements capable of representing complex branching structures in a single lexical statement. These include `if-then-else` statements, `while` statements, and `switch` or `case` statements. When choosing the most appropriate statement, programmers should work to achieve the best possible design while maintaining readability.

If-then-else statements

`If-then-else` statements instruct the computer to engage in decision branching. Different languages will handle this different syntactically, but the idea is the same; a condition statement will follow the initial `if` clause. If the condition is true, the computer will carry out the statement sequence after the `then` clause (or the curly bracket which denotes a block of code in many languages). If the condition is false, the computer will skip the `then` clause and

instead carry out the statement sequence after the `else` clause. Once it has executed one of the clauses, the computer will move to the `end if` statement (or the closing curly bracket). Consider the following program:

In C++, C#, or Java:
```
    if (x < y) {smaller = X;}
        else {smaller = Y;}
```

In Ada:
```
    IF (x < y) THEN
  set smaller to X
    ELSE
        set smaller to Y
    END IF
```

If the x is less than y, the computer will set the smaller value to x. If x is not less than y, the computer will set the smaller value to y.

While statements

`While` statements are a type of branching statement that instructs the computer to perform a repetitive function. A condition statement will follow the `while` clause, and the loop will repeat until the statement is false. Consequently, during the course of a `while` loop, a value must change; otherwise, the loop will repeat into infinity. Consider the following example:

In C++, C#, or Java:
```
X = 100;
while (X > 20)
    X = X - 30;
```
Before entering the `while` loop, X is given a value of 100. Each time through the loop, the value of X is reduced by 30. Once it is less than 20, the next loop will not begin. The final value of X through this loop is 10.

Case statements

A `case` statement (also known as a `select` or `switch` statement) is a type of branching statement used when a logic test could produce multiple outcomes. It instructs the computer to perform a different action for each possible outcome. Consider the following example:

In C++, C#, or Java:

```
    switch (variable) {
  case 1: statement1; break;
  case 2: statement2; break;
  case 3: statement3; break;
  default: statement4;}
```

If logic test '1' is true, perform `statement1`. If logic test '2' is true, perform `statement2`. If logic test '3' is true, perform `statement3`. If something else is true, perform `statement4`. Case statements often provide a means of simplifying `else if` statements.

Comments

Comments are explanatory statements inserted within the program. Their only function is aiding and clarifying a person's understanding of the program code as he or she reads through it. Consequently, translators ignore comments entirely so they don't interfere with execution. There are two common methods of writing comments:

```
    // Comments go here.
    /* Comments go here. */
```

In the first method, '//' marks the becoming of the comment, which takes up the rest the line. In the second method, the comment is inserted between /* and */, and this can span multiple lines. Both methods can be found in Java, C++, and C#. Comments should provide insight rather than redundancy. Consider, for instance, the following program statements:

```
A = B + C;
```

Rather than stating "A is the sum of B and C", the programmer could explain the purpose that A serves in the program. Writing comments about every statement can become confusing to a reader; consequently, it is often better to include all comments about a specific programming unit at the beginning of that unit.

Translator; source program; object program; fixed-format language

A translator is responsible for translating one programming language into another programming language. The translation process consists of three parts: lexical analysis, parsing, and code generation. The source program is the original program before it sent through the translator.

The object program is the new program after it has been translated.

Fixed-format languages require that each program statement occupy a specific position when printed on a page.

Free-format languages do not require program statements to occupy any specific position on a printed page. This allows the programmer to write out the program in such a way that is more understandable to a human reader. Free-format languages rely on *key words* (if, then, else, etc.) and punctuation so that the computer can read the program regardless of its spacing and positioning. Key words are also known as *reserved words* because the programmer must avoid using them for any other purpose.

Lexical analysis

Lexical analysis is the first step of the translation process. The lexical analyzer examines the source code, and determines the symbols that should be grouped into strings. For example, if the

- 126 -

program includes the letter string e-x-e-c-u-t-e, the lexical analyzer will recognize that the letters should lumped into a single word 'execute.' Similarly, if the source code includes the number string 1-7-4-3, it will be interpreted as a single number '1743' rather than four separate numbers (and it will be evaluated as an integer because it is not quote-delimited,

symbol table, which records the name of each variable and its data types.

Syntax diagrams and parse trees

Syntax diagrams are created during the parsing process of translation. They enable the parser to express pictorially the grammatical structure of a

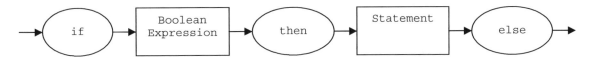

as a string would be). After the lexical analyzer has evaluated each symbol in the source code and determined which strings of symbols should be grouped into a single unit, it will categorize the units by type: numbers, words, operators, etc. The lexical analyzer then creates a token for each unit. The *token* includes the encoded unit and its classification, and is passed on to the parser.

Parsing

Parsing is the second step of the translation process. The parser receives tokens from the lexical analyzer, and groups them into statements. To determine the correct syntax and structure of statements, the parser follows a set of grammar rules specific to the language. For instance, if the program is written in a free-format language, the parser will use *key words* and *reserved words* to determine the grammatical structure for statements. If the program is written in fixed-format, it will follow the order of the statements on the page. The parser describes program statements using *syntax diagrams* and *parse trees*. Once each statement has been identified, the parser separates the declarative statements from the imperative statements. The information within declarative statements is stored within a

programming statement. Consider, for example, the syntax diagram for an if-then-else statement:

Terms that require further description are described as *nonterminal* and enclosed within a rectangle. Terms that do not require further description are described as *terminal* and enclosed within an oval.

Parse trees illustrate how a specific string fits to a syntax diagram. The parse tree begins with a nonterminal expression at the very top, and branches (i.e. decomposes) into progressively simpler expressions until the entire statement is represented as a series of terminal expressions. If a program statement can produce two completely different parse trees, it is described as having *ambiguous grammar*.

Coercion and strongly typed

When a program performs functions (such as addition or subtraction) on multiple variables downloaded from the symbol table, those variables must be compatible data types or the parser will report an error during the translation process. In some cases, the parser will order the code generate to make the variables compatible by converting one variable into a different data type. This approach is called coercion, which is generally avoided because it indicates a poorly written program. Most modern programming languages do not engage in coercion and, instead, require that all functions use innately compatible variable types. This practice is described as being strongly typed.

Code generation is the third and final step of the translation process. A code generator receives statements from the parser, and then translates them into machine-language. An important function in this step is *code optimization,* which is the process of creating the most efficient code possible. For instance, if two statements use the same value, the computer need not reload the value from memory. It can simply retrieve it from the general-purpose registers.

Object-oriented programming, class, instance variable, methods, instance, and constructor

Object-oriented programming, or OOP, derives from the object-oriented paradigm. In OOP, a program consists of numerous active programming units known as *objects*, which contain data and set of instructions determining the object's reaction to a variety of circumstances. The most popular OOP languages include C++, C#, and Java, all of which include statements that describe objects and their behavior.

Class is a program template for a certain kind of object. All objects that rely on this template will possess similar characteristics.

Instance variables are variables contained within objects.

Methods are the set of procedures that govern the actions of the object. Methods are essentially imperative procedures and functions that belong to an object or class.

An instance is a single object from a particular class.

A constructor is a special method that assigns initialization values to objects within a particular class. Any object that derives from this class receives the constructor, and is created by invoking this constructor method.

Inheritance, polymorphism, and encapsulation

Inheritance occurs when one object class gains the properties of another object class. This technique simplifies the process of describing objects with characteristics that are both similar and different. Classes which are children of other classes can inherit the properties of their parents, and thus their objects (instances) can do the same.

Polymorphism is an object's ability to interpret a message in a customized manner, or a way that is unique to the object. Assume, for instance, that two mathematical objects are sent the same 'perform calculations' message. If the mathematical formulas are not the same between objects, each one must execute a different set of functions in order to fulfill the command, even though the command was the same for both objects. Encapsulation limits access to an object's internal properties and features. Access to encapsulated, or *private*, features is limited to the object. Public features can be accessed outside the object. To preserve encapsulation, a developer will often use private properties within an object, and provide public accessor methods only for those properties which he allows others to get, set, or both.

Resolution and resolvent

Resolution is a type of deductive reasoning and one of the inference rules. Using resolution, a person can examine a set of statements, and arrive at a conclusion that must logically follow from those statements. Consider, for instance, the following example of resolution:

> The sun is up or is it nighttime.
> The sun is not up.
> Therefore, it is nighttime.

Resolution statements often use Boolean operators, such OR, AND, NOT, and → (which means "implies). Assume, for instance, that X and Y are assigned the following meanings:

> X means Peter ate a hamburger.
> Y means Paul drank a Pepsi.

X AND Y means that Paul ate a hamburger and Paul drank a Pepsi.
X AND NOT Y means that Paul ate a hamburgers and Paul did not drink a Pepsi.

A resolvent is a conclusion that must logically follow from two previous statements. It is part of the resolution principle. Consider, for instance, the following statements are true:

> X OR Y   (Either X is true or Y is true; consequently, if X is true, Y is false.)

> Z OR NOT Y (Either Z is true or Y is true; consequently, if Y is true, Z is true.)

Based on the above statement, the following conclusion must be true:

> X OR Z   (If X is true, Z is true.)

A resolvent can only be gleaned from two pairs of statements written in clause form. A clause has two pairs statements, each of which is connected by the Boolean operator OR.

Unification and inconsistent

Unification occurs when values are assigned to variables. In doing so, the deductive system applies general statements to specific applications. It is necessary before the system can perform resolution.

An inconsistent group of statements is one in which the statements are self-contradictory, meaning they all cannot possibly be true at the same time. By performing resolution on a group of statements, we can determine its consistency. If the final resolution produces an empty clause (for example, the statement that both X and NOT X are true.), the group is inconsistent. Consider the following example:

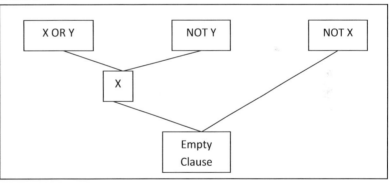

Practice Test

Practice Questions

1. Most software applications include a keyboard shortcut to save the document. What key combination is most often used for saving?
   - a. Ctrl-A
   - b. Alt-S
   - c. Ctrl-S
   - d. Shift-S

2. Which of the following is not a web browser application?
   - a. Internet Explorer
   - b. Squirrel
   - c. Firefox
   - d. Safari

3. In a flowchart, what does the parallelogram symbol represent?
   - a. Start or Stop
   - b. Processing Step
   - c. Input or Output
   - d. Condition or Decision

4. When a programmer finds themselves typing the same set of code more than twice, or just copying and pasting the same code in more than one place, what should be used to improve the efficiency of the code?
   - a. Module or Function
   - b. Compiler
   - c. Assembler
   - d. Clipboard

5. A programming language that uses English words or other types of natural language is what type of language?
   - a. Machine language
   - b. Low-level language
   - c. Assembly language
   - d. High-level language

6. When using a stack input (like cafeteria trays, so that each item added to the stack presses the other items down), what type of input process is described?
   - a. First-in First-out
   - b. First-in Last-out
   - c. First-in Garbage-out
   - d. Garbage-in Garbage-out

7. Which of the following hardware devices could be used to install the Windows Vista operating system on a new personal computer?
   a. CD-ROM
   b. Floppy drive
   c. Scanner
   d. Internal Hard Drive

8. What type of port would be required to connect a digital camera to a personal computer?
   a. Parallel Port
   b. Open Port
   c. Machine Port
   d. USB Port

9. To add a microphone to a personal computer, which of the following ports can be used?
   a. Audio Jack
   b. Serial Port
   c. Firewire
   d. Parallel Port

10. A person maliciously defacing a web page is an example of what?
    a. A virus
    b. Piracy
    c. A worm
    d. Vandalism

11. Downloading a song from a friend or relative without payment or licensing from the song author is an example of what?
    a. A virus
    b. Piracy
    c. A worm
    d. Vandalism

12. A computer program that is written to specifically delete, destroy, or otherwise damage a computer is an example of a(n):
    a. Virus
    b. Act of piracy
    c. Worm
    d. Act of vandalism

13. A computer program that spreads is self-replicating that sends copies of itself to other computers without the need for other programs to attach to is what type of program?
    a. A virus
    b. A pirate program
    c. A worm
    d. A vandal program

14. When a programmer completes writing a computer program, what is required for them to do in order for the program to be protected by copyright?
 a. Send a form to the US copyright office
 b. Nothing
 c. Computer programs cannot be copyrighted
 d. Place the international copyright symbol on the program

15. What key or key combination is most commonly used to obtain help with a computer application?
 a. F1
 b. F2
 c. F3
 d. Ctrl-H

16. Of the following, what type of text alignment is the easiest for people to read?
 a. Justified
 b. Centered
 c. Right-aligned
 d. Top-aligned

17. The standard default layout for a page in a word processor is
 a. Landscape, 8-1/2 x 11
 b. Portrait, 8-1/2 x 11
 c. Landscape, 11 x 8-1/2
 d. Portrait, 11 x 8-1/2

18. Which of the following data types would be best to store real estate house prices that range from $100,000 to $10 million?
 a. Integer
 b. Dollar
 c. Boolean
 d. Double

19. In a standard database, one row represents one
 a. Record
 b. Column
 c. Field
 d. Data type

20. Which of the following applications is best suited to make a presentation that will be shown on an overhead projector?
 a. Microsoft Excel
 b. Microsoft PowerPoint
 c. Microsoft Access
 d. Microsoft Explorer

21. Which of the following applications is best suited to write a memo that will be printed out and passed to many people?
    a. Microsoft Excel
    b. Microsoft PowerPoint
    c. Microsoft Access
    d. Microsoft Word

22. Which of the following applications is best suited to calculate a complex mortgage amortization table, including a graph of the monthly balance?
    a. Microsoft Excel
    b. Microsoft PowerPoint
    c. Microsoft Access
    d. Microsoft Word

23. Which of the following applications is best suited to store information about a classroom that includes the students, their attendance, their grades; and will be able to generate formatted reports showing their attendance and grade progress?
    a. Microsoft Excel
    b. Microsoft PowerPoint
    c. Microsoft Access
    d. Microsoft Word

24. Which of the following is not a commonly-defined learning method that needs to be considered when designing lessons?
    a. Kinesthetic
    b. Auditory
    c. Aural
    d. Evolutionary

25. Which of the following applications or processes would be easiest for beginning computer science students to use to calculate overtime pay?
    a. IBM Assembly Language
    b. Microsoft Visual Basic
    c. Microsoft C++
    d. HTML

26. In the Waterfall model of software development, how many times can the design step be repeated during the entire development for one project?
    a. None
    b. Once
    c. Twice
    d. As many as needed

27. In systems development, which step is the most important?
    a. Maintenance
    b. Programming
    c. Training
    d. Requirements Specifications

28. Which of the following is the best name for a variable that will store the interest rate of a loan?
    a. X
    b. Thisvariablewillstoretheinterestrateofmyloan
    c. dblIntRate
    d. IntRate

29. Adding comments to program code will have which of the following effects?
    a. The code will be more readable
    b. The code will become more difficult to read
    c. The code will become bloated and slower, especially when compiled
    d. It will make the code run faster and more efficiently

30. When writing a program that will receive input from a disk file, which of the following must be done before reading the data?
    a. Sort the data alphabetically
    b. Scan the disk where the files exists for errors
    c. Pause the program
    d. Verify that the data file exists

31. How many bits arc in one byte?
    a. Zero
    b. One
    c. Eight
    d. Sixteen

32. Which of the following is not an operating system?
    a. Windows
    b. O/S 2
    c. IBM
    d. Linux

33. Firmware that is contained in ROM chips which contains the instructions for starting the computer is the _____.
    a. BIOS
    b. Operating System
    c. RAM
    d. Boot Device

34. What does an operating system use to communicate with a hardware device?
    a. Feedback loop
    b. Device driver
    c. String concatenation
    d. Boolean operations

35. What is the core of the operating system that controls files, devices, and managing memory?
    a. Windows
    b. The kernel
    c. RAM.
    d. BIOS

36. Cables used to carry computer network signals that are the same as cables used by cable television are what kind of cables?
    a. Ethernet
    b. RJ-11
    c. Coax
    d. Twisted-pair

37. Which of the following is the standard connector that is used with 8-wire (four twisted pairs) cables?
    a. RJ-45
    b. RJ-11
    c. 568A
    d. Cat-6

38. Which of the following code samples most closely resembles assembly language?
    a. 010010110100101
    b. For intX = 1 to 10
    c. Class myClass { }
    d. MOV AX, #0Ah

39. A program that converts source code into machine language instructions one instruction at a time, then executes them, is a(n)
    a. Interpreter
    b. Compiler
    c. Low-level program
    d. Debugger

40. A program that converts all the source code from a high-level language into machine language at one time is a(n)
    a. Interpreter
    b. Compiler
    c. Low-level program
    d. Debugger

41. When reading a sequential access file, if the program needs to re-read a previous record, what must be done?
    a. Have the program reverse step until it reaches the correct record
    b. Use a function or method that will move back one record
    c. Close the file and start reading again from the start
    d. This process cannot be done with a sequential access file

42. How does a random-access file determine the location of an individual record in the file?
    a. Based on the total number of records stored in the file
    b. Based on the location of the previous record
    c. Based on the method the file was opened
    d. Based on the size of each record

43. In a zero-based one-dimensional array, the third item is stored at what array location (index)?
    a. 0
    b. 1
    c. 2
    e. 3

44. If a particular programming structure has attributes, methods, and events associated with it, what type of structure is it?
    a. An object
    b. A class
    c. A variable
    d. A constant

45. Which of the following is not a common way to concatenate strings?
    a. concatenate function
    b. &
    c. +
    d. !

46. Which of the following is not a logical operator?
    a. BUT
    b. AND
    c. OR
    d. NOT

47. If A is true and B is false, what is the value of A AND B?
    a. It cannot be determined from the information given
    b. True
    c. False
    d. Two

48. If A is true and B is false, what is the value of A OR B?
    a. It cannot be determined from the information given
    b. True
    c. False
    d. Two

49. If a = 2, what is the most likely output of this section of code?
           Print a++; print a;
    a. 2
    b. 3
    c. 23
    d. 32

50. What is the output of the following pseudocode?

```
X = 2
Y = 3
if ( X equals Y)
        X = 3
else
        Y = 2
print Y
```
a. 1
b. 2
c. 3
d. 5

51. What type of sort will this code complete?

```
For X = 1 to n
        For Y = 1 to n-1
                If array(y) > array(y+1)
                        temp = array(y+1)
                        array(y+1) = array(y)
                        array(y) = temp
        Next Y
    Next X
```
a. Selection
b. Bubble
c. Shell
d. Merge

52. What type of sort does this code describe?

```
For X = 1 to n
        minIndex = X
        For Y = x to n
                if array(minIndex) < array(y)
                        minIndex = Y
        Next Y
        temp = array(x)
        array(x) = array(minIndex)
        array(minIndex) = temp
    Next X
```
a. Selection
b. Bubble
c. Shell
d. Merge

53. What type of sort requires splitting the list into two lists before sorting?
a. Selection
b. Bubble
c. Shell
d. Merge

54. What type of sort does this code describe?

```
Gap = n / 2
Do While Gap >= 1
        Do
                done = 1
                For X = 1 to n-Gap
                        If array(X) > array(X + Gap)
                                temp = array(X)
                                array(X) = array(X + Gap)
                                array(X + Gap) = temp
                                done = 0
                Next X
        Until done = 1
        Loop
```

a. Selection
b. Bubble
c. Shell
d. Merge

55. Which of the following does a recursive function always do?
a. Returns a value greater than zero
b. Has a call to itself
c. Returns a value less than zero
d. Calls another function

56. What will be the output of this section of code?

```
function callme(int x)
        if x = 1 then
                return 1
        else
                return callme(x + 1)
print callme(5)
```

a. 5
b. 6
c. 1
d. No output, the code is broken

57. What will be the output of this section of code?

```
Function callme(int x)
        if x = 1 then
                return 1
        else
                return callme(x – 1)
print callme(5)
```

a. 5
b. 6
c. 1
d. No output, the code is broken

58. What will be the output of this section of code?

```
Function callme(int x)
        if x = 1 then
                return 1
        else
                z = x + callme(x-1)
                return z
print callme(5)
```

    a. 15
    b. 5
    c. 1
    d. No output, the code is broken

59. What is the output of this section of code?

```
X = 1
While x < 5 do
        x = x + 1
loop
print x
```

    a. 1
    b. 2
    c. 5
    d. 6

60. What is the output of this section of code?

```
X = 1
While x > 5 do
        x = x + 1
loop
print x
```

    a. 1
    b. 2
    c. 5
    d. 6

61. What is the output of this section of code?

```
X = 1
do
        x = x + 1
until x > 5
print x
```

    a. 1
    b. 2
    c. 5
    d. 6

62. What is the output of this section of code?

```
X = 1
do
        x = x + 1
until x < 5
print x
```

    a. 1
    b. 2
    c. 5
    d. 6

63. Most peripherals will connect to which type of computer port?
    a. USB
    b. Parallel
    c. Serial
    d. MIDI

64. Which of the following is not an example of a magnetic storage device?
    a. Floppy disk
    b. Internal hard drive
    c. Flash drive
    d. Network-attached hard drive

65. What test is applied to computers that is supposed to determine whether a computer is capable of human thought?
    a. Turing Test
    b. Watermelon Test
    c. Intelligence Test
    d. The Super Human Thought Test

66. Which of the following is not studied as part of ergonomics?
    a. Computer monitors
    b. Keyboards
    c. Furniture
    d. Hard drives

67. One kilobyte is exactly how many bytes?
    a. 1
    b. 1,000
    c. 1,024
    d. 10,000

68. Which of the following search patterns will not find the string "Jones"?
    a. *
    b. J*
    c. J*s
    d. J?s

69. The Ctrl-O key combination is most often used for what task?
    a. Opening a new document
    b. Opening a previously saved document
    c. Saving a document
    d. Spell-checking a document

70. The Ctrl-N key combination is most often used for what task?
    a. Opening a new document
    b. Opening a previously saved document
    c. Saving a document
    d. Spell-checking a document

71. The F7 key is most often used for what task?
    a. Opening a new document
    b. Opening a previously saved document
    c. Saving a document
    d. Spell-checking a document

72. A device that was created to replace the mouse on a computer would be most likely protected by what section of law?
    a. Copyright laws
    b. Fair use laws
    c. Patent laws
    d. Trademark laws

73. A software program that was written by an individual would be most likely protected by what section of law?
    a. Copyright laws
    b. Fair use laws
    c. Patent laws
    d. Trademark laws

74. An image that was created by an individual to represent their company or software would be most likely protected by what section of law?
    a. Copyright laws
    b. Fair use laws
    c. Patent laws
    d. Trademark laws

75. Making copies of material for a class on computers would be most likely protected by what section of law?
    a. Copyright laws
    b. Fair use laws
    c. Patent laws
    d. Trademark laws

76. Which of the following font sizes is most readable?
   a. 0
   b. 1
   c. 12
   d. 101

77. For which of the following purposes could the Internet not be used for classroom instruction?
   a. Displaying grades for assignments and the class
   b. Showing video clips of experiments completed in class
   c. Tracking assignment due dates
   d. Watching for students sleeping in class

78. Which of the following would best allow students to continue classroom discussions outside the classroom?
   a. Remote monitoring software
   b. A course web site
   c. A list of additional resources
   d. Online forums

79. In project management, what is the path called that, if changed, will require modification of the end time projection?
   a. Critical path
   b. Path of least resistance
   c. Longest path
   d. Dependence path

80. When teaching a class about web pages with blind students, what hardware item will assist those students the best?
   a. Braille mouse
   b. Screen reader
   c. Large key format keyboard
   d. None of these will help

81. Which of the following office suite applications could not be used to track attendance in classroom?
   a. The Internet
   b. A word processor
   c. A spreadsheet program
   d. A database

82. Which of the following is not a worldwide organization for computers and computing?
   a. IEEE
   b. ACM
   c. CRA
   d. NRO

83. The systems development process that creates a non-working sample project to show how the program will work when completed is which of the following?
    a. JIT
    b. Prototyping
    c. Waterfall
    d. SDLC

84. In a standard flowchart, what does the oval symbol represent?
    a. A process
    b. A decision
    c Start or Stop
    d. Data

85. In a standard flowchart, what does the rectangle with a wavy base represent?
    a. A process
    b. A decision
    c. Start or Stop
    d. A document

86. In a standard flowchart, what does the rectangle symbol represent?
    a. A process
    b. A decision
    c. Start or Stop
    d. Data

87. In a standard flowchart, what does the diamond symbol represent?
    a. A process
    b. A decision
    c. Start or Stop
    d. Data

88. In most programming installations, what is the LIB directory used for?
    a. Libertine files
    b. A temporary directory
    c. Library files
    d. Object files

89. When looking at a web page in a browser, where is the easiest place to locate that web site's URL?
    a. On the status bar
    b. In the source code of the page
    c. In the "Tools" menu
    d. On the address bar

90. Which IEEE standard describes wireless networking?
    a. 802.11
    b. 802.1
    c. 802.802
    d. Wi-Fi

91. Which of the following is a process that assigns IP addresses to client computers?
    a. DHCP
    c. ISP
    c. DNS
    d. FTP

92. Which of the following is a company that provides access to the Internet for individuals and companies?
    a. DHCP
    b. ISP
    c. DNS
    d. FTP

93. Which of the following is a service that converts web addresses from names to IP addresses?
    a. DHCP
    b. ISP
    c. DNS
    d. FTP

94. Which of the following is a method to transfer files over a network?
    a. DHCP
    b. ISP
    c. DNS
    d. FTP

95. Assume A = 1; B = 0; C = true; D = false; E = true; F = 1.
Evaluate: D AND E AND C OR E
    a. True
    b. False
    c. 1
    d. 0

96. Assume A = 1; B = 0; C = true; D = false; E = true; F = 1.
Evaluate: (D AND E) OR NOT (E AND C) AND (C OR (D OR E)) AND D
    a. True
    b. False
    c. 1
    d. 0

97. Assume A = 1; B = 0; C = true; D = false; E = true; F = 1.
Evaluate: 26 * A − 26 * B − 26 * A + 1
    a. True
    b. False
    c. 1
    d. 0

98. Assume A = 1; B = 0; C = true; D = false; E = true; F = 1.
Evaluate: $((A \wedge (3 + A) - B * 99) + 17) * B$
    a. True
    b. False
    c. 1
    d. 0

99. What is the primary language used to build web pages?
    a. Visual Basic
    b. HTML
    c. Windows
    d. Java

100. What "language" should be used to set the formatting, layout, and other design elements of a web page?
    a. CSS
    b. HTML
    c. JavaScript
    d. Visual Basic

Answer Key

Item	Answer	Item	Answer	Item	Answer	Item	Answer
1	C	26	A	51	B	76	C
2	B	27	D	52	A	77	D
3	C	28	C	53	D	78	D
4	A	29	A	54	C	79	A
5	D	30	D	55	B	80	B
6	B	31	C	56	D	81	A
7	A	32	C	57	C	82	D
8	D	33	A	58	A	83	B
9	A	34	B	59	C	84	C
10	D	35	B	60	A	85	D
11	B	36	C	61	D	86	A
12	A	37	A	62	B	87	B
13	C	38	D	63	A	88	C
14	B	39	A	64	C	89	D
15	A	40	B	65	A	90	A
16	A	41	C	66	D	91	A
17	B	42	D	67	C	92	B
18	A	43	C	68	D	93	C
19	A	44	A	69	B	94	D
20	B	45	D	70	A	95	A
21	D	46	A	71	D	96	B
22	A	47	C	72	C	97	C
23	C	48	B	73	A	98	D
24	D	49	C	74	D	99	B
25	B	50	B	75	B	100	A

Answers and Explanations

1. C: While an application designer can write their application to have any key combination complete any task, the standard key combination is Ctrl-S. This standard is followed with all Microsoft products, including Microsoft Word, Excel, and PowerPoint. The shortcut can be found by clicking on the File menu in the application and looking to the right side of the word "Save" in the menu. If the document has not been saved before, a window will pop up to ask the user to name the document to save. Once the document has been saved, pressing Ctrl-S will save the document with the same name, immediately. When working with documents in any type of application, the document should be saved often to guard against loss of data from power losses or other interruptions. Many applications will also automatically save your work, but using the Ctrl-S shortcut will help avoid losing any work.

2. B: Squirrel is not the name of any web browser application currently in use. Internet Explorer is currently the most popular and most used web browser on computers around the world, as it is the web browser that comes installed with most Microsoft Windows operating systems. Internet Explorer accounts for approximately 65-70% of all web browser usage on the Internet. Firefox is used by a large number of more experienced web enthusiasts and makes up as much as 25% of the web browsers used on the Internet today. Firefox is developed and distributed by the Mozilla organization at no charge. Safari is the standard web browser used by the Apple corporation and is the default browser used by Macintosh operating oystems and the iPhone.

3. C: Input or Output. The Start and Stop steps are represented by an oval. Each flow chart may include more than one start and stop point for different processes. All processing steps are rectangles. These are steps that could include an instruction to multiply two numbers or to calculate a sum. The rectangle is the most common flowchart symbol. Input and output steps are represented by the parallelogram symbol. Examples of these steps may be to display a result to the screen or to get input from the keyboard. The condition or decision steps are represented by a diamond and may include binary decisions, where there are just two possible outcomes; or a decision that has many possible outputs such as determining a letter grade from a number.

4. A: Module or Function. When a section of code is repeated in more than one place, it introduces possibilities of different types of errors. If the code contains errors, but is fixed in one place, and not the other, the program will only work when the corrected section is run. By using a module, all the code that completes a certain task is in one place and can be changed in one place. Using a compiler or assembler will just convert the code to assembly language, which will decrease the overall size of the code, but will not replace the identical code segments. The clipboard is used to temporarily store a section of code for copying and pasting, but it will not have any effect on the efficiency of the code itself.

5. D: High-level language. Machine language is the only code that is understood by a computer, but it consists only of numerical codes. Few programmers write code in machine language because it is so difficult to learn and memorize the numerical codes. Assembly language is considered a second generation language and is one step removed from machine language. A low-level language is any programming language that is close to

machine language. Assembly language is an example of a low-level language, as is machine language. High-level languages are any programming languages that are far removed from the machine code and are easier for people to understand. Examples of high-level languages are Microsoft Visual Basic and Logo.

6. B: First-in Last-out. The cafeteria tray example is the most common illustration of how the first-in last-out process works. When you picture placing the first tray on a cafeteria tray stack, the springs will compress and the tray will move down. When you add another tray, the first tray will sink lower and the second tray will remain on top. This will continue as long as you add trays. When a tray is removed from the stack, it will be the tray sitting on top, which is also the last tray that had been added. The very last tray to be removed will be the tray that was added first and has sunk to the bottom of the pile, hence the name "first-in last-out." This process is also known as last-in first out.

7. A: CD-ROM. Microsoft only releases current versions of Windows on two types of media – the CD-ROM and DVD-ROM. The floppy drive is all but obsolete, although that used to be the most common method of software and operating system distribution from the first version of DOS, through Windows 3.11. The scanner is a device that is used to capture an image of documents and to convert hard copies of a document into an image file on the computer. The internal hard drive is where the operating system will be installed to, but it cannot effectively be used as an installation device for Windows without extensive preparation and would only be used in very unusual circumstances such as a series of special non-networked computers that had a specific purpose in mind.

8. D: USB Port. There are a few methods a digital camera can use to connect to a personal computer. All digital cameras can connect to a PC using the common USB port, most with any USB version. Some cameras can also connect using firewire ports. The parallel port is an outdated port that was used to connect printers and other wide devices to the personal computer. Many PCs do not ship with parallel ports anymore. An "Open port" describes any openings for connections on the PC. It does not accurately describe the specific port that is needed for a camera as there are many open ports that cannot be used to connect a camera. A machine port does not exist – there is no such thing.

9: A: Audio jack. Most microphones use the standard analog signals for sound and require an audio jack to connect. Some microphones will also connect to the personal computer with a USB port, but those microphones will only connect with the use of an adapter for USB (or have an adapter built-in to the microphone cord). The serial port is used for devices that will only communicate one signal at a time through a narrow port, and is seldom used in modern computers. Firewire is used for high-speed transfer of audio and visual data and no microphones will plug into that type of port. The parallel port is an outdated port that was used to connect printers and other wide devices to the personal computer.

10. D: Vandalism. Individuals have and give various reasons for defacing web pages, from eco-promotion, to political agendas, to juvenile delinquency. No matter the reason, the act of defacing a web page is legally the same as spray-painting a billboard – simple vandalism. A virus is a software program that is written to intentionally do damage and is typically spread and activated by another user's actions. Few viruses will deface web pages as their primary function. Piracy is the act of stealing software or replicating software without authorized permission. Piracy is a severe crime and is often punished with fines exceeding ten thousand dollars. A worm is a program that is designed to spread from one computer to

another, sometimes carrying a virus payload, sometimes just spreading without doing any additional damage.

11. B: Piracy. When a person records a song, they own the copyright to the song and only the copyright holder can determine where, when, and how additional copies of the song can be made. When a person makes a copy of the song without permission of the copyright holder, even a digital copy, which is the crime of piracy. A virus is a software program that is written to intentionally do damage and is typically spread and activated by another user's actions. A worm is a program that is designed to spread from one computer to another, sometimes carrying a virus payload, sometimes just spreading without doing any additional damage. Vandalism is the intentional and willful destruction of someone else's property, including web pages.

12. A: Virus. Thousands of virus programs are written each day, each one with the primary goal of disrupting data on a computer. These programs can be stand-alone viruses, "Trojan-Horse" viruses that hide inside other programs, or even payload programs that are dropped by fast-spreading worms. Virus programs have been around since the beginning of modern computers. Most viruses can be easily stopped or contained with anti-virus programs that are updated frequently to respond to the growing number of virus programs. An act of piracy involves stealing someone else's property, especially songs or application programs. A worm is a program that is designed to spread from one computer to another, sometimes carrying a virus payload, sometimes just spreading without doing any additional damage.

13. C: A worm. Worms are programs that can spread quickly without user intervention. These types of programs nearly always consume large amounts of bandwidth, sometimes so much that the network or operating system cannot be accessed to stop the spread of the worm. Some worm programs have been designed for good purposes, such as sending out software patches throughout a networked system. A virus is a software program that is written to intentionally do damage and is typically spread and activated by another user's actions. Sometimes a worm program will carry a virus, but the virus program primarily damages files while a worm consumes bandwidth. Piracy is the act of stealing software or replicating software without authorized permission, including operating systems and music files. Vandalism is the intentional and willful destruction of someone else's property, including web pages.

14. B: Nothing. According to the 1886 Berne Convention, copyrights for a created work are automatically put in force at the moment of creation. All countries that subscribe to this convention (including the United States) cannot require any additional action for the creator to own the copyright. As soon as the work is created in a fixed media (in this case, saved to a disk or other device), the author is immediately entitled to all applicable copyright protections. An author can make it easier to defend a copyright if they send a form to register their copyright with the US copyright office, but it is not required. Computer programs, because they are expressions of the creation of a person, most certainly can be copyrighted. The copyright symbol is often used to indicate that a work is copyrighted, but it is not required as the work is copyrighted as soon as it is fixed (saved).

15. A: F1. This is a standard that dates to the 1987 IBM Common User Access documentation. This documentation outlined standards that were to be used by programs to make things more common and more usable across programs. It was quickly adopted by Windows, and all Microsoft programs will allow a user to press F1 to obtain help. When

developing a program, an application programmer can write the program so that any key can have any action, but most users will expect the F1 key to lead them to help in some manner. The F2 does not have a clear, common standard for its use. The F3 key is often used to activate a search function, but still is not as much a standard as the F1 key leading to help. Ctrl-H is not a standard key combination for any use.

16. A: Justified. The text style that is by far the most common in books, magazines, and newspapers is the justified style. This is the style that will ensure that both the left and right sides of text are aligned smoothly. Centered text is useful for highlighting, setting up titles and working with web pages, but is very difficult for users to read in appearances of more than two or three lines. Right-aligned text ensures that the right side of the words are in line, but the left is not. This type of writing is very difficult for the eyes to follow and very hard to read even just two lines. Top-alignment is something that only exists, generally, in spreadsheet applications where the user intends to ensure that text begins at the top of a cell.

17. B: Portrait, 8-1/2 x 11. The most common size paper used in printers today measures 8-1/2 inches wide and 11 inches tall. All standard printers will fit this size of paper, and it is the most common size sold in office supply stores. This is also the same size paper as the standard 3-ring binder and notebook paper. When describing paper, the first number describes the width of the paper, while the second number describes the height. For that reason, both answers that begin with the number 11 are incorrect answers. Portrait and landscape describe the orientation of the paper. A piece of paper in portrait orientation is taller than it is wide. A paper in landscape orientation is wider than it is tall.

18. A: Integer. An integer data type in a 32-bit system will normally store numbers from -2,147,483,648 through 2,147,483,647 (that is, 232 split around the number zero, thus giving -231 through +231). Ten million thus fits easily within these limits. The dollar data type is completely made up and does not actually exist. The boolean data type is designed to store just one bit, either a one or a zero; or a true or a false value. The double data type is usually an eight-bit data type that will store numbers up to ten to the 308th power. This is more memory than we need for this problem, thus being a wasteful programming practice.

19. A: Record. When working with a database, the database will be made up of tables. The tables typically appear as a list of names of the tables. Each table consists of a list of records. Each record is made up of some number of fields that are defined by data types. When working with the data in the database, the fields are displayed in columns, where each field makes up one column. Each field represents one unique piece of information. Combining all the fields in a table makes up one unique item description. On the screen, that one set of fields appears as one row, which is one record.

20. B: Microsoft PowerPoint. Microsoft PowerPoint is an application that is primarily designed to create slide show presentations. These slide shows can be simple, created with a wizard that is part of PowerPoint; or complex, including audio, video, and animation. Microsoft Excel is an application that is used to create spreadsheets. These spreadsheets can be used to do various complex calculations with numbers and charts. Microsoft Access is an application that is used to create and manage databases and work with data. Access can also create reports based on the information stored in the database. Microsoft Word is the application made by Microsoft that is used to write documents. Word can make simple documents like memos, or more complex formatted technical writing.

21. D: Microsoft Word. Microsoft Word is a word processor. Word will allow users to make simple documents like memos, or very complex documents like mailing lists that obtain addresses from a database. Word will also allow complex formatting of documents to create multi-column newsletters, for example. Microsoft Excel is an application that is used to create spreadsheets which can be used to do various complex calculations with numbers and charts. Microsoft PowerPoint is an application that is used to create slide shows and display audio and visual presentations. Microsoft Access is an application that is used to create and manage databases and work with data. Access can also create reports based on the information stored in the database.

22. A: Microsoft Excel. Microsoft Excel is an application that is used to complete calculations. It is a spreadsheet application that can make very complex calculations simple by using functions and formulas. It can also use the data in calculations to show graphs and charts. Microsoft PowerPoint is an application that is used to create slide shows and display audio and visual presentations. Microsoft Access is an application that is used to create and manage databases and work with data. Access can also create reports based on the information stored in the database. Microsoft Word is Microsoft's flagship word processor, used for working with documents. Word can make simple documents like memos, or more complex formatted technical writing.

23. C: Microsoft Access. Microsoft Access is a database management program that can be used to store large amounts of data, but will still work well with small amounts. It can store data, retrieve it, and display the data with complex reports for printing or on-line use. Excel is an application that is used to create spreadsheets. These spreadsheets can be used to perform various complex calculations with numbers and charts. Microsoft PowerPoint is an application that is used to create slide shows and display audio and visual presentations. Microsoft Word is the application made by Microsoft that is used to write documents. Word can create simple documents like memos, or more complex formatted technical writing.

24. D: Evolutionary. There is no such learning type as evolutionary; the answer is made up. Approximately 65% of all learners are visual learners. These students need to see what they are to learn in order to process and learn. This is the method that is used most often, as the majority of people can learn visually. These learners learn best when information is presented visually, such as with an overhead projector or slide show. Approximately 25% of learners are auditory learners. This type of learner needs to hear things to learn them, and functions well with lectures. The remaining 10% of learners are kinesthetic learners. This type of learner does best by doing. They need muscle activity to be able to learn well and do not learn well seated, in a lecture format.

25. B: Microsoft Visual Basic. Visual Basic is a language written by Microsoft that is primarily designed to be a teaching programming language. It is a visual language designed to be very simple to learn and simple to use, but can still be expanded and used to create more complex programs and applications. It is often used as the first language that computer science students learn. IBM Assembly language is a very difficult language to learn and use. It is a low-level language consisting mostly of three-letter mnemonics. Microsoft C++ is a high-level, object-oriented language that requires a good deal of skill to understand and use. It is not a visual language, and therefore all instructions must be typed manually, including creating objects, which is a more advanced computer science skill. HTML is used for web pages and is not actually capable of doing any calculations.

26. A: None. The waterfall development method, first used by manufacturing and applied to software by Winston Royce, is a firm, one-directional process. In this method, each step in the development cycle (requirements, design, implementation, verification, maintenance) must be entirely completed before the next step is started. Once one step is completed, it is not possible to change anything from that step without starting an entirely new process. This method was to be applied to systems like hardware and manufacturing where it was very expensive or impossible to return to a previous step. With most system software, this is an approach that is not used because software, in most cases, can easily be changed and adjusted as the systems development process proceeds through the steps of development.

27. D: Requirements Specifications. In any system development process, the most important part is to determine exactly what must be done. If there is not a clear definition of the requirements, the development process may continue forever, as there is no indication when the work is actually done. In addition, if the requirements specifications are not clear, the other steps will be difficult to define and complete. For instance, the maintenance step is important, but if the requirements are not clear, the process will never reach the maintenance step. Programming is not truly a step in the development process. Instead, it is a part of another step. Training needs to be considered in all systems development processes, but in some cases it may not be needed, depending on the project.

28. C: dblIntRate. Each programming language will have its own syntax and rules that will determine the possible names of variables. When programming, the variable names should be as descriptive as possible while still staying inside the syntax allowed for the specific language. The variable name dblIntRate makes it clear to the programmer that this variable is going to be of type double from the prefix dbl. It is also clear that the variable is going to store the interest rate. Few languages permit spaces in variable names, but most will allow upper- and lower-case letters, which makes the variable clear and more readable. The variable names x and i are commonly used variable names that are short and easy, but far from clear to understand. The variable name thisvariablewillstoretheinterestrateofmyloan is too long and would make the code even more difficult to understand.

29. A: The code will become more readable. When comments are added to the source code in any programming language, it will be easier to understand the code. This can help a new programmer who needs to modify the code, but it can also help the original programmer when debugging their own code. It can also help the original programmer when coming back to a particular project after working on others, when his ideas will be less fresh. The code will not become bloated and slower when compiled, because when source code is compiled into object code, all the comments are removed. Comments will not make the code run faster and more efficiently because comments are only in the source code, and will not affect the operation of the program.

30. D: Verify the file exists. To avoid critical errors that can interrupt program flow, when reading input data from a disk, the first step that needs to be taken is to verify that the file actually exists. If a program attempts to read from a file that does not exist, the error that is generated is nearly always enough to interrupt and end the program. Sorting the data before reading it is often not even possible, and even then can only be done after the file actually exists. Scanning the disk has no effect on reading the data, and thus it will not help the program, especially if the file isn't present. Pausing the program would only slow down the operation of the program, while having no effect on the data read from the file.

31. C: Eight. A bit is the smallest unit of measure in computer science. The bit represents a unit that contains either a one or a zero. No other type or state of information can be stored in a bit, which is the basic building block of all modern computers. In order to store larger pieces of information, such as actual numbers and ASCII text, more than one bit is required. Because bits are binary, a sequence of two bits can store just four possible combinations: 00, 01, 10, or 11. It takes a large number of bits to store any amount of information. A combination of eight bits will provide 256 different possible combinations. This is a common unit of measure and is called a byte.

32. C: IBM. The operating system of a computer is the software that provides the interface between the hardware of the computer and the user. Without an operating system, there is no way for a user to interact with the hardware. The most common operating system in use on PCs today is a version of the Windows operating system, including XP, Vista and Windows 7. O/S 2 is an operating system that was designed by the IBM corporation to compete with Windows. Linux is an open source operating system that was designed after the UNIX operating system, but was developed to be open source and free. IBM is a large corporation that manufactures electronic components and parts.

33. A: BIOS. BIOS stands for "Basic Input/Output System." These are very simple instructions that tell the computer how to start up. When the machine is turned on, the POST test checks all the hardware, electronics and connections, and then the BIOS instructions start. These instructions will check the memory and find instructions for the boot device. They will start the machine and pass off control to the boot sector of the boot device (usually the hard drive with the operating system). The operating system can only start after the BIOS has connected all the devices. RAM is random access memory that can be accessed by the operating system. The boot device is what the BIOS actually locates so the computer can continue to start.

34. B: Device driver. The primary job of the operating system is to provide an interface between the hardware of the computer and the user of the computer. Most pieces of hardware were not manufactured or developed by the manufacturer of the operating system, so the operating system may not understand how the device works. The piece of software called a device driver contains the instructions to the operating system that tell how to communicate with the device. No hardware device will work without a device driver, and most hardware devices come packaged with the device driver for that device. Some hardware will work with generic device drivers. The other answers have nothing to do with operating systems, hardware, or device drivers.

35. B: The kernel. This is the definition of the kernel. All operating systems contain a kernel section that does most of the deep-down work running the system. In proprietary systems, such as Windows operating systems, the kernel is hidden from view and is a well-protected secret. In open source operating systems, such as Linux, the kernel is open and can be modified by users. If the kernel fails at any time, most operating systems will crash immediately, and cannot recover until the entire operating system is restarted. Windows is an example of an operating system that contains a kernel. RAM is random-access memory, and has nothing to do with a kernel. BIOS is the basic input/output system that starts the computer and prepares it for the kernel to use.

36. C: Coax. Coaxial cables, often abbreviated as "coax" are the standard thick cables that cable television uses. These cables have a solid copper wire in the center, a section of thick insulation and a woven metal wire all encased in a plastic coating. This type of cable is sometimes known by its radio grade, RG-58. The cable is used on thin Ethernet applications. Ethernet is a type of networking operation. It is sometimes used as a shorthand to refer to a cable with four twisted pairs that is quite common in many networking applications. RJ-11 is a type of connection including a wall jack and the plug that fits in the wall jack. Twisted pair is any pair of wires that has been twisted together, not just Ethernet.

37. A: RJ-45. The RJ-45 connector is the standard that is used by all 8-wire systems. The jack will be wired in such a way that all eight wires are connected to slides inside the connector, so they will make contact with the RJ-45 jack. The RJ-45 jack may be a wall jack or the standard network cable connection on a personal computer or server. RJ-11 is the connector type that uses only four pairs of wires. This is the standard that is used for telephone cords and telephone jacks. 568A is a standard that is used to wire RJ-45 jacks. 568B is another type of standard that is used to wire RJ-45 jacks. Cat-6 is a type of quality of cable and is not a connector at all.

38. D: MOV AX, #0Ah. Assembly language is a low-level programming language that consists of numerous basic instructions. In this example, the instruction MOV represents move. The instruction requires two parameters to indicate the destination and the value to move. This example instructs the computer to move the numerical value 0A (hex) to the AX register. The string of ones and zeros is just a number, or could also be machine language. The second example is a sample of basic code (for instance, Microsoft Visual Basic). Class myclass {} is an example of an object-based code instruction, such as C++.

39. A: Interpreter. High level languages are designed to be easy for humans to understand so that they can write instructions quickly and easily. The easier the instructions are for humans to understand, the harder they are for the computer to understand. To make software development easier, some programming languages are written so they can be changed into machine language just one line at a time. This process allows the programmer to see the effect of each line of code one at a time. A compiler is similar, but a compiler changes all the source code instructions into machine language at one time before execution. A low-level program is a program that is written in a language similar to machine or assembly language. A debugger is a program that is used to find errors in programs.

40. B: Compiler. High level languages are designed to be easy for humans to understand so that they can write instructions quickly and easily. The easier the instructions are for humans to understand, the harder they are for the computer to understand. Before these high level programs can be executed, they must be changed into a low level program, like machine language. A compiler attempts to read all the source code at one time and then convert that code into object code, which can eventually be executed. Some compilers contain linker programs that can make the object code completely executable. An interpreter is similar, but it converts source code into machine language one line at time. A low-level program is the result of the compiling process. A debugger is a program that is used to find errors in programs.

41. C: Close the file and start reading again from the start. When a file is opened for sequential access, the file can only be read in one direction, one record at a time. All records need to be read sequentially, no matter which record data is desired. Sequential files are

normally used when all the data is needed at one time, such as with a series of transaction processing steps or batch processing. Sequential files can only be read in one direction, from start to finish. There is no way for the program itself to reverse; if a data value is lost, all records must be read again from the start. There are no functions or methods that will allow any sequential access file to back up a record.

42. D: Based on the size of each record. A random access file is a file that is created so that any record in the file can be accessed in any order. On a computer hard drive, the location of each record is based on the size of each record. For example, if the record size is 12KB then record #10 is located 120KB from the start of the file. All records must be exactly the same size in order to use random access files. The total number of records in the file will only determine the file size, not any locations of records. When reading from a random access file, there is no such thing as a previous record, so its location cannot be used to locate another record.

43. C: 2. When using a one-dimensional array, the array may be zero-based or non-zero based. If the array is non-zero based, each element may be sequentially numbered, or there may be another method to determine the array locations. Some arrays may be based on non-sequential numbers. If an array is zero-based, that means that the first item in the array will be stored at array location zero and each item stored after that will be stored in the next sequentially numbered location. Therefore, item one is in location zero, item two is in location one, and the third item will be stored in location two.

44. A: An object. When using an object-oriented language, objects are locations where information can be stored. This information is stored in the attributes of the object. Because the structure is an object, it can both perform actions (methods) and be the recipient of actions (events). A class is the blueprint or description of how the object will act, but the class itself has no attributes, methods, or events itself. A variable is a structure that can normally store just one piece of information and one type (such as integer or string). A constant also can normally store just one piece and type of information, but this particular piece cannot be changed as the program executes.

45. D: !. The exclamation point, in most programming languages where it is used, represents the logical operator NOT. It is seldom associated with strings in any manner. Many programming languages include a method or function that will allow strings to be concatenated. In C, the function is simply strcat(). In Lisp, it is concat(). Many programs and programming languages also allow the ampersand character to be used to combine two strings in numerous instances. A number of languages also allow the plus sign to be used to add two strings. In those cases, the two items to be added either must be strings or must be converted to strings either explicitly or implicitly.

46. A: BUT. Logical operators are operators that result in a single result of true or false. Logical operators will convert the operands to boolean values (true or false) before the logical operation can be carried out. Two binary logical operators are AND and OR. Either of these two operators will accept two boolean values, perform the operation, then return a boolean result. An example of a unary logical operator is the NOT operator. This operator will accept one boolean value as an input and will return the other boolean operator (NOT true is false and NOT false is true).

47. C: False. When using the logical operator AND, the truth table indicates that the answer is true only when both values compared are true. In any other combination of values, the result of an AND operation is false. When using a binary logical operator, there are only four possible combinations of results. The first value can either be true or false, and the second value can only be true or false:

> True and true is true.
> True and false is false.
> False and true is false.
> False and false is false.

48. B: True. When using the logical operator OR, the truth table indicated that the answer is false only when both values compared are false. In any other combination of values, the result of an OR operation is true. When using a binary logical operator, there are only four possible combinations of results. The first value can either be true or false, and the second value can only be true or false:

> True OR true is true.
> True OR false is true.
> False OR true is true.
> False OR false is false.

49. C: 23. The operator in this example, ++, is the postincrement operator. The operator is designed to be shorthand that adds one to the variable. The code x++ can be replaced by x = x + 1. In formal programming languages, the postincrement operator only completes the increment operation after all other operations and functions have been completed on the line. In the problem, the first part requests that the value of the variable x be output (2), and then the postincrement operator performs its operation, increasing the value of x to three. The second instruction then outputs the new value of x, 3. This will result in one line of output containing the numbers two and three.

50. B: 2. The pseudo code first assigns the value of two to the variable location X. It then assigns the value of three to the variable location Y. The next line compares the two values stored in the two variable locations to see if they are equal. The equal comparison operator will return the value false, because the two values are not equal to one another. This causes the program to skip the true portion of the if statement (X = 3) and jump to the false section of the if statement, after the else keyword. Program execution continues from that point, assigning the value of two to the variable location Y. The final line prints the value that is stored in the Y variable location (in this case, two).

51. B: Bubble sort. The bubble sort is a standard sort process that works through an entire array, from the first element to the last, comparing each pair of elements and switching them, if necessary. This will be repeated until the array is sorted. As the sort continues, the correct values "bubble" up to the top of the array. The selection sort finds the smallest element in the array, and then places that item at the end of the array. The process is then completed for the rest of the array, starting with the next element. The shell sort divides the array into chunks and sorts the chunks, then sorts the entire array. As it iterates through the array, the chunks get smaller and smaller until each chunk is one element. The merge sort requires splitting the list into two lists, sorting each of the lists, then merging the two lists back into one sorted list.

52. A: Selection sort. The selection sort finds the smallest element in the array and then places that item at the end of the array. The process is then completed for the rest of the array, starting with the next element. The bubble sort is a standard sort process that works through an entire array, from the first element to the last, comparing each pair of elements and switching them, if necessary. This will be repeated until the array is sorted. The shell sort divides the array into chunks and sorts the chunks, then sorts the entire array. As it iterates through the array, the chunks get smaller and smaller until each chunk is one element. The merge sort requires splitting the list into two lists, sorting each of the lists, and then merging the two lists back into one sorted list.

53. D: Merge sort. The merge sort requires splitting the list into two lists, sorting each of the lists, and then merging the two lists back into one sorted list. The selection sort finds the smallest element in the array, and then places that item at the end of the array. The process is then completed for the rest of the array, starting with the next element. The bubble sort is a standard sort process that works through an entire array, from the first element to the last, comparing each pair of elements and switching them, if necessary. This will be repeated until the array is sorted. The shell sort divides the array into chunks and sorts the chunks, then sorts the entire array. As it iterates through the array, the chunks get smaller and smaller until each chunk is one element.

54. C: Shell sort. The shell sort divides the array into chunks and sorts the chunks, then sorts the entire array. As it iterates through the array, the chunks get smaller and smaller until each chunk is one element. The selection sort finds the smallest element in the array, and then places that item at the end of the array. The process is then completed for the rest of the array, starting with the next element. The bubble sort is a standard sort process that works through an entire array, from the first element to the last, comparing each pair of elements and switching them, if necessary. This will be repeated until the array is sorted. The merge sort requires splitting the list into two lists, sorting each of the lists, then merging the two lists back into one sorted list.

55. B: Has a call to itself. A function or algorithm that is recursive is one that is solved by continuously creating a smaller set of data on which to solve the problem. Each successively smaller set of data makes the problem simpler to solve and will eventually lead to the solution to the problem. For example, determining the nth number in the Fibonacci sequence is difficult. However, determining the n-xth number is simpler. The larger x becomes, the simpler the problem. Using a recursive function that calls itself with a progressively lower number makes the problem easier each time, until eventually the solution to the smaller problem can be obtained, and then that solution can be applied to the larger problem. A recursive function may return any value and may call any other functions.

56. D: No output, the code is broken. In this case, the function sets up an infinite loop with a never-ending recursive function call. The main program at the bottom calls the function callme with a value of 5. That value is passed into the function and placed in the variable x. The if-statement compares this 5 to one and finds them not equal. The else section of the if statement will then be executed, which will recursively call the function with a new value, x+1, which is 6. A new copy of the function is created with an x value of 6, and the process repeats. The value of x will continue to rise. In most programming languages, this will continue until the computer runs of out memory, and then the program will crash.

57. C: One. The main program at the end makes the call to the callme function and sends the value of 5 to the function. The function assigns the 5 to the variable x. The if-statement compares the value of the variable x to 1 and finds that they are not equal. Therefore, the else section of the code executes, which calls the function with the value 4. This repeats until the value of 1 is sent to the function. At that point, the function returns the value of 1. The value of 1 will be returned 5 times (the number of function iterations deep at the point of the solution), until the 1 is returned back to the main program that called the original callme function. This will result in the number 1 being printed to the output device.

58. A: 15. The main program calls the callme function and provides the number 5. The function compares the 5 to 1 and finds them not equal, so it processes the else portion of the if-statement. This assigns to z the value of 5 plus the result of the callme function provided with the number 4 (5-1). The second instance of the callme function takes the 4 and attempts to assign to z the value of 4 plus the result of callme provided with a 3 (4-1). This process will continue until the callme function is called with a value of 1, in which case it will return a 1. The second recursion outward will assign 1+2 to z. The third will assign 3+3, and so on, until the first call returns 5+(4+3+2+1) to the main program, which will print the 15.

59. C: 5. This code snippet starts x with a value of 1. The while-statement compares the 1 to 5 and finds that 1 is less than 5. The loop code executes, which increases x to 2. The code loops and the 2 is compared to 5. Again, 2 is found to be less than 5, and thus the loop code executes again. This time x is increased to 3. This continues until x is increased to 5 inside the loop. At that time, the while statement compares 5 to 5 and finds that 5 is not less than 5, so the loop code ends and the program continues to the line after the loop statement. The next line of code prints the contents of x—in this case, 5.

60. A: 1. This is an example of a poorly prepared loop. The code begins by assigning the value of 1 to the variable x. The next line has the while statement compare that value of x—1—to 5. The computer will find that 1 is not greater than 5, so the code will transfer control to the next statement after the loop statement. That line prints the value of x to the output device—in this case, that value is just 1. The code inside the loop will never be executed in this section of code. It is likely that in this section of code, the greater-than sign was actually intended to be a less-than sign.

61. D: 6. The code starts out by assigning the number 1 to the variable x. The loop is a post-test loop, so the next instruction that is completed is the code inside the loop that increments the value of x by 1. The until line will compare that new value of x to 5 and find that 2 is not greater than 5, so the loop will repeat. The second time through the loop, the value of x will be increased to 3, and so on. When the value of x is 5, the until line will still determine that 5 is not greater than 5, so the code will execute again, increasing x to 6. At that point, the until line will determine that 6 is greater than 5, so the loop will end and the value of x will be printed.

62. B: 2. The code first assigns the value of 1 to the variable x. The loop is a post-test loop, so the code inside the loop is executed next. One is added to the value of x, storing a 2 in the location of x. The until line of code then compares the 2 to 5 and will find that 2 is less than 5, and the loop will end. The next line will output the value of x, in this case 2. When using a post-test loop like this one, the code inside the loop will always be executed at least one time, no matter what the condition is on the until line of code.

63. A: USB. While most modern computers have a number of different ports included, few are used as much as the USB port. The port is flexible and many manufacturers of computer products have adapted their hardware to use the USB port. The parallel port is used for parallel items, previously mostly a printer. Few printers are capable of using the parallel port anymore because of the volume of data sent to the printers. The serial port is a port that looks similar to the parallel port, but is smaller. It used to be used for a number of devices including mice and game controllers, but has almost no practical use today. The MIDI port is used to connect special electronic musical instruments to the computer and is a very specialized port.

64. C: Flash drive. Magnetic storage devices are popular and reliable storage devices that rely on a magnetically-charged surface and a drive that moves tiny magnets around to store data. This data is stored as ones and zeros in the form of the orientation of the magnetic material on the device. The floppy drive has a magnetic disk inside the case, as does the hard drive, whether the hard drive is internal to the computer, external, or attached as a network drive. The flash drive, however, is an electronic device that has no moving parts and no magnetic parts.

65. A: Turning Test. Alan Turing was an English mathematician. He worked with the British during WWII and broke many German codes. He also created the Universal Turing machine, the first digital computer. He developed a test in 1950 called the Turing Test. This was a test to determine whether a computer was capable of human thought by setting up a scenario where a human judge could not determine the difference between human responses and a computer's responses. The Turing test and Alan Turing's research has been used as a basis for a great deal of research in the areas of artificial intelligence.

66. D: Hard drives. Ergonomics is the study of human engineering, or the physical interaction between computers and humans. Specifically, ergonomics is usually concerned with reducing or eliminating stress on the human body and repetitive stress injuries that can be caused by computers and computer layouts. Ergonomics will study everything physical about computer-human interaction, from the layout of the desk and chair to the location and height of the monitor. The location, layout, and shape of the mouse and keyboard are also part of the study of ergonomics. Hard drives have no effect on the person using the computer, so studying the location, layout, or other characteristics of the hard drive is not concerned with the field of ergonomics.

67. C: 1024. In computer measurements, one location that can store either a one or a zero (and no other value) is called a bit. Storing just one piece of information serves little value, so larger storage spaces are needed. Eight bits is called a byte, and contains enough information to store the alphabet (28, or 256, combinations are enough to store the alphabet and a great number of numerical and special characters). As computers handle more and more tasks, more and more storage space is needed, and the amount of storage space increases in powers of two. Two to the eighth power is 256. Two to the ninth is 512. Two to the tenth is 1024. The unit of measure associated with the 1024 is kilo, so in computing the notation K actually represents 1,024 units of measure, as opposed to the 1,000 units of measure in standard mathematics.

68. D: J?s. When using a search pattern, standard wild cards are used to make the search more efficient and to search for unknown data. The two most common wild card characters

are the asterisk and the question mark. The asterisk is a replacement for any number of characters, including zero character. It will locate anything in that position in the search string. The question mark represents exactly one character and will only locate a single character in that location. In the question, answers A-C all use the asterisk wild card, which will match any combination of character. In the last answer, J?s, the search pattern will only find 3-letter combinations that begin with the letter J and end with the letter s.

69. B: Opening a previously saved document. When a programmer writes a program, they are free to make any key combination complete any task. However, to make programs more usable, common key presses should complete common, standard actions. Throughout the development of programs, the Ctrl-O combination is most often used to open a document that has already been saved to the disk. All Microsoft and Sun applications use this standard, as do most other common applications. This combination does not open a new document, as that task is most often reserved for Ctrl-N. Saving a document is usually the Ctrl-S key combination, while F7 is used for spell checking.

70. A: Opening a new document. When a programmer writes a program, they are free to make any key combination complete any task. However, to make programs more usable, common key presses should complete common, standard actions. Throughout the development of programs, the Ctrl-N combination is most often used to create a new document. All Microsoft and Sun applications use this standard, as do most other common applications. This combination does not open an existing document, as the Ctrl-O key combination is reserved for that task. Saving a document is usually the Ctrl-S key combination, while F7 is used for spell checking.

71. D: Spell checking a document. When a programmer writes a program, they are free to make any key combination complete any task. However, to make programs more usable, common key presses should complete common, standard actions. Throughout the development of programs, the F7 key is most often used to begin spell checking a document. All Microsoft and Sun applications use this standard, as do most other common applications. This combination does not open an existing document, as the Ctrl-O key combination is reserved for that task. Saving a document is most often the Ctrl-S key combination.

72. C: Patent laws. A patent is used when a physical device has been invented by a person. These patents are registered with the US Patent office and the invention cannot be re-created by anyone else using the same process for 20 years. Copyright laws protect "original works of authorship" that include creations of writing, drama, music and other such activities, like programming. The creation of the copyright is automatic and exists as soon as the work has been created (the work must be created, as you cannot copyright an idea). Fair use laws exist to allow the use of copyrighted material without permission, but limits that use to academic or review settings and situations. A trademark is a "word, phrase, symbol or design" that represents a certain person, thing, or company.

73. A: Copyright laws. Copyright laws protect "original works of authorship" that include creations of writing, drama, music and other such activities, like programming. The creation of the copyright is automatic and exists as soon as the work has been created (the work must be created, as you cannot copyright an idea). Fair use laws exist to allow the use of copyrighted material without permission, but limits that use to academic or review settings and situations. A patent is used when a physical device has been invented by a person. These patents are registered with the US Patent office and the invention cannot be re-

created by anyone else using the same process for 20 years. A trademark is a "word, phrase, symbol or design" that represents a certain person, thing, or company.

74. D: Trademark laws. A trademark is a "word, phrase, symbol or design" that represents a certain person, thing, or company. Copyright laws protect "original works of authorship" that include creations of writing, drama, music, and other such activities, like programming. The creation of the copyright is automatic and exists as soon as the work has been created (the work must be created, as you cannot copyright an idea). Fair use laws exist to allow the use of copyrighted material without permission, but limits that use to academic or review settings and situations. A patent is used when a physical device has been invented by a person. These patents are registered with the US Patent office and the invention cannot be re-created by anyone else using the same process for 20 years.

75. B: Fair use laws. Fair use laws exist to allow the use of copyrighted material without permission, but limits that use to academic or review settings and situations. Copyright laws protect "original works of authorship" that include creations of writing, drama, music, and other such activities, like programming. The creation of the copyright is automatic and exists as soon as the work has been created (the work must be created, as you cannot copyright an idea). A patent is used when a physical device has been invented by a person. These patents are registered with the US Patent office and the invention cannot be re-created by anyone else using the same process for 20 years. A trademark is a "word, phrase, symbol or design" that represents a certain person, thing, or company.

76. C: 12. Font sizes in computers and typography are typically measured in points. Each point is a unit of measure. The standard in computers is the Desktop Publishing point of 1/72 of one inch, or 0.0139 inches. A font of size 12 is approximately 1/6 of an inch or 0.17 inches for the average size character, or about 50 lines per page. A font size of 0 would not exist. A font size of 1 would have the characters on the page about 0.0139 inches tall – or 611 lines on one page. A font size of 101 would be characters that are 1.4 inches tall each, allowing only six lines on a page. The easiest fonts for people to read are size 10, 12, or 14.

77. D: Watching for students sleeping in class. The Internet has the ability to connect computers around the globe, including those in local classrooms. Most students have access to the Internet, either at home, at school, or at a library. The Internet can be used in many ways to expand the classroom beyond the four walls of the school room. A web site could be maintained for each class that would allow students (or parents) to log in and see the progress of the student on any and all assignments. Videos could be taken in class and posted to the web to show students how different experiments turn out, or to offer tutorials, in general.

78. D: Online forums. There are numerous software manufacturers who will enable the set up of online forums. Many of these are free and allow the administrator to manage the forums and moderate the forum discussions. Threads can be set up to allow discussions based on individual days or specific topics. This can allow a great deal of classroom discussion, especially helpful for those students who may not speak up in class. Remote monitoring software will have no effect on the classroom discussion. A course web site might provide information to the students about the class, but will seldom help with discussions. Again, additional resources are helpful, but may or may not stimulate discussion.

79. A: Critical path. When developing a project and the project path in project management, each task is listed along with the prerequisites for the task. When all the tasks are assembled in one location or screen, each task will appear on the list after all its prerequisite tasks. In most cases, this setup will show that some tasks can be started at different times and completing certain tasks will have no effect on the final time line. However, a path can be traced through the project management organization sheet that will show the longest period of time that is required, based on the list of prerequisites. That path is known as the critical path because changes to any of those task times will result in a change in the final delivery date of the project.

80. B: Screen reader. There are a large number of hardware devices that have been developed for the personal computer that will help disabled students learn. The screen reader is a piece of hardware or software that will attempt to read the text and words on the screen to the user. This will work with Internet web pages, as the device will simply read the page to the user. It will also play audio clues indicating hot links to other pages, enabling the user to interact with the web page much as any other user might. There is no such thing as a braille mouse. A large format keyboard could help those with limited vision, or those with fading vision, but it would do little to help someone who is entirely blind.

81. A: The Internet. While the Internet can be used in a variety of ways and can be used to expand the classroom outside the four walls of the school building, it cannot, by itself, do much to track anything. In addition, the Internet is not actually part of any office suite program. A word processor could be used with tables and calculations in those tables to track and print grades and attendance. A spreadsheet might work even better, as a spreadsheet program is designed to do calculations and can keep detailed records of anything requiring mathematical calculations. A database is the most complex of these, but may be able to do the most work for the user, including printing detailed, accurate reports.

82. D: NRO. The NRO is National Reconnaissance Office. This US government organization exists to build and operate US Reconnaissance satellites for the CIA and Department of Defense. The IEEE is the Institute of Electrical and Electronics Engineers, retaining its IEEE name despite their expanding into more areas of knowledge, specifically including computers and computing. The ACM is the Association for Computing Machinery, an organization that develops and expands knowledge in computers. Members seeks to advance computing as a science and a profession. The CRA is Computing Research Association, an organization that seeks to strengthen research and advanced education in computers and related fields.

83. B: Prototyping. When a prototype is created, it is created quickly and with various plugs and stubs that will allow the program to appear to work but it will not actually be completed or working. This is often done to provide the customer with a model of what the project might look like. This will help ensure the goals of the project are being met before a large time period is spent in thorough development. JIT is just-in-time, which is normally associated with the delivery of inventory in inventory management processes. Waterfall is a software development method where each step is completed before the next step is started. SDLC refers to the overall process of the system development lifecycle and does not apply to just one specific type of development.

84. C: Start or stop. The flowchart is used to create a visual representation of a process and the structures associated with the process. In many cases in computing, drawing a flowchart is completed before programming in order to make the steps for programming clear to the

computer programmer. A process in the flow chart is represented by the rectangle symbol. This can represent any simple process, including adding, subtracting, and other calculations. A decision is represented by the diamond symbol. This can be used to represent an if-statement or other set of options. The start or stop process is represented by an oval symbol. In most flow charts, there will be one starting, or entry point, and one exit, or ending point. Data, usually input data for the program, will appear in a parallelogram.

85. D: A document. The flowchart is used to create a visual representation of a process and the structures associated with the process. In many cases in computing, drawing a flowchart is completed before programming in order to make the steps for programming clear to the computer programmer. Any document in the flow chart is represented by the rectangle with a wavy base. This can represent any type of document, but is usually an external document or source of information. A decision is represented by the diamond symbol. This can be used to represent an if-statement or other set of options. The start or stop process is represented by an oval symbol. In most flow charts, there will be one starting, or entry point, and one exit, or ending point. Data, usually input data for the program, will appear in a parallelogram.

86. A: Process. The flowchart is used to create a visual representation of a process and the structures associated with the process. In many cases in computing, drawing a flowchart is completed before programming in order to make the steps for programming clear to the computer programmer. A process in the flow chart is represented by the rectangle symbol. This can represent any simple process, including adding, subtracting, and other calculations. A decision is represented by the diamond symbol. This can be used to represent an if-statement or other set of options. The start or stop process is represented by an oval symbol. In most flow charts, there will be one starting, or entry point, and one exit, or ending point. Data, usually input data for the program, will appear in a parallelogram.

87. B: Decision. The flowchart is used to create a visual representation of a process and the structures associated with the process. In many cases in computing, drawing a flowchart is completed before programming in order to make the steps for programming clear to the computer programmer. A process in the flow chart is represented by the rectangle symbol. This can represent any simple process, including adding, subtracting, and other calculations. A decision is represented by the diamond symbol. This can be used to represent an if-statement or other set of options. The start or stop process is represented by an oval symbol. In most flow charts, there will be one starting, or entry point, and one exit, or ending point. Data, usually input data for the program, will appear in a parallelogram.

88. C: Library files. Library files are files that are used in more than one program, or even just used more than once in one program. These files are usually modules or sections of code that will be easily accessible to the program. They will be used more than once and will be fully tested and debugged before use. "Libertine files" is a nonsense term. The temporary directory is most often named "temp" or "tmp." Object files are temporary files that are created by compiler as an intermediate step in the compilation process. They are usually stored in a directory called "obj" or "object."

89. D: On the address bar. The URL is the uniform resource locator for the web page. This is the common name for a web page, designed for people to understand. Behind the scenes, the URL has to be changed into an IP address in order to locate the actual web page and return it from the server. The URL is also known as a URI, or universal resource indicator.

The status bar is at the bottom of the screen and is used to display the status or messages about the web pages. The source code of the web page may or may not display the URL of the web page; it depends on the web page. The tools menu on different browsers will have various different options, but all of those options are unlikely to show the URL of the web page.

90. A: 802.11. The IEEE 802.11 standard describes all sorts of network, with the 802.11a, 802.11b, 802.11g, and 802.11n are all different standards for increasing faster wireless network connections. These are used by wireless cards in PCs, laptops, and in various wireless routers. The manufacturers of these devices must adhere to these standards if they want their devices to be able to interface with other devices. The 802.1 standard describes wired ports that access network devices. The 802.802 standard does not actually exist. Wi-Fi is slang to describe wireless devices or networks, and has nothing to do with the IEEE standards.

91. A: DHCP. DHCP stands for dynamic host configuration protocol. This is a process that normally runs on the server of a network and contains a list of valid IP addresses for the network. When a client computer starts up, the DHCP process responds and provides an IP to the requesting computer. ISP stands for Internet Service Provider. These are companies that have access to the Internet backbone and provide a connection to that backbone, usually for a fee. DNS stands for Domain Name System (or Domain Name Services). This is the process that converts a web address (like www.domain.com) to an IP address (like 192.168.2.173). FTP stands for File Transfer Protocol, a method that can be used to move files over any type of network.

92. B: ISP. ISP stands for Internet Service Provider. These are companies that have access to the Internet backbone and provide a connection to that backbone, usually for a fee. DHCP stands for dynamic host configuration protocol. This is a process that normally runs on the server of a network and contains a list of valid IP addresses for the network. When a client computer starts up, the DHCP process responds and provides an IP to the requesting computer. DNS stands for Domain Name System (or Domain Name Services). This is the process that converts a web address (like www.domain.com) to an IP address (like 192.168.2.173). FTP stands for File Transfer Protocol, a method that can be used to move files over any type of network.

93. C: DNS. DNS stands for Domain Name System (or Domain Name Services). This is the process that converts a web address (like www.domain.com) to an IP address (like 192.168.2.173). DHCP stands for dynamic host configuration protocol. This is a process that normally runs on the server of a network and contains a list of valid IP addresses for the network. When a client computer starts up, the DHCP process responds and provides an IP to the requesting computer. ISP stands for Internet Service Provider. These are companies that have access to the Internet backbone and provide a connection to that backbone, usually for a fee. FTP stands for File Transfer Protocol, a method that can be used to move files over any type of network.

94. D: FTP. FTP stands for File Transfer Protocol, a method that can be used to move files over any type of network. DHCP stands for dynamic host configuration protocol. This is a process that normally runs on the server of a network and contains a list of valid IP addresses for the network. When a client computer starts up, the DHCP process responds and provides an IP to the requesting computer. ISP stands for Internet Service Provider.

These are companies that have access to the Internet backbone and provide a connection to that backbone, usually for a fee. DNS stands for Domain Name System (or Domain Name Services). This is the process that converts a web address (like www.domain.com) to an IP address (like 192.168.2.173).

95. A: True. This exercise tests the knowledge of logical operators. When two items are combined with the AND operator, the result is true only when both operands are true. If either of the two operands is false, the result is false. When using the OR operator, the result is false only when both operands are false. In any other condition, the result is true. The statement that was provided for evaluation would be evaluated by the computer from left to right, one pair of operands at a time. However, examining the end of the problem will quickly give the result of true because the last operation is blank OR true. It does not matter what the rest of the statement evaluates to, as the end result will be true because of that OR operator.

96. B: False. This exercise tests the knowledge of logical operators. When two items are combined with the AND operator, the result is true only when both operands are true. If either of the two operands is false, the result is false. When using the OR operator, the result is false only when both operands are false. In any other condition, the result is true. The statement that was provided for evaluation would be evaluated by the computer from left to right, one pair of operands at a time. However, examining the end of the problem will quickly give the result of false because the end of the statement is blank AND false. No matter what the rest of the statement evaluates to, the end result will be false because of that AND operation.

97. C: 1. The exercise tests the knowledge of order of operations. When more than one mathematical operator appears in a statement, the order of operations will determine in what order the different operators will be applied. In the case of multiplication, subtraction, and addition, the multiplication will take precedence over the addition and the subtraction, and then the addition and subtraction will be completed from left to right. In the equation provided, all the multiplication will be completed first, resulting in the equation: 26 – 0 – 26 + 1. The last step will be to evaluate the addition and subtraction from left to right, resulting in 1.

98. D: 0. The exercise tests the knowledge of order of operations. When more than one mathematical operator appears in a statement, the order of operations will determine in what order the different operators will be applied. In the case of multiplication, subtraction, and addition, the multiplication will take precedence over the addition and the subtraction, and then the addition and subtraction will be completed from left to right. Exponents take precedence over multiplication and will be completed before multiplication. In addition, parentheses will take precedence over all other operations and will always be evaluated first. In the provided equation, knowledge of the order of operations can make solving the equation quick and easy. Noting that the end of the equation ends with times zero, the end result will be zero.

99. B: HTML. HTML stands for hypertext markup language. This is the basic language that has been used for writing web pages since the popular advent of the Internet. It is a very simple language that is completely text-based in order to make transfer times as fast as possible. All web pages must contain simple, text HTML instructions for a web browser to understand the page. More advanced options and technologies have been added to make the Internet do more, but HTML is still the basic technology which makes web pages. Visual

- 165 -

Basic is a programming language that was developed by Microsoft as a language to teach beginning programmers how to program computers. Windows is an operating system that helps control a computer and has nothing to do with the Internet. Java is a programming language that is used in client-server computing and can be included with web pages, but only through the use of HTML tags.

100. A: CSS. CSS stands for cascading style sheets. These style sheets can be used on all modern browsers. The purpose of the style sheets are to allow the web page designer to use the HTML tags of the Internet to describe the content of the tags (such as an address or a paragraph), and then describe the color, layout, or other descriptive features of the items using the style sheet. Most browsers will allow HTML to describe the layout of the page, but this is an outdated process and shows poor form. JavaScript is an object-oriented language that can be used on web pages to complete calculations and process information, but cannot describe the layout of the page without the assistance of HTML or CSS. Visual Basic is a programming language that was developed by Microsoft as a language to teach beginning programmers how to program computers.

Secret Key #1 - Time is Your Greatest Enemy

Pace Yourself

Wear a watch. At the beginning of the test, check the time (or start a chronometer on your watch to count the minutes), and check the time after every few questions to make sure you are "on schedule."

If you are forced to speed up, do it efficiently. Usually one or more answer choices can be eliminated without too much difficulty. Above all, don't panic. Don't speed up and just begin guessing at random choices. By pacing yourself, and continually monitoring your progress against your watch, you will always know exactly how far ahead or behind you are with your available time. If you find that you are one minute behind on the test, don't skip one question without spending any time on it, just to catch back up. Take 15 fewer seconds on the next four questions, and after four questions you'll have caught back up. Once you catch back up, you can continue working each problem at your normal pace.

Furthermore, don't dwell on the problems that you were rushed on. If a problem was taking up too much time and you made a hurried guess, it must be difficult. The difficult questions are the ones you are most likely to miss anyway, so it isn't a big loss. It is better to end with more time than you need than to run out of time.

Lastly, sometimes it is beneficial to slow down if you are constantly getting ahead of time. You are always more likely to catch a careless mistake by working more slowly than quickly, and among very high-scoring test takers (those who are likely to have lots of time left over), careless errors affect the score more than mastery of material.

Secret Key #2 - Guessing is not Guesswork

You probably know that guessing is a good idea - unlike other standardized tests, there is no penalty for getting a wrong answer. Even if you have no idea about a question, you still have a 20-25% chance of getting it right.

Most test takers do not understand the impact that proper guessing can have on their score. Unless you score extremely high, guessing will significantly contribute to your final score.

Monkeys Take the Test

What most test takers don't realize is that to insure that 20-25% chance, you have to guess randomly. If you put 20 monkeys in a room to take this test, assuming they answered once per question and behaved themselves, on average they would get 20-25% of the questions correct. Put 20 test takers in the room, and the average will be much lower among guessed questions. Why?

1. The test writers intentionally write deceptive answer choices that "look" right. A test taker has no idea about a question, so picks the "best looking" answer, which is often wrong. The monkey has no idea what looks good and what doesn't, so will consistently be lucky about 20-25% of the time.

2. Test takers will eliminate answer choices from the guessing pool based on a hunch or intuition. Simple but correct answers often get excluded, leaving a 0% chance of being correct. The monkey has no clue, and often gets lucky with the best choice.

This is why the process of elimination endorsed by most test courses is flawed and detrimental to your performance- test takers don't guess, they make an ignorant stab in the dark that is usually worse than random.

$5 Challenge

Let me introduce one of the most valuable ideas of this course- the $5 challenge:

You only mark your "best guess" if you are willing to bet $5 on it.
You only eliminate choices from guessing if you are willing to bet $5 on it.

Why $5? Five dollars is an amount of money that is small yet not insignificant, and can really add up fast (20 questions could cost you $100). Likewise, each answer choice on one question of the test will have a small impact on your overall score, but it can really add up to a lot of points in the end.

The process of elimination IS valuable. The following shows your chance of guessing it right:

If you eliminate wrong answer choices until only this many remain:	Chance of getting it correct:
1	100%
2	50%
3	33%

However, if you accidentally eliminate the right answer or go on a hunch for an incorrect answer, your chances drop dramatically: to 0%. By guessing among all the answer choices, you are GUARANTEED to have a shot at the right answer.

That's why the $5 test is so valuable- if you give up the advantage and safety of a pure guess, it had better be worth the risk.

What we still haven't covered is how to be sure that whatever guess you make is truly random. Here's the easiest way:

Always pick the first answer choice among those remaining.

Such a technique means that you have decided, **before you see a single test question**, exactly how you are going to guess- and since the order of choices tells you nothing about which one is correct, this guessing technique is perfectly random.

This section is not meant to scare you away from making educated guesses or eliminating choices- you just need to define when a choice is worth eliminating. The $5 test, along with a pre-defined random guessing strategy, is the best way to make sure you reap all of the benefits of guessing.

Secret Key #3 - Practice Smarter, Not Harder

Many test takers delay the test preparation process because they dread the awful amounts of practice time they think necessary to succeed on the test. We have refined an effective method that will take you only a fraction of the time.

There are a number of "obstacles" in your way to succeed. Among these are answering questions, finishing in time, and mastering test-taking strategies. All must be executed on the day of the test at peak performance, or your score will suffer. The test is a mental marathon that has a large impact on your future.

Just like a marathon runner, it is important to work your way up to the full challenge. So first you just worry about questions, and then time, and finally strategy:

Success Strategy

1. Find a good source for practice tests.
2. If you are willing to make a larger time investment, consider using more than one study guide- often the different approaches of multiple authors will help you "get" difficult concepts.
3. Take a practice test with no time constraints, with all study helps "open book." Take your time with questions and focus on applying strategies.
4. Take a practice test with time constraints, with all guides "open book."
5. Take a final practice test with no open material and time limits

If you have time to take more practice tests, just repeat step 5. By gradually exposing yourself to the full rigors of the test environment, you will condition your mind to the stress of test day and maximize your success.

Secret Key #4 - Prepare, Don't Procrastinate

Let me state an obvious fact: if you take the test three times, you will get three different scores. This is due to the way you feel on test day, the level of preparedness you have, and, despite the test writers' claims to the contrary, some tests WILL be easier for you than others.

Since your future depends so much on your score, you should maximize your chances of success. In order to maximize the likelihood of success, you've got to prepare in advance. This means taking practice tests and spending time learning the information and test taking strategies you will need to succeed.

Never take the test as a "practice" test, expecting that you can just take it again if you need to. Feel free to take sample tests on your own, but when you go to take the official test, be prepared, be focused, and do your best the first time!

Secret Key #5 - Test Yourself

Everyone knows that time is money. There is no need to spend too much of your time or too little of your time preparing for the test. You should only spend as much of your precious time preparing as is necessary for you to get the score you need.

Once you have taken a practice test under real conditions of time constraints, then you will know if you are ready for the test or not.

If you have scored extremely high the first time that you take the practice test, then there is not much point in spending countless hours studying. You are already there.

Benchmark your abilities by retaking practice tests and seeing how much you have improved. Once you score high enough to guarantee success, then you are ready.

If you have scored well below where you need, then knuckle down and begin studying in earnest. Check your improvement regularly through the use of practice tests under real conditions. Above all, don't worry, panic, or give up. The key is perseverance!

Then, when you go to take the test, remain confident and remember how well you did on the practice tests. If you can score high enough on a practice test, then you can do the same on the real thing.

General Strategies

The most important thing you can do is to ignore your fears and jump into the test immediately- do not be overwhelmed by any strange-sounding terms. You have to jump into the test like jumping into a pool- all at once is the easiest way.

Make Predictions

As you read and understand the question, try to guess what the answer will be. Remember that several of the answer choices are wrong, and once you begin reading them, your mind will immediately become cluttered with answer choices designed to throw you off. Your mind is typically the most focused immediately after you have read the question and digested its contents. If you can, try to predict what the correct answer will be.

You may be surprised at what you can predict.

Quickly scan the choices and see if your prediction is in the listed answer choices. If it is, then you can be quite confident that you have the right answer. It still won't hurt to check the other answer choices, but most of the time, you've got it!

Answer the Question

It may seem obvious to only pick answer choices that answer the question, but the test writers can create some excellent answer choices that are wrong. Don't pick an answer just because it sounds right, or you believe it to be true. It MUST answer the question. Once you've made your selection, always go back and check it against the question and make sure that you didn't misread the question, and the answer choice does answer the question posed.

Benchmark

After you read the first answer choice, decide if you think it sounds correct or not. If it doesn't, move on to the next answer choice. If it does, mentally mark that answer choice. This doesn't mean that you've definitely selected it as your answer choice, it just means that it's the best you've seen thus far. Go ahead and read the next choice. If the next choice is worse than the one you've already selected, keep going to the next answer choice. If the next choice is better than the choice you've already selected, mentally mark the new answer choice as your best guess.

The first answer choice that you select becomes your standard. Every other answer choice must be benchmarked against that standard. That choice is correct until proven otherwise by another answer choice beating it out. Once you've decided that no other answer choice seems as good, do one final check to ensure that your answer choice answers the question posed.

Valid Information

Don't discount any of the information provided in the question. Every piece of information may be necessary to determine the correct answer. None of the information in the question is there to throw you off (while the answer choices will certainly have information to throw you off). If two seemingly unrelated topics are discussed, don't ignore either. You can be confident there is a relationship, or it wouldn't be included in the question, and you are probably going to have to determine what is that relationship to find the answer.

Avoid "Fact Traps"

Don't get distracted by a choice that is factually true. Your search is for the answer that answers the question. Stay focused and don't fall for an answer that is true but incorrect. Always go back to the question and make sure you're choosing an answer that actually answers the question and is not just a true statement. An answer can be factually correct, but it MUST answer the question asked. Additionally, two answers can both be seemingly correct, so be sure to read all of the answer choices, and make sure that you get the one that BEST answers the question.

Milk the Question

Some of the questions may throw you completely off. They might deal with a subject you have not been exposed to, or one that you haven't reviewed in years. While your lack of knowledge about the subject will be a hindrance, the question itself can give you many clues that will help you find the correct answer. Read the question carefully and look for clues. Watch particularly for adjectives and nouns describing difficult terms or words

that you don't recognize. Regardless of if you completely understand a word or not, replacing it with a synonym either provided or one you more familiar with may help you to understand what the questions are asking. Rather than wracking your mind about specific detailed information concerning a difficult term or word, try to use mental substitutes that are easier to understand.

The Trap of Familiarity

Don't just choose a word because you recognize it. On difficult questions, you may not recognize a number of words in the answer choices. The test writers don't put "make-believe" words on the test; so don't think that just because you only recognize all the words in one answer choice means that answer choice must be correct. If you only recognize words in one answer choice, then focus on that one. Is it correct? Try your best to determine if it is correct. If it is, that is great, but if it doesn't, eliminate it. Each word and answer choice you eliminate increases your chances of getting the question correct, even if you then have to guess among the unfamiliar choices.

Eliminate Answers

Eliminate choices as soon as you realize they are wrong. But be careful! Make sure you consider all of the possible answer choices. Just because one appears right, doesn't mean that the next one won't be even better! The test writers will usually put more than one good answer choice for every question, so read all of them. Don't worry if you are stuck between two that seem right. By getting down to just two remaining possible choices, your odds are now 50/50. Rather than wasting too much time, play the odds. You are guessing, but guessing wisely, because you've been able to knock out some of the answer choices that you know are wrong. If you are eliminating choices and realize that the last answer

- 171 -

choice you are left with is also obviously wrong, don't panic. Start over and consider each choice again. There may easily be something that you missed the first time and will realize on the second pass.

Tough Questions

If you are stumped on a problem or it appears too hard or too difficult, don't waste time. Move on! Remember though, if you can quickly check for obviously incorrect answer choices, your chances of guessing correctly are greatly improved. Before you completely give up, at least try to knock out a couple of possible answers. Eliminate what you can and then guess at the remaining answer choices before moving on.

Brainstorm

If you get stuck on a difficult question, spend a few seconds quickly brainstorming. Run through the complete list of possible answer choices. Look at each choice and ask yourself, "Could this answer the question satisfactorily?" Go through each answer choice and consider it independently of the other. By systematically going through all possibilities, you may find something that you would otherwise overlook. Remember that when you get stuck, it's important to try to keep moving.

Read Carefully

Understand the problem. Read the question and answer choices carefully. Don't miss the question because you misread the terms. You have plenty of time to read each question thoroughly and make sure you understand what is being asked. Yet a happy medium must be attained, so don't waste too much time. You must read carefully, but efficiently.

Face Value

When in doubt, use common sense. Always accept the situation in the problem at face value. Don't read too much into it. These problems will not require you to make huge leaps of logic. The test writers aren't trying to throw you off with a cheap trick. If you have to go beyond creativity and make a leap of logic in order to have an answer choice answer the question, then you should look at the other answer choices. Don't overcomplicate the problem by creating theoretical relationships or explanations that will warp time or space. These are normal problems rooted in reality. It's just that the applicable relationship or explanation may not be readily apparent and you have to figure things out. Use your common sense to interpret anything that isn't clear.

Prefixes

If you're having trouble with a word in the question or answer choices, try dissecting it. Take advantage of every clue that the word might include. Prefixes and suffixes can be a huge help. Usually they allow you to determine a basic meaning. Pre- means before, post- means after, pro - is positive, de- is negative. From these prefixes and suffixes, you can get an idea of the general meaning of the word and try to put it into context. Beware though of any traps. Just because con is the opposite of pro, doesn't necessarily mean congress is the opposite of progress!

Hedge Phrases

Watch out for critical "hedge" phrases, such as likely, may, can, will often, sometimes, often, almost, mostly, usually, generally, rarely, sometimes. Question writers insert these hedge phrases to cover every possibility. Often an answer choice will be wrong simply because it leaves no room for exception. Avoid answer choices that have definitive words like "exactly," and "always".

Switchback Words

Stay alert for "switchbacks". These are the words and phrases frequently used to alert you to shifts in thought. The most common switchback word is "but". Others include although, however, nevertheless, on the other hand, even though, while, in spite of, despite, regardless of.

New Information

Correct answer choices will rarely have completely new information included. Answer choices typically are straightforward reflections of the material asked about and will directly relate to the question. If a new piece of information is included in an answer choice that doesn't even seem to relate to the topic being asked about, then that answer choice is likely incorrect. All of the information needed to answer the question is usually provided for you, and so you should not have to make guesses that are unsupported or choose answer choices that require unknown information that cannot be reasoned on its own.

Time Management

On technical questions, don't get lost on the technical terms. Don't spend too much time on any one question. If you don't know what a term means, then since you don't have a dictionary, odds are you aren't going to get much further. You should immediately recognize terms as whether or not you know them. If you don't, work with the other clues that you have, the other answer choices and terms provided, but don't waste too much time trying to figure out a difficult term.

Contextual Clues

Look for contextual clues. An answer can be right but not correct. The contextual clues will help you find the answer that is most right and is correct. Understand the context in which a phrase or statement is made. This will help you make important distinctions.

Don't Panic

Panicking will not answer any questions for you. Therefore, it isn't helpful. When you first see the question, if your mind goes blank, take a deep breath. Force yourself to mechanically go through the steps of solving the problem and using the strategies you've learned.

Pace Yourself

Don't get clock fever. It's easy to be overwhelmed when you're looking at a page full of questions, your mind is full of random thoughts and feeling confused, and the clock is ticking down faster than you would like. Calm down and maintain the pace that you have set for yourself. As long as you are on track by monitoring your pace, you are guaranteed to have enough time for yourself. When you get to the last few minutes of the test, it may seem like you won't have enough time left, but if you only have as many questions as you should have left at that point, then you're right on track!

Answer Selection

The best way to pick an answer choice is to eliminate all of those that are wrong, until only one is left and confirm that is the correct answer. Sometimes though, an answer choice may immediately look right. Be careful! Take a second to make sure that the other choices are not equally obvious. Don't make a hasty mistake. There are only two times that you should stop before checking other answers. First is when you are positive that the answer choice you have selected is correct. Second is when time is almost out and you have to make a quick guess!

Check Your Work

Since you will probably not know every term listed and the answer to every question, it is important that you get credit for the ones that you do know. Don't miss any questions through careless mistakes. If at all possible, try to take a second to look back over your answer selection and make sure you've selected the correct answer choice and haven't made a costly careless mistake (such as marking an answer choice that you didn't mean to mark). This quick double check should more than pay for itself in caught mistakes for the time it costs.

Beware of Directly Quoted Answers

Sometimes an answer choice will repeat word for word a portion of the question or reference section. However, beware of such exact duplication – it may be a trap! More than likely, the correct choice will paraphrase or summarize a point, rather than being exactly the same wording.

Slang

Scientific sounding answers are better than slang ones. An answer choice that begins "To compare the outcomes..." is much more likely to be correct than one that begins "Because some people insisted..."

Extreme Statements

Avoid wild answers that throw out highly controversial ideas that are proclaimed as established fact. An answer choice that states the "process should be used in certain situations, if..." is much more likely to be correct than one that states the "process should be discontinued completely." The first is a calm rational statement and doesn't even make a definitive, uncompromising stance, using a hedge word "if" to provide wiggle room, whereas the second choice is a radical idea and far more extreme.

Answer Choice Families

When you have two or more answer choices that are direct opposites or parallels, one of them is usually the correct answer. For instance, if one answer choice states "x increases" and another answer choice states "x decreases" or "y increases," then those two or three answer choices are very similar in construction and fall into the same family of answer choices. A family of answer choices is when two or three answer choices are very similar in construction, and yet often have a directly opposite meaning. Usually the correct answer choice will be in that family of answer choices. The "odd man out" or answer choice that doesn't seem to fit the parallel construction of the other answer choices is more likely to be incorrect.

Special Report: What Your Test Score Will Tell You About Your IQ

Did you know that most standardized tests correlate very strongly with IQ? In fact, your general intelligence is a better predictor of your success than any other factor, and most tests intentionally measure this trait to some degree to ensure that those selected by the test are truly qualified for the test's purposes.

Before we can delve into the relation between your test score and IQ, I will first have to explain what exactly is IQ. Here's the formula:

Your IQ = 100 + (Number of standard deviations below or above the average)*15

Now, let's define standard deviations by using an example. If we have 5 people with 5 different heights, then first we calculate the average. Let's say the average was 65 inches. The standard deviation is the "average distance" away from the average of each of the members. It is a direct measure of variability - if the 5 people included Jackie Chan and Shaquille O'Neal, obviously there's a lot more variability in that group than a group of 5 sisters who are all within 6 inches in height of each other. The standard deviation uses a number to characterize the average range of difference within a group.

A convenient feature of most groups is that they have a "normal" distribution- makes sense that most things would be normal, right? Without getting into a bunch of statistical mumbo-jumbo, you just need to know that if you know the average of the group and the standard deviation, you can successfully predict someone's percentile rank in the group.

Confused? Let me give you an example. If instead of 5 people's heights, we had 100 people, we could figure out their rank in height JUST by knowing the average, standard deviation, and their height. We wouldn't need to know each person's height and manually rank them, we could just predict their rank based on three numbers.

What this means is that you can take your PERCENTILE rank that is often given with your test and relate this to your RELATIVE IQ of people taking the test - that is, your IQ relative to the people taking the test. Obviously, there's no way to know your actual IQ because the people taking a standardized test are usually not very good samples of the general population- many of those with extremely low IQ's never achieve a level of success or competency necessary to complete a typical standardized test. In fact, professional psychologists who measure IQ actually have to use non-written tests that can fairly measure the IQ of those not able to complete a traditional test.

The bottom line is to not take your test score too seriously, but it is fun to compute your "relative IQ" among the people who took the test with you. I've done the calculations below. Just look up your percentile rank in the left and then you'll see your "relative IQ" for your test in the right hand column-

Percentile Rank	Your Relative IQ		Percentile Rank	Your Relative IQ
99	135		59	103
98	131		58	103
97	128		57	103
96	126		56	102
95	125		55	102
94	123		54	102
93	122		53	101
92	121		52	101
91	120		51	100
90	119		50	100
89	118		49	100
88	118		48	99
87	117		47	99
86	116		46	98
85	116		45	98
84	115		44	98
83	114		43	97
82	114		42	97
81	113		41	97
80	113		40	96
79	112		39	96
78	112		38	95
77	111		37	95
76	111		36	95
75	110		35	94
74	110		34	94
73	109		33	93
72	109		32	93
71	108		31	93
70	108		30	92
69	107		29	92
68	107		28	91
67	107		27	91
66	106		26	90
65	106		25	90
64	105		24	89
63	105		23	89
62	105		22	88
61	104		21	88
60	104		20	87

Special Report: What is Test Anxiety and How to Overcome It?

The very nature of tests caters to some level of anxiety, nervousness or tension, just as we feel for any important event that occurs in our lives. A little bit of anxiety or nervousness can be a good thing. It helps us with motivation, and makes achievement just that much sweeter. However, too much anxiety can be a problem; especially if it hinders our ability to function and perform.

"Test anxiety," is the term that refers to the emotional reactions that some test-takers experience when faced with a test or exam. Having a fear of testing and exams is based upon a rational fear, since the test-taker's performance can shape the course of an academic career. Nevertheless, experiencing excessive fear of examinations will only interfere with the test-takers ability to perform, and his/her chances to be successful.

There are a large variety of causes that can contribute to the development and sensation of test anxiety. These include, but are not limited to lack of performance and worrying about issues surrounding the test.

Lack of Preparation

Lack of preparation can be identified by the following behaviors or situations:

Not scheduling enough time to study, and therefore cramming the night before the test or exam
Managing time poorly, to create the sensation that there is not enough time to do everything
Failing to organize the text information in advance, so that the study material consists of the entire text and not simply the pertinent information
Poor overall studying habits

Worrying, on the other hand, can be related to both the test taker, or many other factors around him/her that will be affected by the results of the test. These include worrying about:

Previous performances on similar exams, or exams in general
How friends and other students are achieving
The negative consequences that will result from a poor grade or failure

There are three primary elements to test anxiety. Physical components, which involve the same typical bodily reactions as those to acute anxiety (to be discussed below). Emotional factors have to do with fear or panic. Mental or cognitive issues concerning attention spans and memory abilities.

Physical Signals

There are many different symptoms of test anxiety, and these are not limited to mental and emotional strain. Frequently there are a range of physical signals that will let a test taker know that he/she is suffering from test anxiety. These bodily changes can include the following:

Perspiring
Sweaty palms
Wet, trembling hands
Nausea
Dry mouth
A knot in the stomach
Headache
Faintness
Muscle tension
Aching shoulders, back and neck
Rapid heart beat
Feeling too hot/cold

To recognize the sensation of test anxiety, a test-taker should monitor him/herself for the following sensations:

The physical distress symptoms as listed above
Emotional sensitivity, expressing emotional feelings such as the need to cry or laugh too much, or a sensation of anger or helplessness
A decreased ability to think, causing the test-taker to blank out or have racing thoughts that are hard to organize or control.

Though most students will feel some level of anxiety when faced with a test or exam, the majority can cope with that anxiety and maintain it at a manageable level. However, those who cannot are faced with a very real and very serious condition, which can and should be controlled for the immeasurable benefit of this sufferer.

Naturally, these sensations lead to negative results for the testing experience. The most common effects of test anxiety have to do with nervousness and mental blocking.

Nervousness

Nervousness can appear in several different levels:

The test-taker's difficulty, or even inability to read and understand the questions on the test
The difficulty or inability to organize thoughts to a coherent form
The difficulty or inability to recall key words and concepts relating to the testing questions (especially essays)
The receipt of poor grades on a test, though the test material was well known by the test taker

Conversely, a person may also experience mental blocking, which involves:

Blanking out on test questions
Only remembering the correct answers to the questions when the test has already finished.

Fortunately for test anxiety sufferers, beating these feelings, to a large degree, has to do with proper preparation. When a test taker has a feeling of preparedness, then anxiety will be dramatically lessened.

The first step to resolving anxiety issues is to distinguish which of the two types of anxiety are being suffered. If the anxiety is a direct result of a lack of preparation, this should be considered a normal reaction, and the anxiety level (as opposed to the test results) shouldn't be anything to worry about. However, if, when adequately prepared, the test-taker still panics, blanks out, or seems to overreact, this is not a fully rational reaction. While this can be considered normal too, there are many ways to combat and overcome these effects.

Remember that anxiety cannot be entirely eliminated, however, there are ways to minimize it, to make the anxiety easier to manage. Preparation is one of the best ways to minimize test anxiety. Therefore the following techniques are wise in order to best fight off any anxiety that may want to build.

To begin with, try to avoid cramming before a test, whenever it is possible. By trying to memorize an entire term's worth of information in one day, you'll be shocking your system, and not giving yourself a very good chance to absorb the information. This is an easy path to anxiety, so for those who suffer from test anxiety, cramming should not even be considered an option.

Instead of cramming, work throughout the semester to combine all of the material which is presented throughout the semester, and work on it gradually as the course goes by, making sure to master the main concepts first, leaving minor details for a week or so before the test.

To study for the upcoming exam, be sure to pose questions that may be on the examination, to gauge the ability to answer them by integrating the ideas from your texts, notes and lectures, as well as any supplementary readings.

If it is truly impossible to cover all of the information that was covered in that particular term, concentrate on the most important portions, that can be covered very well. Learn these concepts as best as possible, so that when the test comes, a goal can be made to use these concepts as presentations of your knowledge.

In addition to study habits, changes in attitude are critical to beating a struggle with test anxiety. In fact, an improvement of the perspective over the entire test-taking experience can actually help a test taker to enjoy studying and therefore improve the overall experience. Be certain not to overemphasize the significance of the grade - know that the result of the test is neither a reflection of self worth, nor is it a measure of intelligence; one grade will not predict a person's future success.

To improve an overall testing outlook, the following steps should be tried:

Keeping in mind that the most reasonable expectation for taking a test is to expect to try to demonstrate as much of what you know as you possibly can.
Reminding ourselves that a test is only one test; this is not the only one, and there will be others.
The thought of thinking of oneself in an irrational, all-or-nothing term should be avoided at all costs.
A reward should be designated for after the test, so there's something to look forward to. Whether it be going to a movie, going out to eat, or simply visiting friends, schedule it in advance, and do it no matter what result is expected on the exam.

Test-takers should also keep in mind that the basics are some of the most important things, even beyond anti-anxiety techniques and studying. Never neglect the basic social, emotional and biological needs, in order to try to absorb information. In order to best achieve, these three factors must be held as just as important as the studying itself.

Study Steps

Remember the following important steps for studying:

Maintain healthy nutrition and exercise habits. Continue both your recreational activities and social pass times. These both contribute to your physical and emotional well being.
Be certain to get a good amount of sleep, especially the night before the test, because when you're overtired you are not able to perform to the best of your best ability.
Keep the studying pace to a moderate level by taking breaks when they are needed, and varying the work whenever possible, to keep the mind fresh instead of getting bored.
When enough studying has been done that all the material that can be learned has been learned, and the test taker is prepared for the test, stop studying and do something relaxing such as listening to music, watching a movie, or taking a warm bubble bath.

There are also many other techniques to minimize the uneasiness or apprehension that is experienced along with test anxiety before, during, or even after the examination. In fact, there are a great deal of things that can be done to stop anxiety from interfering with lifestyle and performance. Again, remember that anxiety will not be eliminated entirely, and it shouldn't be. Otherwise that "up" feeling for exams would not exist, and most of us depend on that sensation to perform better than usual. However, this anxiety has to be at a level that is manageable.

Of course, as we have just discussed, being prepared for the exam is half the battle right away. Attending all classes, finding out what knowledge will be expected on the exam, and knowing the exam schedules are easy steps to lowering anxiety. Keeping up with work will remove the need to cram, and efficient study habits will eliminate wasted time. Studying should be done in an ideal location for concentration, so that it is simple to become interested in the material and give it complete attention. A method such as SQ3R (Survey, Question, Read, Recite, Review) is a wonderful key to follow to make sure that the study habits are as effective as possible, especially in the case of learning from a textbook. Flashcards are great techniques for memorization. Learning to take good notes will mean that notes will be full of useful information, so that less sifting will need to be done to seek out what is pertinent for studying. Reviewing notes after class and then again on occasion will keep the information fresh in the mind. From notes that have been taken summary sheets and outlines can be made for simpler reviewing.

A study group can also be a very motivational and helpful place to study, as there will be a sharing of ideas, all of the minds can work together, to make sure that everyone understands, and the studying will be made more interesting because it will be a social occasion.

Basically, though, as long as the test-taker remains organized and self confident, with efficient study habits, less time will need to be spent studying, and higher grades will be achieved.

To become self confident, there are many useful steps. The first of these is "self talk." It has been shown through extensive research, that self-talk for students who suffer from test anxiety, should be well monitored, in order to make sure that it contributes to self confidence as opposed to sinking the student. Frequently the self talk of test-anxious students is negative or self-defeating, thinking that everyone else is smarter and faster, that they always mess up, and that if they don't do well, they'll fail the entire course. It is important to decreasing anxiety that awareness is made of self talk. Try writing any negative self thoughts and then disputing them with a positive statement instead. Begin self-encouragement as though it was a friend speaking. Repeat positive statements to help reprogram the mind to believing in successes instead of failures.

Helpful Techniques

Other extremely helpful techniques include:

Self-visualization of doing well and reaching goals
While aiming for an "A" level of understanding, don't try to "overprotect" by setting your expectations lower. This will only convince the mind to stop studying in order to meet the lower expectations.
Don't make comparisons with the results or habits of other students. These are individual factors, and different things work for different people, causing different results.
Strive to become an expert in learning what works well, and what can be done in order to improve. Consider collecting this data in a journal.
Create rewards for after studying instead of doing things before studying that will only turn into avoidance behaviors.
Make a practice of relaxing - by using methods such as progressive relaxation, self-hypnosis, guided imagery, etc - in order to make relaxation an automatic sensation.
Work on creating a state of relaxed concentration so that concentrating will take on the focus of the mind, so that none will be wasted on worrying.
Take good care of the physical self by eating well and getting enough sleep.
Plan in time for exercise and stick to this plan.

Beyond these techniques, there are other methods to be used before, during and after the test that will help the test-taker perform well in addition to overcoming anxiety.

Before the exam comes the academic preparation. This involves establishing a study schedule and beginning at least one week before the actual date of the test. By doing this, the anxiety of not having enough time to study for the test will be automatically eliminated. Moreover, this will make the studying a much more effective experience, ensuring that the learning will be an easier process. This relieves much undue pressure on the test-taker.

Summary sheets, note cards, and flash cards with the main concepts and examples of these main concepts should be prepared in advance of the actual studying time. A topic should never be eliminated from this process. By omitting a topic because it isn't expected to be on the test is only setting up the test-taker for anxiety should it actually appear on the exam. Utilize the course syllabus for laying out the topics that should be studied. Carefully go over the notes that were made in class, paying special attention to any of the issues that the professor took special care to emphasize while lecturing in class. In the textbooks, use the chapter review, or if possible, the chapter tests, to begin your review.

It may even be possible to ask the instructor what information will be covered on the exam, or what the format of the exam will be (for example, multiple choice, essay, free form, true-false). Additionally, see if it is possible to find out how many questions will be on the test. If a review sheet or sample test has been offered by the professor, make good use of it, above anything else, for the preparation for the test. Another great resource for getting to know the examination is reviewing tests from previous semesters. Use these tests to review, and aim to achieve a 100% score on each of the possible topics. With a few exceptions, the goal that you set for yourself is the highest one that you will reach.

Take all of the questions that were assigned as homework, and rework them to any other possible course material. The more problems reworked, the more skill and confidence will form as a result. When forming the solution to a problem, write out each of the steps. Don't simply do head work. By doing as many steps on paper as possible, much clarification and therefore confidence will be formed. Do this with as many homework problems as possible, before checking the answers. By checking the answer after each problem, a reinforcement will exist, that will not be on the exam. Study situations should be as exam-like as possible, to prime the test-taker's system for the experience. By waiting to check the answers at the end, a psychological advantage will be formed, to decrease the stress factor.

Another fantastic reason for not cramming is the avoidance of confusion in concepts, especially when it comes to mathematics. 8-10 hours of study will become one hundred percent more effective if it is spread out over a week or at least several days, instead of doing it all in one sitting. Recognize that the human brain requires time in order to assimilate new material, so frequent breaks and a span of study time over several days will be much more beneficial.

Additionally, don't study right up until the point of the exam. Studying should stop a minimum of one hour before the exam begins. This allows the brain to rest and put things in their proper order. This will also provide the time to become as relaxed as possible when going into the examination room. The test-taker will also have time to eat well and eat sensibly. Know that the brain needs food as much as the rest of the body. With enough food and enough sleep, as well as a relaxed attitude, the body and the mind are primed for success.

Avoid any anxious classmates who are talking about the exam. These students only spread anxiety, and are not worth sharing the anxious sentimentalities.

Before the test also involves creating a positive attitude, so mental preparation should also be a point of concentration. There are many keys to creating a positive attitude. Should fears become rushing in, make a visualization of taking the exam, doing well, and seeing an A written on the paper. Write out a list of affirmations that will bring a feeling of confidence, such as "I am doing well in my English class," "I studied well and know my material," "I enjoy this class." Even if the affirmations aren't believed at first, it sends a positive message to the subconscious which will result in an alteration of the overall belief system, which is the system that creates reality.

If a sensation of panic begins, work with the fear and imagine the very worst! Work through the entire scenario of not passing the test, failing the entire course, and dropping out of school, followed by not getting a job, and pushing a shopping cart through the dark alley where you'll live. This will place things into perspective! Then, practice deep breathing and create a visualization of the opposite situation - achieving an "A" on the exam, passing the entire course, receiving the degree at a graduation ceremony.

On the day of the test, there are many things to be done to ensure the best results, as well as the most calm outlook. The following stages are suggested in order to maximize test-taking potential:

Begin the examination day with a moderate breakfast, and avoid any coffee or beverages with caffeine if the test taker is prone to jitters. Even people who are used to managing caffeine can feel jittery or light-headed when it is taken on a test day.
Attempt to do something that is relaxing before the examination begins. As last minute cramming clouds the mastering of overall concepts, it is better to use this time to create a calming outlook.
Be certain to arrive at the test location well in advance, in order to provide time to select a location that is away from doors, windows and other distractions, as well as giving enough time to relax before the test begins.
Keep away from anxiety generating classmates who will upset the sensation of stability and relaxation that is being attempted before the exam.
Should the waiting period before the exam begins cause anxiety, create a self-distraction by reading a light magazine or something else that is relaxing and simple.

During the exam itself, read the entire exam from beginning to end, and find out how much time should be allotted to each individual problem. Once writing the exam, should more time be taken for a problem, it should be abandoned, in order to begin another problem. If there is time at the end, the unfinished problem can always be returned to and completed.

Read the instructions very carefully - twice - so that unpleasant surprises won't follow during or after the exam has ended.

When writing the exam, pretend that the situation is actually simply the completion of homework within a library, or at home. This will assist in forming a relaxed atmosphere, and will allow the brain extra focus for the complex thinking function.

Begin the exam with all of the questions with which the most confidence is felt. This will build the confidence level regarding the entire exam and will begin a quality momentum. This will also create encouragement for trying the problems where uncertainty resides.

Going with the "gut instinct" is always the way to go when solving a problem. Second guessing should be avoided at all costs. Have confidence in the ability to do well.

For essay questions, create an outline in advance that will keep the mind organized and make certain that all of the points are remembered. For multiple choice, read every answer, even if the correct one has been spotted - a better one may exist.

Continue at a pace that is reasonable and not rushed, in order to be able to work carefully. Provide enough time to go over the answers at the end, to check for small errors that can be corrected.

Should a feeling of panic begin, breathe deeply, and think of the feeling of the body releasing sand through its pores. Visualize a calm, peaceful place, and include all of the sights, sounds and sensations of this image. Continue the deep breathing, and take a few minutes to continue this with closed eyes. When all is well again, return to the test.

If a "blanking" occurs for a certain question, skip it and move on to the next question. There will be time to return to the other question later. Get everything done that can be done, first, to guarantee all the grades that can be compiled, and to build all of the confidence possible. Then return to the weaker questions to build the marks from there.

Remember, one's own reality can be created, so as long as the belief is there, success will follow. And remember: anxiety can happen later, right now, there's an exam to be written!

After the examination is complete, whether there is a feeling for a good grade or a bad grade, don't dwell on the exam, and be certain to follow through on the reward that was promised...and enjoy it! Don't dwell on any mistakes that have been made, as there is nothing that can be done at this point anyway.

Additionally, don't begin to study for the next test right away. Do something relaxing for a while, and let the mind relax and prepare itself to begin absorbing information again.

From the results of the exam - both the grade and the entire experience, be certain to learn from what has gone on. Perfect studying habits and work some more on confidence in order to make the next examination experience even better than the last one.

Learn to avoid places where openings occurred for laziness, procrastination and day dreaming.

Use the time between this exam and the next one to better learn to relax, even learning to relax on cue, so that any anxiety can be controlled during the next exam. Learn how to relax the body. Slouch in your chair if that helps. Tighten and then relax all of the different muscle groups, one group at a time, beginning with the feet and then working all the way up to the neck and face. This will ultimately relax the muscles more than they were to begin with. Learn how to breathe deeply and comfortably, and focus on this breathing going in and out as a relaxing thought. With every exhale, repeat the word "relax."

As common as test anxiety is, it is very possible to overcome it. Make yourself one of the test-takers who overcome this frustrating hindrance.

Special Report: Retaking the Test: What Are Your Chances at Improving Your Score?

After going through the experience of taking a major test, many test takers feel that once is enough. The test usually comes during a period of transition in the test taker's life, and taking the test is only one of a series of important events. With so many distractions and conflicting recommendations, it may be difficult for a test taker to rationally determine whether or not he should retake the test after viewing his scores.

The importance of the test usually only adds to the burden of the retake decision. However, don't be swayed by emotion. There a few simple questions that you can ask yourself to guide you as you try to determine whether a retake would improve your score:

1. What went wrong? Why wasn't your score what you expected?

Can you point to a single factor or problem that you feel caused the low score? Were you sick on test day? Was there an emotional upheaval in your life that caused a distraction? Were you late for the test or not able to use the full time allotment? If you can point to any of these specific, individual problems, then a retake should definitely be considered.

2. Is there enough time to improve?

Many problems that may show up in your score report may take a lot of time for improvement. A deficiency in a particular math skill may require weeks or months of tutoring and studying to improve. If you have enough time to improve an identified weakness, then a retake should definitely be considered.

3. How will additional scores be used? Will a score average, highest score, or most recent score be used?

Different test scores may be handled completely differently. If you've taken the test multiple times, sometimes your highest score is used, sometimes your average score is computed and used, and sometimes your most recent score is used. Make sure you understand what method will be used to evaluate your scores, and use that to help you determine whether a retake should be considered.

4. Are my practice test scores significantly higher than my actual test score?

If you have taken a lot of practice tests and are consistently scoring at a much higher level than your actual test score, then you should consider a retake. However, if you've taken five practice tests and only one of your scores was higher than your actual test score, or if your practice test scores were only slightly higher than your actual test score, then it is unlikely that you will significantly increase your score.

5. Do I need perfect scores or will I be able to live with this score? Will this score still allow me to follow my dreams?

What kind of score is acceptable to you? Is your current score "good enough?" Do you have to have a certain score in order to pursue the future of your dreams? If you won't be happy with your current score, and there's no way that you could live with it, then you should consider a retake. However, don't get your hopes up. If you are looking for significant improvement, that may or may not be possible. But if you won't be happy otherwise, it is at least worth the effort.

Remember that there are other considerations. To achieve your dream, it is likely that your grades may also be taken into account. A great test score is usually not the only thing necessary to succeed. Make sure that you aren't overemphasizing the importance of a high test score.

Furthermore, a retake does not always result in a higher score. Some test takers will score lower on a retake, rather than higher. One study shows that one-fourth of test takers will achieve a significant improvement in test score, while one-sixth of test takers will actually show a decrease. While this shows that most test takers will improve, the majority will only improve their scores a little and a retake may not be worth the test taker's effort.

Finally, if a test is taken only once and is considered in the added context of good grades on the part of a test taker, the person reviewing the grades and scores may be tempted to assume that the test taker just had a bad day while taking the test, and may discount the low test score in favor of the high grades. But if the test is retaken and the scores are approximately the same, then the validity of the low scores are only confirmed. Therefore, a retake could actually hurt a test taker by definitely bracketing a test taker's score ability to a limited range.

Special Report: Additional Bonus Material

Due to our efforts to try to keep this book to a manageable length, we've created a link that will give you access to all of your additional bonus material.

Please visit http://www.mometrix.com/bonus948/texescompsci to access the information.